A

FRENCHMAN'S WALK
THROUGH
IRELAND
1796·7

A

FRENCHMAN'S WALK
THROUGH
IRELAND
1796-7

Translated from the French of

DE LATOCNAYE

by

JOHN STEVENSON

1917

with an Introduction by

JOHN A. GAMBLE FRGS

1984

THE
BLACKSTAFF
PRESS

A Frenchman's Walk *through* IRELAND 1 7 9 6-7

(Promenade d'un Français dans l'Irlande)

Translated from the French of

DE LATOCNAYE

by

JOHN STEVENSON

BELFAST:
McCAW, STEVENSON & ORR, LTD.
The Linenhall Press.

DUBLIN:
HODGES, FIGGIS & CO., LTD.
104 Grafton Street.

First published in English by M. Harris of Cork, 1798
This edition, published by The Blackstaff Press in
1984, is a photolithographic facsimile of the 1917
edition of McCaw, Stevenson & Orr
Reprinted in 1985
The Blackstaff Press
3 Galway Park, Dundonald, Belfast BT16 0AN, Northern Ireland
and
51 Washington Street, Dover, New Hampshire 03820 USA
in association with
Emerald Isle Books, Belfast

Printed in Northern Ireland by
The Universities Press Limited

British Library Cataloguing in Publication Data

Latocnaye, De
A Frenchman's walk through Ireland 1796–7
1. Ireland – Description and travel – 1701–1800
1. Title   II. Promenade d'un Français dans l'Irlande. English
914.15'04507   DA972
ISBN 0 85640 308 3

INTRODUCTION

The idea of a Frenchman walking round Ireland in the turbulent days before the 1798 Rebellion is not so incongruous as it may at first appear. Le Chevalier de La Tocnaye, or to give him his full title, Jacques Louis de Bougrenet (Chevalier de La Tocnaye), was a French Royalist Officer of Cavalry, of Breton origin, who with thousands of other Royalists was forced to become an émigré from his native land because of the Revolution in France. La Tocnaye, as I shall call him according to the correct style of his time, came to England in 1792. At twenty-five years of age, tired of doing nothing in London, he travelled through England and into Scotland, with a view to writing a book. He remained in Scotland for two years, and his *Promenade dans La Grande Bretagne* was published in Edinburgh in 1795, (reprinted Dublin 1797). He then decided to travel to Ireland and, arriving at Waterford with letters of recommendation from the Rt Hon W.B. Conyngham to Lord Camden the Viceroy and many other influential people, he was assured of hospitality (although Mr Conyngham died in May 1796). His arrival was opportune for us today, as we have a graphic and descriptive first-hand account of the state of Ireland on the eve of the 1798 Rebellion. Other travellers, such as Rev John Wesley, Arthur Young and Richard Twiss, have given us accounts of the state of Ireland in the eighteenth century, but none so close to the Rebellion as La Tocnaye.

The first edition of this work *Promenade d'un français dans l'Irlande* was published at Dublin in 1797. Further details of his writings will be found, together with those of John Stevenson of Coolavin, Belfast, the translator of the 1917 edition, in the bibliography and reading list.

The edition which we have used for this reprint is the translation by John Stevenson, to whom we are indebted for a good text, though in his original preface he leaves the reader in no doubt about his own limitations and about the uncertain style of La Tocnaye's French. He omitted the swear words used by La Tocnaye, and also left out other portions of the French original, mainly some of the fanciful conjectures on the history of Ireland quoted by La Tocnaye from the writings of General Charles Vallancey (1721–1812). Stevenson states that the French text printed in Dublin was full of errors to start with, and that he has modified some of the 'little sallies in the French manner'. On working through the French text and comparing it with the English edition of 1799, and that of 1917, it would appear that Stevenson either did not know of the English edition of 1799 or chose to ignore it, e.g. at page 273 Stevenson includes a ten-line reference to Voltaire which is absent from the 1799 English edition. We concluded that in so doing Stevenson chose to work unaided from the original French text. Stevenson's easy-flowing English, despite errors in the text, such as naming Sir Richard instead of Sir James Ware, makes the work very readable and enjoyable as we walk with La Tocnaye on his journey of over one thousand miles around the maritime and some inland counties of Ireland for approximately a year, in 1796/7.

La Tocnaye was indebted to General Vallancey, Commandant of the port of Cove, an Englishman of Huguenot ancestry, who theorised on the history, language and literature of Ireland, publishing essays on the Celtic language without having read the original chronicles of Ireland. La Tocnaye exercises a wry humour when writing of Vallancey, calling him a man of value to the state, and father of forty-three children. However, Vallancey's generosity to La Tocnaye was considerable, and he gave La Tocnaye, whose budget was somewhat strained, the four engraved plates found in the first edition of 1797.

Despite the adverse comments which La Tocnaye passed about Cork, he must have had other good friends there apart from General Vallancey, because the first edition of his book in English was published in Cork in 1798. It is of considerable rarity, and although there is no copy in the British Library there are three copies in the National Library of Ireland (one defective). The London edition did not come out until the following year, 1799. The pagination and format of the Cork and London editions are identical and only the imprint differs on the London edition. We discovered that the paper used for the title page of the London edition differs from the text paper, and one uncut copy in original boards showed clear evidence of a cancel title page being substituted. It is my opinion that, in fact, the Cork edition did not sell well in 1798 and that the sheets were transferred to London where the publication was taken over by Robinsons. It is obvious that the translator of the Cork edition had a strong connection with Cork, and despite its being the year of the Rebellion, was prepared to publish the Chevalier's narrative. Unfortunately we do not know who the translator was, but we conjecture that he could have been motivated to the task by General Vallancey, who had considerable linguistic interests. The translator, working through the Rebellion year of 1798, saw fit to record the philosophical comment: 'should his observations tend to the diminution of party spirit and religious bigotry, the translator will not think his time unprofitably employed'. He cited Goldsmith on the advantages of travel on foot, and was very enthusiastic about La Tocnaye's independent thinking and observations, signing himself 'An Irishman' on the title page.

We also learn that La Tocnaye wrote up his journals while resident in Dublin, and that he had finished them prematurely because of the turbulent state of the country: he had hoped to follow the course of all the canals and to visit the coalmines of Kilkenny and Leitrim, and include an account of these in his book.

The author's daily journey was about twenty-two Irish miles, which corresponds to twenty-eight English Statute miles, the English mile being approximately three-quarters of an Irish mile. His colourful appearance must have aroused great curiosity as he walked around Ireland, his possessions slung across his shoulder in three bundles on top of his sword cane. La Tocnaye's personality, with his ready wit, *joie de vivre*, thoughts of adventure and astute powers of observation, would have made him a welcome guest in the homes which he visited, in both the upper and lower ranks of society. As well as the Viceroy and the Conynghams, he met people like Peter La Touche, the Wicklow banker, John C. Walker the antiquarian and Lord and Lady Londonderry of Mount Stewart. His description of the extraordinary lifestyle of the Earl Bishop of Derry is worth noting.

At Waterford he was mistaken for Count Rumford, who was due to arrive to give advice to the local administration on the better running of their house of industry. Mr Stevenson described Count Rumford (1753–1814) as an Englishman, though in fact he was born in Massachusetts, his real name being Benjamin Thompson, later Sir. He was a member of the Royal Irish Academy, and his inventive genius was put to good use in improving the heating of houses. He was, in fact, the first scientist to determine that 'heat is a mode of motion'. He founded the Royal Institution of London which was chartered in 1799. La Tocnaye revelled in this case of mistaken identity.

In Connemara he visited the estate of Colonel Richard Martin, 'the King of Connemara', who was otherwise known as 'Humanity Dick' (he became one of the founders of the National Society for the Prevention of Cruelty to Animals), and also as 'Hairtrigger Dick' because of the prodigious number of duels he fought.

La Tocnaye provides an important contemporary account of the unfortunate refugees who were coming to Connemara and Mayo as a result of the religious and political quarrels chiefly between the Protestant 'Orange Boys' and the Catholic 'Defenders' in Co. Armagh, when

iv

many families received a card telling them they had so many days to sell their belongings and 'go to Connaught or Hell'. (Some historians believe this expression dates from this time.) The Belfast newspaper, the *Northern Star*, in 1796 writes of 700 families being driven from their homes and, about the close of that year, a report from Co. Mayo gave the number of refugees from the disturbed North as 1,360.

In Enniskillen he enjoyed the hospitality of the celebrated Dr Joseph Stock who had just been appointed headmaster of Portora Royal School, Enniskillen, in 1795, and who, in 1798, became Bishop of Killala, Co. Mayo, where he was imprisoned by General Humbert, leader of the invading French Army, after the landing at Killala on 22 August 1798. The Bishop later published an impartial and authentic record of the historic events of the French invasion. La Tocnaye's mention of the inscription on the gate of Enniskillen, 'The Glorious First of July', is interesting, as 1 July 1690 was the old-style date of the Battle of the Boyne. Because of the calendar change in 1752 this became 12 July, now the date celebrated by Orangemen to commemorate the victory of King William III over King James II at the Boyne.

The author must have asked many questions, as we find good descriptions of contemporary secret societies. In Co. Wexford he gives a good description of the 'White Boys', an agrarian secret society founded in 1761. He also encountered other groups such as the 'Orange Boys', the 'Defenders', the 'United Irishmen' and the 'Peep o' Day Boys'. This was in the Wexford district of Forth and Bargy, where, he says, the people spoke a language akin to Flemish. Some scholars refer to it as 'Chaucerian' and William Barnes and Poole wrote an interesting book about this dialect in 1867.

La Tocnaye's observations on the state of religion in Ireland are very explicit. He refers to the staunch Catholic observance of fast days, and writes about the Catholic people and priests, giving his own opinion that the Government should befriend the Catholics of Ireland. This

v

is very illuminating, written in the days immediately after the Catholic Relief Act of 1793 which gave Catholics the vote.

Of great historic interest is the unusual description of a group of people raising potatoes for a man because, says La Tocnaye, they felt friendly towards him. This euphemism is more likely interpreted as one of the 'Diggings' carried out by sympathisers of the United Irishmen, in which information was passed under the guise of working the land. The author felt nervous in the North, but one is full of admiration for his courage and fortitude, as the imminence of the Rebellion in the region was by now fast becoming apparent. The French Revolution had a very unsettling influence on the Presbyterians of Belfast, with many citizens celebrating the French victories. The Society of United Irishmen had been founded at Belfast in 1791: naturally, as a French Royalist, La Tocnaye does not mention this, but he described Belfast as a rather pretty town, and one with which he felt an affinity because of the French Huguenot establishments in the area.

He returned to Dublin a little more than a year after leaving it, and decided to quit Ireland, probably feeling himself in considerable danger because of the political situation. The Rebellion broke out on 23 May 1798.

To conclude this introduction, we add a note relating to the author's spelling of Irish words. They have been retained in his original spelling, although many are incorrect. There are other anomalies in the text, relating to place names, so we have supplied a short index of Irish place names at the end. The reader should note in Chapter XI that Londonderry is not on the River Derg but on the River Foyle, and at page 256 that Primate Robertson is, of course, Archbishop Richard Robinson (Lord Rokeby), who built the Observatory at Armagh.

John A. Gamble FRGS, ABA
April 1984

Thanks are expressed to Mrs Barbara Kelly, BA,
to Professor A.T.Q. Stewart, Professor Desmond Bowen,
Dr Kenneth Taylor and to Mr Hugh Russell
and Mr Roger Dixon of Belfast Central Reference Library
for their kind assistance.

CONTENTS

CHAPTER I

CHAPTER II

CHAPTER III

CONTENTS

CHAPTER IV

CHAPTER V

CHAPTER VI

CHAPTER VII

CONTENTS

CONTENTS

A FRENCHMAN'S
WALK THROUGH IRELAND,
1796-7

CHAPTER I

LONDON—QUIBERON

AFTER a sojourn of more than two years in Scotland, the famous ' Land of Cakes,' well treated by everybody, but, like Partridge, ' often in danger of starving in the midst of compassionate friends,' the late Lord Dreghorn, who had had the goodness to read my observations on the country, persuaded me to print them.

The idea of publishing *in* Scotland a book *on* Scotland may be thought singular. ' Why should you take it on you to instruct us about our own country ? ' said some. ' We know Scotland only too well,' said others. After much reflection I came to the conclusion that talk about ourselves is precisely what we do like, and so I published my book, which succeeded perfectly.

Lord Dreghorn was kind enough to read the proof-sheets as they passed through the press. I was not in the best of humours at the time, and so there met his eyes a good many would-be satirical remarks. My good old judge was lenient. ' This is very funny, very original,' he said, ' everybody will laugh, ourselves excepted. My advice to you is, " Don't make the dogs bark until you are out of the village,"' and so I corrected and cut away until at last he himself could smile at the joke.

It was just at the time when the news came of that cursed expedition to the shores of France, in which so many of our exiles perished uselessly ; and I resolved at once to go and see my friends at London, to bemoan our case and console those who were bereaved. My way lay through Berwick, where I met the good folk who welcomed me when I came to Scotland, and was glad to find that they had not forgotten me.

Two English companies who have leased the Tweed salmon fisheries maintain a service of smacks—light little vessels—from this port. Some of them have salt-water wells in the hold—these are supposed to carry the salmon alive to London, but many die on the way. Others take the salmon packed in ice, in deal cases—the fish in these arrive in good condition, although the voyage is one of more than four hundred miles.

In order to get a little profit out of these forced journeys, the proprietors carry a few passengers, who are not badly fed, getting tea twice a day and a good bed in the cabin for the very small sum of fifteen shillings. To make any money at this rate, the companies must calculate that the majority of the passengers, being unaccustomed to the sea, will be sick for three days, which is the average duration of the voyage.

I engaged a berth in one of these smacks, and made the voyage with the salmon. Unfortunately, bad weather and contrary winds delayed us, giving me occasion to tell the captain, after I had recovered from my sickness, that if he did not hurry I would certainly ruin him.

We were eight days *en route*, and during that time sailed often so near to the shore that the coast towns were easily distinguished. First appeared Flamborough; then Scarborough, one of those towns famous for the idlers who flock to it under pretence of sea-bathing; its castle situated on a rock is a striking and beautiful object. Off Yarmouth the sea was covered with boats passing to and fro like barges in a canal.

Several times when the vessel struck out for open sea I regretted having adopted this way of travel. It would have been disagreeable to have fallen in with Carmagnoles, who would have done me the kindness to take me to Paris when I wanted to go to London—it is always annoying to have one's travelling plans disarranged. It was with much pleasure then that, at last, I saw opening before us the mouth of the Thames, and as the customs authorities take no account of smacks, we kept straight ahead and disembarked at the Tower of London. It was a great joy to me to find myself once more in a city where I had so many relations and friends, after two years of separation spent entirely among strangers.

However, the time of my arrival was anything but gay. The news of the frightful disaster at Quiberon had just arrived; there was hardly a French family in London that had not to deplore the loss of a father, a husband, or a brother: people shunned each other—

3

all the bonds of society seemed to be broken ; a blind
and sullen grief seemed to alienate the few friends
who remained. These had divided into two parties,
the one supporting M. D'Hervilly and the other M. de
Puisaye, and mutually accused each other, or defended
him whose cause they had adopted. I was a neutral,
and could admire the fiery courage of the one without
believing the other to be a traitor, although I was far
from approving his conduct. Certain it is that what
he promised was executed almost to the letter ; only
the relief which was to effect the junction between
the disembarked and a great number of Chouans
failed to arrive. This disastrous expedition cost the
lives of a great part of the nobility of Brittany and of a
very great number of former officers of the French
navy who were uselessly sacrificed.

It appeared that when the corps made prisoners
had laid down their arms, the intention of the republican
chiefs was not to put them to death ; there were more
than fifteen hundred of them, while their escort was a
guard of only three hundred men. The night was very
dark, and to keep themselves from losing their way
they held on to each other by the skirts of their tunics ;
some, however, did get out of touch, and were obliged
to cry out loud and long before any came to secure
them. Some republican officers, who foresaw what the
fate of the captured would be, suggested, I am told,
to several of their acquaintances—prisoners—that they
should make escape, but these, having given their
word, did not wish to profit by the kindness of the
captors making the proposal. They were taken to
Vannes and kept there, prisoners on parole, for a few
days ; but at last the order for their death arrived,

4

and after the mockery of a trial they were shot. A few, however, succeeded in escaping, and it is from these that the details of the bloody tragedy have been learned.

It appears from their story that the inhabitants of the town and the troops were horrified at their fate. The Chouans were masters of the country, but nevertheless a handful of strangers (Liègeois), ministers of the barbarous wills of the tigers employing them, succeeded by the terror they inspired in sending the prisoners to their doom. Thus it is that the most atrocious acts of the revolutionists have been committed. The nations of Europe have marvelled oft at the bravery and energy of the people of Paris— it is rather its cowardice and weakness that should astonish them. The bulk of mankind is a vile herd always ready to run at the bark of the dog whose bite they fear. Who can doubt that of the soldiers who assisted at the martyrdom of Louis XVI, seven-eighths of the number would have seen him escape with pleasure, and among the remaining eighth there were very many indifferent ? It may seem paradoxical if I say that I do not believe that more than a dozen men were eagerly set on his slaughter, and the ardour of these twelve, which served the rage and ambition of a few, was, perhaps, not their own. I shall have cast up to me, of course, the astonishing victories and brilliant successes of the republican armies. But did we not see, before there was any French Revolution, the great Frederick beat the kings of Europe with their own subjects? Do we forget the 40,000 Saxons, his prisoners of war, enrolled, in spite of themselves, among his troops ? When the armies face each other the opinions

5

of individuals composing them go for nothing—they must fight for personal safety ; the dangers of desertion are so great that, unless in very special circumstances, few will dare to brave them. Besides it was no longer a case of war for or against the king, it was, unfortunately, obvious that it was for or against France. In this case *every* individual had a powerful interest in defending his country, no matter what may have been the colour of his political opinions.

Reports of the expedition to Quiberon brought emigrants from the four corners of the earth, alas ! only to hear, on arrival, the harrowing tale of its disastrous termination. The king's brother came from the heart of Germany, and learned the news only when he set foot on English shores. Nevertheless, the Vendean war went on, and the brave defenders of royalty eagerly demanded the assistance so long promised. An expedition in their aid was at last decided on— had the forces lost at Quiberon been sent at first to them they would have effected a considerable diversion in their favour.

It does not seem that the project was taken very seriously. Certain landowners of this country offered their services as volunteers for the fleet, intending simply to be landed and then to endeavour to do something for the arming of the peasantry ; but they were told that their offers must be refused unless they made a definite engagement. However the expedition did, at length, get away and carried the prince to l'Isle-Dieu, and then, after much fatiguing exertion, the fleet returned two months later without striking a blow. Spite of all sources of trouble, I found the emigrants in London, to my great astonishment, much better off

6

than at the time of my departure for the north and
Scotland two years earlier. In whatever situation
Providence may see fit to place us, time and resigna-
tion make our case supportable. Some I found occupied by little industries which supplied the means for
existence ; the ladies embroidered, and the Government
allowed them a small pension, as they did also to the
priests and to persons over fifty years of age. Those
who suffered most were the (formerly) rich landlords of
France who, accustomed to live on their large revenues
without work, and without thought for the morrow,
were without the resourcefulness which developed in
their poorer compatriots.

After a short time devoted to renewal of acquaint-
anceships my genius for observation would not permit
me to rest. I frequented all places where men assemble,
from tavern to parliament-house, from church to
street-crowd, and everywhere, like Solomon, I found
only vanity and vexation of spirit.

I was possessed of kindly-given letters of recommendation, some of them to men of great wealth. Oh
the droll faces of some when I approached them !—
they didn't like the name of *émigré*, and to a certainty
it was still more displeasing to me.

Several, however, who had read my ' Walk through
Great Britain ' suggested that I should go to Ireland
and write a book about my travels in that country.
I had nothing to do, it was a new country for me,
magnificent passports and letters of recommendation
were forthcoming, and I was tempted.

Before my departure I wished to find out what
those amiable and learned (?) gentlemen, the book-
sellers, had done with my books, and I soon learned to

distinguish the character of my man at the first step
in his shop.   If the bookmonger met me with a smile
and an honest look, I did no more than put my question
and take my departure.   If, on the contrary, he treated
me to sour looks, I was sure that he had sold my
books, and refused to leave him until he paid up.

I was witness of the civil way the king was received
by Parliament at the beginning of 1796.   The frenzy
of the populace surprised me greatly, it seemed to me
that the consequences must be alarming.   I had with
me an old English officer.   'It's nothing,' said he,
'they will be as quiet as ever in a short time; it's only
their way of expressing their good will to His Majesty.'
The yells were appalling, and two rather pretty young
woman, frightened at the row, threw themselves,
tremblingly, into our arms.   After having examined
the one who fell to mine I kissed her cordially by
way of reassurance; as for my English friend he put
his two hands into his pockets immediately, evincing
fear and surprise: I am inclined to take the different
actions on this occasion as fairly representative of the
manners of the two peoples.

I found myself one day in a political club of a kind
abounding in London.   After having regulated the
destinies of Europe, one of the speakers remarked
in a loud voice, 'This Clairfaix must be a clever fellow,
he has saved Germany by taking the Rhine'; then,
turning with an important air to me, the self-revealed
foreigner, he added, 'You have been in these parts,
no doubt, and will know that it is a very strongly
fortified town.'   'It is certainly a great place for
water,' I replied.   One of the company, laughing
immoderately at this, put on a wise air and, addressing

me, said, ' Will you please tell me what was the name of the French admiral on this occasion ? '

When I let them know that the Rhine was a river not much wider than the Thames at Chelsea, they were astonished that they had heard so much about it—' for,' said they, with much sagacity, ' there's nothing easier than crossing a river in a boat.'

By coach I made my way to Beacon's Fields and there, at the house of Mr. Blair, spent a very agreeable week. From here I went to Bath, where I gladly found amusement in the attractions and distractions of the gay city. But, spite of all that was done for them, I noticed that the idlers were bored to death, yawning from the springs to the card-table, from the card-table to the ball, from the ball to the bookseller's, and from the bookseller's to their beds, where, perhaps, for a few hours they cease to feel the burden of their existence.

This city, infinitely agreeable in so many respects, ceases to be so after a short stay, if one has not made or found friends. Everybody runs so much after pleasure that pleasure runs from everybody—and nobody seems to be able to catch it.

I found at Bath a few of my exiled compatriots doing much better than at London, where they only worried each other. I noticed how much the city had been enlarged since my previous visit—entirely new quarters on magnificent scale had been built, proving that the place is still growing in favour with the dwellers in Great Britain.

Leaving Bath I travelled to Bristol, intending to embark at once for Ireland, but the wind being contrary I was obliged to stay for a few days. To occupy

9

my time I went to one of the fashionable assemblies, where at once I found myself on familiar terms with the company. I was asked to play cards with the ladies ; I accepted and—lost.

Tired of waiting for the wind I went after it. The machine which carried us with the mails, and with as little ceremony as was accorded to the mail-bags, rattled along with such speed that I saw on this long journey little or nothing, and wished that it had entered into the heart of the powers to make a decent road and a convenient port for the arrival and departure of the boat.

This part of Wales is broken up into little hills and shallow valleys which seem to be very fertile. The peasant women wear, ordinarily, a man's old coat over their petticoats, and a big straw hat which shades them entirely. The houses are not unlike those of the Highlands of Scotland ; the language is a form of Celtic with a strong resemblance to our low Breton.

Swansea is a port of considerable size, and serves for Bristol and the South of England. All that I was able to remark in the way of special manners in these parts is, that at Carmarthen the inhabitants use for salmon fishing a boat, or rather a basket, covered with horse skin. They sit in the middle and preserve equilibrium very cleverly, and, fishing over, they carry the boat home with them, where it serves as a cradle for the children.

The cemeteries also attracted my attention. Instead of filling them with an incongruous assortment of tombstones with ridiculous inscriptions, the relations of the lost cultivate on their graves flowers and plants,

coming often to care for them, so that the cemeteries
are more like gardens than homes of the dead. People
practising such a custom must be of gentle manners,
and I was very sorry that I could not live for a while
among them. But I was on my way to Ireland, and
hurried on to Milford Haven, an ugly hole in which
the anxious traveller may eat up to his last penny
while waiting for a favourable breeze. Three or four
times we set sail, and as many times were we forced
by the waves to return to port. On the fourth endeavour we stopped at Deal, a little village at the
mouth of the bay, and there we stuck for eight long
days.

In the ordinary course of affairs, how impatiently
I should have chafed at the delay, spite of the sight
of the large and beautiful bay and singular country!
But chance had settled that I should engage a place
in the same boat as that which was to carry an amiable
Scotch family, and an Irishman who had served a
long time in France, and I found myself in such good
company that I began to fear, rather than to desire, a
favourable wind. We made the crossing at last, and
rather rapidly, for we reached the Irish coast within
twenty-four hours.

The customs officers claim tribute on both sides
of the water, demanding from the passengers half a
crown per head, for the permission to ship or disembark
their luggage. One who refused to pay had his bag
tumbled and turned over in a cruel manner. The
price of the passage is exorbitant—a guinea and a
half in the cabin—and the packet was far from being
either comfortable or clean. I had chosen the route
from motives of economy, and found the charges to

mount to double those of the Holyhead route. We
entered the river Suir, at the mouth of which is a
strong castle seated on a rock jutting out into the sea.
Mr. Latin, who travelled in the boat, was kind enough
to ask me to his house at Drumdouny, and so from
the very first day I spent on Irish soil I had the good
fortune to enjoy Irish kindness and hospitality.

CHAPTER II

THE banks of the Suir are lined with pleasant-looking country-houses, and the water is deep as far as Waterford, a town with a great trade in salted meat, and which seems to be very prosperous. There is a quay which might be a very ornamental feature had the authorities not thought fit to place some boat-building yards on it, along with several tasteless sheds for the public service. It would have been infinitely better for the workers to have had the ship-building industry on the other side of the river, and its settlement there would have left the quay an uninterrupted sweep, and saved the neighbouring houses from the unpleasantness of the overpowering odour of tar—but *O! sweet smell of gain.*

The bridge is the first in Ireland to be constructed in its manner—the wood piles have thirty feet of water round them at high-water. The beauty and solidity of the structure and adaptability to such deep water reflect great credit on the architect, who has designed several others on the same plan.

There was at the time, in the river, an American vessel, with passengers from Nantes for New York, which had suffered shipwreck on the Irish coast within a few days from leaving France. The inhabitants

13

subscribed money and furnished provisions for the benefit of the poor voyagers. I questioned a few of the passengers about the country they had left— they were for the greater part artisans—but they could tell me nothing, except that bread was very dear, that they were very miserable, and that they were going to New York in the hope of finding work.

As it was my intention to reach Dublin as quickly as possible, I took place in a coach to convey me to Gorum, where I expected to join the Cork mail. Unfortunately when this arrived every place was occupied, and I was left in this miserable village with no way of proceeding with my luggage except by hiring what they call a *car*. Their car is a species of low cart on wheels two feet in diameter, made out of one or two pieces of wood, attached to a great axle of wood or iron turning with them. This singular construction seems to be well fitted for carrying heavy loads, but not for the country work in which they are commonly employed. I take it to be a farmer's invention.

Having then made a bargain with a driver to take me six miles at the price of a post-chaise, I mounted beside my luggage. My man stopped at every public-house to drink or talk, leaving me in the middle of the road exposed to the rain. Two or three times I begged him, civilly, to proceed, but as he did not appear to pay the slightest attention to my requests, I commenced to repeat those eloquent compliments which one may learn about the docks and markets of London, and was pleased to see that I had, at last, impressed him, for I heard him say, when quitting some of his friends, ' By ——, I'm sure he's a gentleman for he swears most confoundedly.' After this little lesson

I had not the least trouble with my charioteer, but the rain, and some annoyances due to my position at the horse's tail, put me in such bad humour that I vowed never again to expose myself to such discomfort.

I stopped at Carlow, where there has been established recently a seminary for Catholic priests. This town is situated on the Barrow, which joins with the Grand Canal of Ireland. Wishing to see something of this waterway I went to Athy, from whence every day there is a service of public boats to Dublin. At the entrance to the village I was stopped by four or five persons who asked for charity—they explained that it was to be used to give decent burial to a poor wretch who had died of hunger. I replied that since he was dead he wanted nothing. This answer did not appear to satisfy them, and so I contributed to the funereal pomp, the occasion being, perhaps, the only one in which the poor fellow's friends were interested in his concerns.

The canal boats are very comfortable, being indeed very like those of Holland, but the cost here is nearly double. The one in which I travelled carried a large number of political talkers of the type known in France as *mouchards*. Seeing that I was a foreigner, one of them spoke to me several times on delicate and difficult matters affecting the Government. Fearing false interpretations I responded in ambiguous terms, and in the end found it politic to feign sleep—a very good way of getting out of such difficulties.

The canal is a magnificent piece of work, crossing immense tracts of moor, where ten or twelve feet of peat have had to be removed before reaching earth in which the waterway could be cut. Several aqueducts have been necessary, one of them of really prodigious length and height.

Dublin is a very considerable city, about one-fourth the size of London, of which it is the image in little—even the streets bear the same names; the beauty of the buildings may dispute for precedence with those of the capital; one is astonished at their magnificence and number. The Parliament House does honour to the nation's representatives; it is an immense circular building surrounded by a magnificent colonnade.

It is worthy of remark that the place where the deputies or representatives of the greatest nation assemble is commonly an old, irregular, ugly building, for which there is such attachment or affection that nobody thinks of displacing it by a new and more commodious structure.

The Bourse or Royal Exchange is somewhat like the Mansion House in London, but smaller. The Customs House is much too fine for its work, and the new building which they call the Four Courts of Justice gives Themis the pleasure to see herself decently lodged, a rare thing in European countries. Her old residence was a frightful place, as much on account of the members as by reason of the lugubrious and sombre appearance of the cave where they practised. I amused myself often by walking among them, and as it was extremely unlikely that I, in my circumstances, should ever have anything to do with them, I could laugh at their big wigs, in which the face is so buried that only a long nose protrudes. They reminded me of hawks dressed to pounce on their

16

prey, with the beaks only visible. If rumour is to be believed, attorneys here yield in nothing to their brethren of our courts ; indeed, from certain stories I have heard it would seem that they are even cleverer.

The squares are large and well built, only the port seems to me to be unworthy of the city. There has just been constructed an immense dock, which will make good certain shortcomings when some houses have been built to protect it from wind. It is singular that the inhabitants have never thought of building a beautiful church here ; the churches are all old and without the least decoration. Among them all there are but two miserable bell-towers, and this want prevents the city from having the fine appearance it should exhibit from a distance.

As my object is not to give a topographical description of this great city, I shall not attempt to describe the Castle and the beautiful buildings associated. The splendid carriages and the apparent wealth of the principal houses render the more displeasing the sight of the beggars, whose abject poverty is horrible. They may be seen hanging on for hours to the railings of basement stories, forcing charity by depriving those who live in these places of light and air. Some of them are insolent, seeking to get in some fashion, by force, what is not forthcoming by good-will. These disgusting scenes harden the heart little by little, and I never felt less disposed to alms-giving than after having lived some time in Dublin.

I occupied my leisure in the early days of my sojourn as I do ordinarily in such times elsewhere, by moving from one place to another, and mixing as much as possible with the crowd. I joined one which seemed, on a certain day, to be expecting something with impatience, and found myself among them in front of a large building which had something of the look of an old castle. There was a little platform at the level of a window in the second storey ; two men of somewhat disagreeable look made their appearance on it, and I thought I was about to witness some peculiar ceremony. But I was promptly disabused of this idea, for one of them passed a loop of rope round the neck of the other and fastened the cord to a bar of iron above him. I turned to get away, but the crowd was too dense for movement ; the poor wretch stood for a moment, alone, in view of the people, then a bolt slipped, and the little platform on which he stood fell against the wall. The Irish have, perhaps, got the better of their neighbours in the matter of hanging people with grace, but to me it appears a great cruelty to make a sort of parade of the death of a man, and in diminishing the horror of the punishment crime is increased and executions multiplied. I think I am not far wrong in assigning this as the reason why there are more people hung in Great Britain and Ireland than in all the rest of Europe.

The crowd seemed to move steadily in one direction, and I followed again—this time to be led to Phœnix Park, where there was a horse race. I really could not say which of the two—execution or race—gave the greater pleasure to the hundred-headed monster.

Although the part of the city where the well-to-do people live is perhaps as beautiful as anything similar in Europe, nothing anywhere can compare with the dirt and misery of the quarters where the lower classes

vegetate. They call these quarters ' The Liberties '
of Dublin, and this made me think often of ' liberties '
of France under Robespierre, than which there was
nothing more disgusting in the universe.

Among those to whom I had letters of recommendation were generals and doctors, bishops, and curates,
bankers and authors, lords and professors, barristers
and solicitors. Mr. Burton Conyngham was one of
those who welcomed me most warmly ; he was kind
in encouraging me to carry out my plan. He was a
most honourable man, a friend of the public good, a
supporter of every effort made for the benefit of his
country. I can say this now without fear of being
accused of flattery, for he is dead. To him I owe my
introduction to various learned societies, and the
friendship of some of their members. There were
among them some very amiable and highly educated
men—there was not among them one without something peculiar or original in his manner.

In natural history collections the cabinet of which
Mr. Kirwan has charge merits the attention of the
curious. There will be found in it a most interesting
assemblage of all known stones and minerals. Lord
Charlemont's library is a gem of elegance and taste.

From seeing Irishmen abroad one would imagine
them to be most gallant and incapable of living without
society. The very same men who appear to find so
much pleasure in dancing attendance on our ladies
allow cavaliers to flirt with their own. When an
Irishman presents himself at the door of a Jacques
Roastbeef in England, the latter fears immediately
an attack on his purse, his wife, his daughter, or his
wine. In revenge Dublin is shy in receiving the

foreigner. One would say that the Dubliners remember their own faults of youth.

There are few social functions except those that are called *routs*. With reason I might describe them as *déroutes*. Where a house might comfortably entertain twenty persons, sixty are invited, and so in proportion. I have seen routs where, from vestibule to garret, the rooms were filled with fine ladies beautifully dressed, but so crushed against each other that it was hardly possible to move. A foreigner has cause for embarrassment in these too brilliant assemblies, for he may here see really charming women in greater number than in most cities, and he thinks it a pity to see them lose on a stairway the time which might be passed much more agreeably with a small number of appreciative friends.

Nearly all the rich, I am told, spend more than their incomes, and so are obliged to resort to ruinous expedients in order to keep up style. In most European countries such prodigality is not so injurious to society, in that the expense goes to encourage art and talents, which serve to make life agreeable. Here in Ireland there is no such redeeming result, for the things on which the money is spent are not products of the country, and those who practise the fine arts, being without encouragement, and being, indeed, despised, seek other lands where their work is more highly appreciated. To nobles who are bent on ruining themselves, I counsel the spending of their means on Irish-made goods. That would be real patriotism.

When it was known that I intended to write the trifles which occupy the attention of the reader at the moment, several people exerted themselves to procure for me entry to various establishments where never before had foreigner been admitted.

I was warned by the case of a certain Mr. Twiss to be careful as to what I should put on paper. This Twiss was an Englishman, not wanting in wit, but still an Englishman of a commonly-seen type, full of prejudice in favour of his own country and considering all peoples of other lands as very inferior species. After having travelled over the greater part of Europe he came to Ireland, and had the imprudence to express discontent when several persons for whom he had letters of recommendation did not invite him to their houses. He should have remembered that the usage had been copied from England, where people will sometimes pay you the compliment of inviting you to an inn and leave you to pay your own charges. Such treatment was, perhaps, responsible for some dry responses at which he was much mortified. Thereupon he proceeded on his travels, and found in the towns what I have myself experienced—that is to say, a too ceremonious hospitality, the person to whom you have presented your letter paying you a visit of ceremony and then sending you on the day following an invitation for three or four days ahead. Surely it is a curious compliment to oblige a traveller to remain so long in a little town, where he has neither friend nor acquaintance, in order that he may, at last, have the pleasure to see much beautiful silver shining beautifully on the sideboard, servants in livery, and a huge piece of beef on the end of the table with hungry executioners round it. But it is the custom, and those who practise it think they are acting with great politeness in not asking you on the first day. However, in all towns there are folk who follow the good old custom, and the thing to do is to avoid having letters for the other sort, then one can pass the time very agreeably.

This style of entertainment displeased Mr. Twiss very much, and as in the world disagreeableness is a coin which can be given as well as received, his retaliations were as bad as the provocations he had received. He finished his journey very quickly, and immediately on his return published a record, not of what he had observed, but of what had been told by travellers four or five hundred years ago, and certainly set down some things not generally known, as, for example, the manner of baking bread by Cork girls in the year 1400. He permitted himself certain pleasantries about the skins of potatoes and the legs of ladies—this latter is a delicate subject to treat, and one about which the narrator should keep to himself the observations he has been fortunate enough to make. The Irish were extremely displeased by his remarks, going so far as, childishly, to represent him pictorially in a very undignified position. What may, perhaps, console him for the contumely with which he has been treated, is that his work, which had no great merit, had so much attention called to it by this angry fuss that the sales were good, and a copy could hardly be found in Dublin unsold. As for me, I have no spite against anyone ; the prejudices of this country are foreign to me ; the political and religious quarrels which have rent it for so long are as little to me as those of the Chinese. That being the case, why should I not say what I think, and what merit would my book have if I stooped to flattery on any occasion whatsoever.

DUBLIN

One of my friends took me to the Society Theatre, assuredly the most sumptuous thing of the kind which I have seen anywhere. The house is very fine, the company numerous and select—the number of beautiful women seen there is something bewitching, and the only kind of crowd by which I don't mind being squeezed is one like that which here fills the hall where coffee is served after the performance. Nevertheless, I must say that this playhouse does a great injury to the public theatre, for the rich young folk who ruin their fortunes in trying to be actors at the Society Theatre will certainly not encourage their rivals at the public playhouse, and we cannot there expect good actors unless they are well supported and adequately paid. Men are not admitted to the Society Theatre unless they are subscribers, and the subscription runs to about a guinea per representation. Each gentleman subscribing may bring two ladies, and on the day of my admission this rule gave occasion to a young blade to rig himself out in petticoats, and find his way in as a lady through the introduction of one of his friends. Unfortunately, he was a bit merry and came out with some oaths of ill accord with femininity, which scandalised the hearers and occasioned his ejection. Some of the actors played their parts passably well, but I must say I do not take kindly to the sight of men of rank on the theatrical stage before the public, for the assembly was numerous enough to allow my use of the term.

The public playhouse is ugly enough, the theatre being poorly attended, and the actors nothing better than what are to be found in a little provincial town.

23

They have devised in Dublin a rather singular form of entertainment, the proceeds of which are applied to the maintenance of a Maternity Hospital. It is called a Promenade, and the name made me wish to go and see one. The visitors walk in a circular hall called the Rotunda, and while there is somewhat more freedom than that which obtains at private entertainments, people only mix with, and speak to, members of their own circle. After a certain time a bell sounded, and the company hurried through a door just opened, and groups of friends settled round tea-tables. My society consisted of myself, and being unable to join any party I had opportunity to scan the various groups : everywhere there reigned a kind of quiet enjoyment which gave me much more pleasure than I had expected to find. The good mammas were not very numerous, and those who were present appeared to be absent-minded. The young folk, on the other hand, were very numerous and making good use of their time—I think, perhaps, the Promenade attained its object along more lines than one. The cash result is nearly all the hospital has to depend on for maintenance ; balls are given sometimes, and for these the hall seems to be better suited than for Promenades.

There are several other hospitals, all maintained by subscriptions as in England. I hate to see the aid given to the poor depend on the caprice or fashion of the moment. If it were not here the fashion to subscribe, what would become of all these establishments ! Formerly they had the revenues from lands to support them, but at the time of the Reformation these were taken possession of by certain rich families, in order to avoid malpractices of which the former administrators were accused.

The Hospital for old men does honour to the inhabitants of this city. Here are maintained a great number of aged men, fallen on evil times, near the end of their lives.

The House of Industry is a large establishment containing about 1700 poor folk who, in part, support themselves by their labours. Their food is infinitely better than that found on the tables of the peasantry. They have meat once a week; bread, potatoes, and other vegetables every day; very clean beds; only their clothes remain as they were before entry. Any poor person has the right of entry; those who come of their own accord are allowed to go out one day weekly. Notwithstanding these advantages, the love of liberty is so rooted in the heart of man there are very few who come of their own will, and the others are constantly trying to escape. Artizans and tradesmen are generally occupied in making things foreign to their experience, and perhaps to this cause is to be attributed the mediocrity of the most of the goods manufactured.

While I was in Dublin it was the fashion for people of high style to attend the charity sermons of a famous preacher, Mr. Kirwan. It has happened often at these services that the collections have amounted to a thousand or twelve hundred pounds, the money being applied to the support of Schools for Orphans. The Dublin ladies carry on little industries, providing the materials at their own charges, and selling the finished products for the benefit of the same schools. In most of the rich houses to which I was admitted I found the

ladies occupied in this way. As the class below the
highest is always disposed to imitate its superiors,
charity sermons are very frequent all over the city.

To my mind Mr. Kirwan is a perfect preacher,
joining to excellent discourse an eloquence far from
common. He draws from the purse of the sinner that
aid which cold charity alone could never extract.
And yet I must say that the fervour of his expressions
and the animation of his gestures do not work for
good of the pulpit of Dublin. They have tended
to produce a breed of imitators, who by their ridiculous
frenzies might well make the weaker folk of the con-
gregations think the devil had tricked himself out in a
chasuble to preach to them. Strange how fashion
rules the world !—here in Dublin, to imitate a favourite
preacher who certainly has great merit, the mob of
preachers affect a declamation and gesture more than
theatrical, while at Edinburgh, where Mr. Greenfield,
the favourite minister, has adopted an entirely different
manner, they stand motionless, eyes with a fixed
stare, and articulate a cold sermon in a cold way, so
lifeless and cold indeed, that the pulpit might as
well be occupied by a billet of wood clothed in the
Presbyterian cassock,—in both cases influenced by
the desire to imitate a man admired, with reason,
by the public. The excuse given by Mr. Greenfield
for his immobility is that Nature has so built him
that, if in the course of his sermon his eye caught sight
of anything in the least degree absurd or ridiculous
he could not abstain from bursting into laughter,—
surely one of the most curious reasons ever heard of.
Did any man less gifted offer such an explanation of
his manner he would not be believed. Be that as

it may, there is no reason for the herd to copy him in it at Edinburgh and to out-Herod Herod in the case of Mr. Kirwan at Dublin.

Justice is dispensed here very much in the same manner as in England. The cost of law and, I may add, of medicine is exorbitant—not only are the poor absolutely deprived of the help of the latter, but even those of moderate means cannot afford it. The middle classes can hardly expect to see one of Messieurs, the disciples of Hippocrates, under a guinea or two guineas per visit. However, it must be admitted that doctors often make it a duty to visit, for nothing, folk who cannot pay anything, and among these latter are some very well-educated and respectable persons.

There are also arrangements for facilitating the procuring of justice for the poor, but these means cannot be employed decently except by the man who has nothing at all. It is difficult for the poor pleader to bring his cause to the ear of a judge ; nevertheless, there are examples of poor men obtaining justice, and quickly, but in the main these are cases where rich men have taken their cause and made it their own.

The profession of barrister in the three kingdoms is held to be very honourable, its members well educated and of good families. Whatever may be said of the attorneys they are not such devils as is shadowed forth by their blackness. I have known some very honest and amiable men in this class. Nevertheless, I have been assured that if you must have any transactions with them, whether at London or at Dublin, it is well to say your good-bye in the street, otherwise it will be chalked up against you as a consultation, and they say if you ask one to dinner it may happen that he will charge you for the wear of his teeth.

I have heard of one of these gentlemen who regularly charged his client for having thought about him while at dinner. While I was in Dublin, one of them was asked by a lady in the country to take charge of a letter for her sister in Dublin. Arrived in town he called a carriage, and drove to the lady's house. Not finding her at home he returned, daily, for fifteen days, when, having found the consignee and delivered his letter, he presented a bill for fifteen guineas for his trouble and charges. I should never finish if I started to tell all the stories in circulation about Dublin lawyers. To them one might apply the answer of Lord Chesterfield, when Miss Chardleigh (afterwards Duchess of Kingston) complained to him that people were going about seeking to destroy her reputation by saying that she had brought twins into the world. ' Oh,' said he, ' don't let that bother you. You know that people should only believe half of what they hear.'

It seems to me that in English jurisprudence too much is made of the oath—it appears at every point —and much importance, it appears, is attached to swearing of witnesses, &c. Is it not plain that the unscrupulous man will make very little of charging his conscience with an additional crime, if he thinks he is going to gain anything by it, and the good man has no need for the formality? Here is a little story which illustrates my views in this matter :

Pierre avait emprunté le chaudron
De son voisin Lucas ; puis le trouvant très bon
Ne voulut pas le rendre, et lui chercha querelle !
De propos insultans une longue kyrielle
S'en suivit : après quoi le juge déclara
Qu'il fallait que Pierre jurât
N'avoir pas du voisin emprunté la marmite !
'De tout mon cœur,' s'écria l'hypocrite,
Et, sur le champ en l'air sa dextre il lui montra.
'Mais, méchant,' dit Lucas, 'tu vas perdre ton âme.'
'Toi, ton chaudron,' lui repartit l'infâme.[1]

The Court of the Viceroy at Dublin is nearly as brilliant as that of the King at London, and the castle in which it is held is an ancient structure with an appearance as good at least as that of St. James' Palace. Mr. Burton Conyngham was good enough to present me to Lord Camden, who, having been informed of my plans, believed he could help me much, and urged me to put them at once into execution. Greatly encouraged by this, I set myself seriously to the task, and began to read all the books I could find dealing with the country's history.

If one believes all that is written by these old Irish authors he will find it difficult to imagine that what he reads relates to this island ; the pompous descriptions of the High King and of the numberless kings who composed his Court make it appear that

[1] Peter had borrowed a kettle from his neighbour Lucas. Finding it very useful, he wished to keep it, and set himself to pick a quarrel with the lender. Hence a whole litany of insulting remarks. Peter was called on by the judge to swear to the truth of his statement that he had not borrowed the kettle. 'With all my heart,' he said, and held up his right hand. 'O wicked one,' cried Lucas, 'you are about to lose your soul.' 'And you your kettle,' answered Peter.

the splendour of this Grand Monarch was like that of Alexander after the conquest of Asia.[1]

. . . .

I went one day to a grand review in Phœnix Park. They fired cannon and made the air thick with noises of sorts. For me, I had seen quite too much of stepping and wheeling soldiers, and so I left the sillies to look at them while I reveiwed the ladies who were crowded on the parapet of the garden. There were three yellow bonnets forming a battery much more attractive than that of the General, while nearly as formidable. If I had not the fate of poor Twiss before me, oh what could I not say ! Let it suffice, ladies, to tell you that never was place better than your perch for demonstrating to the whole earth how greatly you were caluminated by the infamous Twiss when he spoke ill of your ——; but I must be discreet.

I was present at the opening of the new dock—the importance of such a considerable work added interest to the pomp and ceremony. The Viceroy's yacht was the first to pass the gates to the sound of volleys of cannon, and when the centre of the dock was reached his lordship knighted, on the vessel, the contractor who had built, and furnished part of the cost of, this superb national work which completes on this side the junction of the canals with the sea.

[1] At this point are omitted several pages of imperfectly digested history dealing with the Tuatha de Danaan, the Milesians, the Danes, and Brian Boromhe's victory over the last-mentioned. Following this account are some pages devoted to the language theory of the author's friend, General Vallancey, who had satisfied himself that the language of ancient Carthage and Irish of its period were alike. The author finishes the tale of his reading with the story of St. Patrick and the venomous beasts. This second-hand matter is of no modern interest.—Tr.

DUBLIN

The Viceroy was afterwards rowed from one end of the dock to the other in an elegant barge, followed and preceded by the acclamations of the people. The enthusiasm of the immense crowd surrounding the basin made me fear that many would be crowded into the water, or, what I should have liked still less, that I should be pushed in myself. In all countries the populace is easily electrified by the sentiment of public joy, especially when there is reasonable motive for it, as on this occasion.

The party spirit, political [1] or religious, has weakened very much of late, and I would dare to hope that in ten years it will have ceased to exist. The Catholic religion has very many more followers than has the dominant, which is indeed only the religion of the rich. All the lower classes all over Ireland, the north excepted, are Catholics. They observe Lent and the fast days with a regularity perfectly horrible to a man who wishes only to fast after the manner of the Scotch. On Holy Saturday, by way of rejoicing, some butchers promenaded the streets bearing a gaily decorated herring, which they belaboured with a stick at every cross-road, while a crowd of children followed them, crying baa, baa, baa, like a flock of sheep.

The common folk call the English shilling a hog, and the sixpence a pig. As the English shilling is worth a halfpenny more than the Irish, a distinguishing title is needed, and so they have given it the name of the commonest and most useful animal to be found in Ireland. The Irish are very friendly with the pig ; he lives on equal footing with the folk in the country, and often when nurses wish to say sweet things to

[1] I speak of Jacobite party spirit.—*Note by Author.*

31

their little brats, they jump them up in their arms, singing ' my dear little pig, pig, pig, sweet little pig,' meaning it as a most endearing expression, somewhat as one of our bourgeois will call his wife ' *mon chou*,' ' *ma poule*,' or ' *mon rat*.'

There is a famous university at Dublin, its chairs almost too richly endowed—a statement which will not find favour with the professors, who number among them some very learned and very agreeable men. Before the Reformation one had probably to be a priest to gain a chair, as the professors were not allowed to marry. By a caprice singular for an old maid, Queen Elizabeth made the same stipulation in the new charter which she granted to the College. Although nearly all the professors are married, they make a show of compliance with the old law, for their wives do not bear their husbands' names.

There is a fine library at the College, well furnished with books and rare manuscripts, many of these in the Irish language. There is also a cabinet of Natural History and one of Anatomical specimens. In this latter is the skeleton of a man the whole of whose joints had ossified, and even a part of his flesh. In this way he lived for years until, at last, the malady attacked the vital parts.

They drink infinitely less in Dublin, and, indeed, all over Ireland, than I could have believed. Generally, in the principal houses, an hour, or perhaps only half an hour, after the ladies have quitted the dining-room, the master of the house pushes his glass to the middle of the table and rises. I am not going to deny that there are such things as drinking parties where one may get straightforwardly drunk ; I have indeed seen a somewhat original example of the outcome of one of these. Returning home one evening I saw a tipsy, rather, I should say, a drunk, man elbow a passer-by, and the latter standing the shock stiffly, the reaction carried the drunkard off his feet. In a fury the incapable arose, seized the man he had jostled by the collar, demanded his name, tendered his own, and insisted on fighting. The assaulted refused, and answered the challenger very coldly. ' I see you're not the man to fight like a gentleman ' said the aggressor. ' Well, I'll box you for sixpence.' The other appeared to consent, and then, as one must strip to box, the tipsy man let go his hold of the collar of his adversary, and the latter immediately slipped through the crowd and disappeared. When the warrior had stripped, he looked for his antagonist, and not finding him he began to swear and shout, ' Where is the lousy rascal ? Where is the lousy rascal ? ' and he went through the crowd asking, ' Are you the lousy rascal ? ' Having exhausted his rage—no one deemed it his duty to answer such a discourteous question—he looked for his clothes and found the shirt had disappeared. For boxing in earnest to be in order bets must be deposited, otherwise the vanquisher must accept responsibility for consequences. But if a bet has been made, you may with safety, and with an easy conscience, punch out the eye or break the jaw of your opponent.

After having seen all that was curious or interesting in Dublin, and having made such arrangements as would ensure the success of my project, I proceeded to put it into execution. Mr. Burton Conyngham was kind enough to procure a passport from the Lord Lieutenant for me, and to give me a number of letters addressed to his friends in the country. He engaged me to communicate results from time to time, and made me promise to begin my promenade from his house in the county of Wicklow. The Commandant-in-Chief, General Cunningham, also gave me a general letter of recommendation, and I fixed on May 25 as the day of my departure.

I intended to start in the forenoon, but I was asked to dinner by a charming family, and pretty women and a good dinner are two things I never could resist.

CHAPTER III

HAVING then definitely made my resolution, my baggage in my pocket, and my stick in my hand, gaily I commenced my voyage. It was a happy thing that I had this stick in my hand, for without it one of the children of St. Patrick would have broken his head on the pavement.

As I was making my way along one of the footpaths, I saw a young boy near me amusing himself by jumping over the iron railings along the way, and jumping back again. In one of these leaps his foot caught on a sharp point of the railings. With such force had he jumped that, if the foot had remained on the spike, his head would certainly have struck the pavement, and with a killing blow. With a sudden and violent blow with the stick from below, I disengaged the foot, just in time, and he fell on his feet. Examining the wound I found that the foot was nearly pierced through. I carried the poor boy to an apothecary's where the wound was bound up, and giving the sufferer a shilling, I told him not to be such a fool another time. My walk, I said to myself, is going to be fortunate, since at the very commence-

35

ment I have saved a young creature's life. I looked
on this incident as a happy omen and pursued my
way.

I stopped at the door of a house to ask my way
from a man on horseback, who was holding a conversation with a friend. When I had proceeded for
about half an hour, the horseman joined me on the way
and called out, ' I am an old soldier, I am going your
way, if a share of my horse suits you it is at your
service.' ' Monsieur,' I answered, ' I am a young
soldier and I am very much obliged to you.' I had
barely finished the words when I was already up behind
him, and we had some interesting chat about the
old wars. It was with great regret that I separated,
later, from this good creature. I have not the slightest
idea of who he was.

I had not taken the trouble to calculate distances
very carefully in starting, and now, late in the evening,
I found myself still eight miles from my destination—
and eight miles Irish count for something. It was
past eleven o'clock when I arrived at the house where
I expected to be received. The doors were locked,
and to my distress I found that the owner, who had
invited me to his house, was not at home. Further,
that there was no inn nearer than four miles distant,
and that on the side of Dublin which I had left. To
go back on my way was a hateful idea—I preferred
rather to go ten miles forward than four back—and so
I went on. At half-past twelve I found myself in a
village, its name unknown to me. Everybody seemed
to be asleep ; however, at the last, I found a cabin
with a light in the window, the dwelling of some poor
labourers who had returned late from the city. I

entered, asked for hospitality, and had placed before
me immediately what was in the house. For rest I
passed the night on a three-legged stool, my back
leaning against the wall. This for the first day of my
travels was not a very agreeable beginning, but I had
to take troubles as they came.

There was no need to wake me in the morning.
At dawn of day all the animals in the cottage, sleeping
pell-mell with their masters, acquainted me with the
fact that the sun was up, and I rose from my stool
and left this unfortunate house of want. How profitable this night would have been to me had I been
always the favoured child of fortune ! I would advise
parents to force their children thus to pass several
nights in their youth ; it would be more advantageous
to them than years at school. Really to have compassion on the poor, and to have a real desire to help
them requires that they should be approached ; the
careless rich, who have never seen the poor near at
hand, think of them with disgust and turn away their
eyes from the sight of poverty.

About four o'clock in the morning I came to the
camp at Bray, and was able at leisure to admire the
good order and even elegance of the barrack arrangements. Excepting a few sentinels no one stirred.
I was scandalised to see the soldiers so lazy while I
was up so early. However, after having made a tour
of the enclosure a number of times, I felt tired, and
sitting down at a little distance at the foot of a tree,
I fell asleep myself. At seven o'clock in the morning
I felt a hand fumbling in my pockets, while a voice
said ' Are you dead, Sir ? ' ' Yes,' I answered, and
the apparition, who must have been none other than

the devil in person, or at any rate some ragamuffin of the camp, fled.

I quitted my hard bed without regret, and being informed that the residence of Mr. Burton Conyngham was not in the immediate neighbourhood, I started for a walk of three miles. I arrived at last at Rochestown, but it was still only half-past eight, and I could scarcely find anyone to speak to. They told me that the master of the house was sick, and that the breakfast hour was eleven o'clock. Patience was evidently necessary; one does not know the value of a good breakfast who has been lying in bed all morning, but after the night I had spent, and a light supper before it, I knew.

Mr. Burton Conyngham I found surrounded by his family and by an army of apothecaries, surgeons, and doctors. I was not allowed even to speak to him. This seemed to me very strange for a simple cold, but I was not otherwise uneasy. When a man is rich, I said to myself, and has a cut finger, his entourage puts on a sad air, and if he has a cold the doctor will gravely fill him with medicines in order to acquire a certain reputation, and to prolong the cough which fortunately fills his pockets. I was wrong, however, in this case, for the malady was mortal. There was nothing for it now but to pursue my way, and crossing the wild mountains which seemed to overhang Dublin, I arrived, after three or four miles of walking, at Enniskerry, where I was received by Mr. Walker, who has made great researches in the matter of Irish antiquities. This little town belongs to Lord Powerscourt. His park and his house are among the greatest curiosities near the capital. It is through this park that the

LA LAGÉNIE OR LEINSTER, ETC.

River Dargle flows in a charming valley to which it
has given its name, a valley of which the inhabitants
are proud with just reason. In this park also is the
Powerscourt waterfall, which strangers come from afar
to view. The mass of water is not very considerable,
and it does not detach itself much from the rock, but
the fall of the water is great, and to me it seemed to
resemble the wind-blown, snowy hair of a venerable
old man. This may not be a remarkably happy
comparison, but it expresses what I felt. The valley
into which it falls is, without contradiction, the most
romantic and the best wooded in all Ireland.

It was spring, the trees were fully covered with new
leafage, the charming verdure invited to repose. I
fell into a dreamy state, and in it was safely delivered of
the following rondeau. It has nothing to do with my
travels, but let that pass :

> À votre aise vous pouvez rire
> Du torment que cause l'amour :
> Vous connaîtrez à votre tour
> Qu'aimer est un cruel martyre
> Quand on n'attend pas de retour.
>
> Il me semble entendre en ce jour
> Pour vos mechants traits de satyre
> Le dieu d'amour, piqué, vous dire
> À votre aise.
>
> De ce dieu, charmante . . .
> Craignez sur vous d'attirer l'ire,
> Aimez, que votre cœur soupire;
> Que pour moi son feu vous inspire
> Et je vous dirai sans détour.
> À votre aise.

I have seen so many beautiful books in which the author has been gracious enough to present his loved one to the public, that I hope I may be excused for this short apostrophe, and that the public will be pleased that I have not lingered longer over the fine qualities, the white skin, the black eyes, and the fingers full of roguishness of my Maria, Lodoïska, or Carolina.

The innkeeper at Enniskerry is a representative of the O'Tooles who owned this territory in the far past, and who lost their lands because they refused to submit to the English yoke. He has taken for sign the arms of the new proprietors.

If ever the exiles return to France, and if their estates are not returned to them, I am certain of this, that it is not on my own lands that I shall become innkeeper.

From the heights above the town one can see one of the singular openings which nature has made at several places in the mountains of this country. The road is carried through these *chasms,* as they are called, as they are the only places at which it is possible to cross the heights without climbing to the top. Returning eastward, nearly over the ground I had traversed, I fell in with a peasant who explained a number of things about the country with a good deal of sense. Generally the inhabitants of County Wicklow are very intelligent, and their country well cultivated, especially near the coasts. The low mountains and the numerous well-built houses give the district a very agreeable aspect.

I came at last to Hollybrook, where I was received by Lord Molesworth, of whose goodness I had already had experience during my sojourn at Dublin. Here laurel, arbutus, holly, and even myrtle abound, although they do not appear to fruit well, the fact being, I suppose, that to ripen berries more heat is required than is provided in this climate.

It was here that there lived Robert Adair, so famous in Scotch and Irish song. I have seen his portrait ; he is the ancestor of Lord Molesworth and of Sir Robert Hodson, to whom Hollybrook belongs. They told me a curious story about him. A Scotch-man, a champion drunkard apparently, having heard of the Bacchic prowess of Robert Adair, came from Scotland expressly to challenge him to drink with him. He had no sooner disembarked at Dublin than he demanded from everybody he met in his Scotch jargon —' Ken ye ane Robin Adair ' ? and in the end he found his man. He demanded a sight of him, and gave his challenge. Robert Adair was actually at table, and offered to begin the contest there and then ; but the Scotchman declined, and invited him to where all was ready at the inn in Bray.

In due time the champions appeared on the field of battle, but after ten bottles the Scotchman fell under the table. Thereupon Robert Adair rang the bell, ordered another bottle, and in presence of the domestics set himself astride the poor Scotchman, in which position he drank off the eleventh bottle without drawing breath, and gave loud huzzas for his victory.

When the Scotchman recovered he returned to his own country, but the story had preceded him, and wherever he went he was met with the mocking question, ' Ken ye ane Robin Adair ? ' And to this his invariable answer was ' I ken the de'il.'

Following the windings of a romantic valley, shut in by steep mountains which were for the greater part clothed with verdure to the summit, I arrived at Bellevue, the home of Mr. Peter Latouche. Madame Latouche holds here a school for twenty-four young girls, who are maintained at her charges. She herself acts as school-mistress. When the girls come of age, she gives them a dowry, and marries them to labourers of good character. This is one of the most noble and most reasonable amusements of the rich that I have ever met with. Nothing in the world is more likely to change the face of a country than a succession of young and virtuous women accustomed to industry and the well-being which attends it.

According to my usual custom I walked a good deal about the neighbourhood, entering into the cabins of the peasants and talking with them. This is the way to find, often, the falsity of certain reputations for benevolence ; but it is also the way to find out the truth about other reputations, which have solid foundation in goodness. Many of the houses here are very clean and well kept, honest industry has brought comfort, and even the peasants who have not been amenable to influence exercised, blessed Providence for having here placed riches in good hands.

There is in the parish church a superb monument in white marble, erected to the memory of David Latouche by his three sons. This David came from France at the time of the Revocation of the Edict of Nantes, and, by continuous industry exerted for forty years, he acquired a very considerable fortune. Although a banker he was humane and charitable. They tell that, in his last days, he never went out without filling his pockets with shillings, which he gave to the poor as he met them. It was represented to him that if he gave to all who asked he was certainly giving to unworthy subjects. ' I know,' he said ; ' but if my shilling falls right once in ten times that is enough.'

The church which contains his monument was built by him. Over the portal is engraved this touching inscription, ' Of Thy own, O my God, do I give unto Thee.'

It was at Bellevue that I received the sad news of the death of Mr. Burton Conyngham. Although I was now at the twelfth day of my march, and had really covered much ground, I was not, at this point, more than seventeen miles from Dublin, and I was much embarrassed as to the course which I ought to pursue. I saw clearly that after this misfortune I should have much labour and fatigue without any advantage to myself ; in the end, however, after full reflection, the idea of the utility of which I believed my project to be susceptible made me set aside any personal considerations, and I determined to pursue my journey vigorously, and leave the rest to Providence. I resolved to present the letters of recommendation which Mr. Burton Conyngham had given me, even although the recipients might look upon them as messages from the other world.

Here I paid my respects to the oldest and biggest tree to be found, not only in Ireland, but I should say in the mountains of Nice or of Provence. It is to be found in the beautiful garden of Mount Kennedy. The body of the tree is at least three feet in diameter, and wind and time having bent it to the ground, it took root in this situation, and has sent out branches of extraordinary size, so that in itself it is a little wood. Leaving here I buried myself in the passes of the arid mountains of the County of Wicklow, and came to Loughilla, one of the houses of Mr. Peter Latouche. One is surprised to find such a house in such a wild and lonely place. The next house to it is at a distance of five or six miles. There are not even peasants' cabins in the neighbourhood. It is seated on a little bit of fertile earth near a beautiful lake, a bit of earth as distinct from the rest of the country as an island is from the water which surrounds it. Following the course of the stream which flows from the lake, I came to Glendalough, a word which means the valley of the two lakes. It is singular that there is not a single ancient name in this country which has not its special signification. The appropriateness here is evident, for there are really two lakes, which join at the portion of the valley called ' The Seven Churches.'

It is here in this desert place that are to be found the most ancient remains of the devotion of past centuries, remains whose antiquity reaches back to the early ages of Christianity. St. Kevin here founded a monastery in the third or fourth century of the Christian era, probably on the ruins of a temple of the Druids, who sought always the wildest places for the practice of their cult. This was for long a bishopric, but now it is united to that of Dublin. Here are still to be seen the ruins of seven churches, and one of those round towers of unknown origin which are so common in Ireland. They are all alike, having a door fifteen or twenty feet from the ground, generally opening east-ward, some narrow windows, and inside not the slightest remains of a staircase, unless this may be found in a few projecting stones which may have served to support floors in which there must have been trap doors to allow of passing from one to another by means of ladders. These towers are always found at some distance from a church, and entirely isolated. The one which is to be seen at Brechin in Scotland is exactly of the same character.

I remember reading in the story of certain travels in the North of Asia a description of similar towers. The traveller, as far as I know, had no knowledge whatever of Ireland; he had escaped from Siberia, where, perforce, he had been living for years, and he reports having seen these extraordinary towers in that part of Tartary which lies to the north-east of the Caspian Sea. He gives a little engraving of one of them, with the ruins which are near, which ruins he says are those of ' a house of prayer near which these towers are always to be found.' If it were not for the dress and faces of the figures appearing in the picture, one would say that the illustration was that of an Irish ruin.

Whatever these ancient buildings may have been, the Irish have now for them the greatest possible veneration. They come here from afar for pilgrimages and penitences, and on the day of the Saint, which is June 3, they dance afterwards and amuse themselves until nightfall. In this sacred enclosure are to be found remedies for many ills. Have you a pain in your arm ?—it suffices to pass the limb through a hole worked in a stone, and you are free from your trouble. There is another stone on which for another ailment you shall rub your back, and another one against which you shall rub your head. And there is a pillar in the middle of the cemetery which, if you can embrace, will make you sure of your wife. The Saint's Bed is a hole about six feet long, hollowed in the rock—a very special virtue belongs to it. It is only to be reached after much trouble in scaling a steep slope of the mountain above the lake, but whoever has enough strength and resolution to climb to it, and will lie down in it, is sure never to die in childbirth. Belief in this virtue makes a great number of wives, and of girls who hope to become wives, come here to pay their devotions.

All this seemed to come in very fitly at the beginning of my travels. I pushed my arm through the hole in the stone. I rubbed my back against the rock which cures the troubles of the back, and my head against another, thus ensuring my health for the remainder of my journey. I even tried to embrace the pillar, but I cannot tell with what result. As to the Saint's Bed, I thought there was little danger of my dying from the malady against which it insures, and therefore I did not climb.

Rathdrum is a little town at some distance from this famous place. It seems to me fairly prosperous, for they make there a prodigious quantity of flannel, and the peasantry seem to be more industrious and more comfortably off than elsewhere. On the first Monday of each month there is held a market, and I am assured that flannel to the value of £4000 sterling is sold on one of these market days. Lord —— (I do not remember his name) has built, at his own charges, a warehouse in which the material can be deposited. He it is who has encouraged this new manufacture. The action does him honour, and in the end it will be advantageous to his estate.

I found the peasantry very curious as to the time of day. Every minute women and children would run from cabins by the wayside to ask the traveller what o'clock it was, perhaps for the pleasure of seeing a watch, or of having a chat.

There is in this neighbourhood a very considerable copper mine. The first expenditure on it amounted to £60,000 sterling before the company had any return whatever. It is at present in a great state of activity, and employs about three hundred workers. The water which is taken from the mine is made to pass over certain metal plates which partly dissolve the copper and hold it. They make use here of a rather ingenious plan for renewing the air in the bottom of the mine. The course of a little stream has been altered so as to make it fall into the opening over faggots of thorn, and the water falling as a fine rain induces a current of air.

The gold mine about which so much noise was made in 1795 is only about six or seven miles from here across the mountains. I had to ask my way to it pretty often, and my questions always seemed to excite the most lively curiosity. Peasants quitted their labours in the fields to answer me, and, in turn, put to me a thousand questions, wishing to know if I were going to work at the mine, if the Government had sent me, &c., &c. ; and they told me how a certain Peter had sent his children to search for gold one Sunday morning after rain, and that they had brought him back more than twenty guineas worth. It is always the case that we hear about the lucky finds, but nothing is said about the many who have lost their time and even their lives in unfruitful searches. There are many workers who have passed days and nights in hard labour without finding anything to reward them for their trouble, and when at last, overcome by fatigue, they have returned to their families, they have died almost immediately.

On my way I came to a rather rapid river of several feet depth, which it was necessary to ford, or make a detour of four or five miles to find a bridge. The weather was warm, and I profited by the occasion to take a bath. A peasant, rather well-clothed, who had been talking to me about the gold mine, was much interested in this matter, and in order to have the pleasure of talking with me longer, he imitated my example, and was good enough to carry my clothes to the other side.

The place where the peasants have dug in search of gold is at the foot of a rather high mountain, called *Cruachan*, in the bed of a stream or rather of a torrent. Apparently the idea did not occur to any of them to dig on the slopes of the mountain, from whence it would seem that the gold had been washed into the stream.

This torrent is called in Irish ' The Golden Stream ' and in English ' The Poor Man's Stream,' and from this it may be gathered that gold had been found long ago.

I had a letter given me by my late friend, Mr. Burton Conyngham, for the officer of the regiment which the Government has placed here to guard the mine, and prevent the peasants from working. He walked over the ground with me several times. The number of holes which the thirst for gold has been the means of digging in this stream is inconceivable—some persons have assured me that they have seen as many as four thousand men at work at once. There is not a single one of these holes from which something has not been taken, although often it was not the worker who profited, but the women and children running about from one to the other who had nothing to do but use their eyes.

The total value of what has been found in this mine is estimated at three or four thousand pounds sterling. The largest piece of gold taken weighed twenty-two ounces, and is supposed to be worth over eighty guineas. It would seem that this piece had been in a state of fusion, and had been carried from the mountain by the torrent, with the stones, peat, and trees which are washed down with the stream. It was attached to a stone, as if it had been melted round it, and the labourer who found it could only detach it by hammering blows. The Government has entirely forbidden any work here for some time ; if they had not done so, all the vagabonds, not only of Ireland, but of England, and perhaps the Continent, would have been here in crowds, and the most of them, finding so much less than they expected, would have finished by ravaging the country for the means to live. There is always a guard of twenty or thirty men at some distance, and a sentinel at the mine to prevent any attempt at digging. As to whether the ground would pay for proper exploitation, nothing is yet known. The Government certainly cannot always maintain a force here, and it is quite certain that as soon as the men are removed the peasantry will return to work. Even if the mine were properly worked, the profit would hardly pay the Government, for I am convinced that the expenses would be more considerable than would be covered by the value of the gold found, unless, indeed, it were possible, as in Peru, to employ slaves.

After having satisfied my curiosity I made a frugal dinner of potatoes and water in the neighbourhood, then turning eastward I came to Arklow, where I was received with great kindness by the Rev. Mr. Bailly, rector of the village He had the good nature to write out for me the following observations about the gold mine, and the large nugget of which I have spoken :

'The gold is found in marshy spots by the side of a small stream, in a gravelly stratum and in the clefts of the rock which lie beneath. It is of all forms and sizes, from the large nugget described down to the smallest perceptible pieces, all bearing the appearance of having been in a state of fusion. When the mud and gravel are carefully washed, they afford a considerable quantity of gold dust. The large nugget is the property of eight poor labourers, who agreed to share in the result of the search.

'The secret of the mine was discovered about eleven or twelve years ago by some poor people in the neighbourhood, who have since occasionally collected considerable quantities. It was not, however, publicly known until the beginning of September 1795 ; from that time several hundreds, sometimes thousands of the country people have been daily employed in the search. It is computed that gold to the value of several thousand pounds has been collected. On October 14 two companies of the Kildare Militia marched into Arklow, and on the following day proceeded to guard the mine on the part of His Majesty.'

The country round the little town of Arklow is very pretty, well wooded, and diversified by mountain and plain. The company working the copper mines has the intention to render the river navigable as far as Rathdrum. It is a work which may be of the greatest utility, but the expenses are so very great that, unless the Government will come to the aid of the company, I do not think it will be possible to proceed. The port of Arklow, besides, is bad : rather, indeed, is it a roadstead, for the shore is flat, and vessels are obliged to remain nearly a mile out at sea and to set sail on the least appearance of bad weather.

Walking in a torrent of rain, and with nothing to protect me from it beyond a piece of waxed cloth which I had bought in Dublin, and which doubtless appeared a strange garment to the inhabitants of the villages through which I passed, I stopped for a moment at Ferns to examine a little round tower near the ruins of the cathedral, and the old castle. The Bishop's Palace here was much larger than the largest town of his bishopric. I accosted a man who appeared to me a good sort of creature, and asked him some questions. Instead of answering, he looked me over from head to foot, and then asked if I had been born in an out-of-the-way corner of the kingdom. As I am always prepared for such questions, I answered, smilingly, in broad Scotch, 'I dinna ken, I dinna mind,' on which he required to know from whence I came and whither I was going. 'I come hence,' I replied, pointing to the north, 'and I gang there,' I continued, pointing to the south. 'I know your

language,' said he, and tapping me on the shoulder
he went on, ' You are a d——d canny Scot. You are
come to this country to make your fortune ; well, well,
we shall hear of you, for you are a d——d lucky set.'
' Ne'er fash, mon,' I replied, smilingly, and after I
had asked my way, he indicated it with good grace.

I used here a little ruse which has often been
serviceable to me in my travels. Indeed, it rarely
fails. Country folk could easily distinguish that I
was a stranger, but they could not fix the nation to
which I belonged, and when I addressed them a few
words in broad Scotch, they always set me down as
a Scotchman.

The Irish are pretty well accustomed to see people
of every class coming from Scotland, and making, by
the end of a few years, a very considerable fortune. It
is really when he is abroad that the character of the
Scotchman is remarkable. It is sufficient that there
should be in a town one of them who has made a little
money, to attract a great number of his compatriots.
They range themselves round the first-comer, and he
pushes them forward, protects them, helps them with
credit, and starts them in the way of well-doing, and
I suppose there is hardly any considerable town in
Europe in which you will not find a Scotchman who
has worked his way into a good position, and others
of his country who have followed, attracted by this
' smell of the roast.' It is all very creditable to them,
and a foreigner who sees them at home has great difficulty in imagining how they can be so attached and
so serviceable to each other far from their native
hearths.

The rain in this country is terrible ; it seems to

penetrate to the bones, and would make you shiver with cold in the middle of summer. Happily, the succeeding wind nearly always dries you. This is what happened to me as I entered Enniscorthy, after having been wet all day as if I had been walking through a river. I did not stop in this town (which is one of some considerable size and with many manufactures) longer than to rest myself, and, this accomplished, I proceeded three miles farther, to Wilton, where the hospitality of Mr. Alcock soon made me forget my fatigue. I found there an old *irrigateur*, who was going from house to house with a plan for watering meadows. The good man was cute enough to exact for his services a guinea per day in addition to food for himself and his horse. He claimed to having been secretary to Pope Ganganelli. Unless a man like this has got a touch of the charlatan about him, it is safe to bet that he will have no success in this country.

From here I proceeded to Wexford, and without wishing it harm, I may say that it is one of the ugliest and dirtiest towns in the whole of Ireland. The excessive exercise in which I had indulged, and to which I had not been accustomed for a long time, compelled me to remain here eight days with a fever ; and to make matters worse, the greater number of the letters I had for this town were those of my dead friend, Mr. Burton Conyngham. However, I received certain attentions. Wexford is situated on a large bay, which at low tide is almost entirely dry. Six or seven thousand acres of ground could here be reclaimed, and there would be an additional advantage of making out of the deepened river an important port. At Wexford I found the longest bridge I had ever seen joining two portions of land. I spent seven minutes walking from one end to the other, and from that I assumed that it is at least one-third of an Irish mile in length. This is a favourite walk with the belles of the neighbourhood. There are chairs on which folk may rest on Sundays, and there is a band which attracts a great many people and makes the promenade agreeable. Fortunes in this neighbourhood appear to be more equally divided than elsewhere; there are not to be found any of those monstrous whales of wealth who devour, for their needs, the produce of a province. On the other hand, there are many people in comfortable circumstances, and none excessively rich. The greater part of the proprietors are descendants of Cromwell's soldiers, but as these were numerous in this part of the country, it was necessary to make their lots smaller in order to give something to everybody.

It was in this neighbourhood that Strongbow disembarked some of his troops to help the King of Leinster, MacDermot, who had been dethroned by his countrymen. We know what was the pretext for the invasion by Henry II, King of England, a little later, and how he compelled the different kings and princes of the island to render homage. Nevertheless, the English had to remain within strictly limited territory for more than three hundred years, and did not make themselves masters of the whole island until the time of Queen Elizabeth. The inhabitants of the Barony of Forth, near Wexford, are the descendants of the first followers of Strongbow. They have never mixed with the Irish, and still speak a singular language, which is more akin to Flemish than to modern English. They are like the Flemish also in manner, and marry among themselves. Their houses are cleaner and more comfortable than those of the other inhabitants, and they are also so much more clean in person that they appear quite as a different race.

In the month of July 1793 the White Boys experienced here a complete defeat, and since that time they have not shown themselves. As a great deal has been said and written about them, I believe it will be of interest if I give a few details about their existence. In every country of the world the peasant pays tithe with reluctance ; everywhere it is regarded as an onerous impost, prejudicial to the spread of cultivation, for the labourer is obliged to pay on the product of his industry. In Ireland it seems to me a more vexatious tax than elsewhere, for the great mass of the people being Catholic, it seems to them hard that they should be obliged to maintain a minister who is often the only Protestant in the parish, and who exacts his dues with rigour. Beyond the ordinary tithe he has a right, over nearly the whole of Ireland, to one-tenth of the milk of a cow, one-tenth of the eggs, and one-tenth of the vegetables of the gardens. One can easily understand that these conditions may be very severe when the minister exacts his dues in kind, and especially when it is considered that these poor miserable folk have, as well, to supply a subsistence for their own priests. They have often made complaints and claims in connection with this subject, and to these it was hardly possible to give attention without overturning the whole of the laws of the Establishment, as it is called ; that is to say, the Established religion. From complaints and claims the peasants came to threats, and from threats to the execution of the things threatened. They assembled at night in great numbers in certain parts of Ireland, and in order that they might recognise each other safely, they wore their shirts outside their clothes, from whence came the name of White Boys. In this garb they overran the country, breaking the doors and gates of ministers' houses, and if they could catch the cattle they mutilated them by cutting off their tails and ears. All the time they did no other violent act, and a traveller might have gone through the country with perfect security. For different offences of the kind indicated the magistrates of Wexford arrested a score or so of the culprits, and immured them in the town prison. Their comrades demanded their liberation, and were not able to obtain it. They threatened then to come and free them by force, and advanced on the town to the number of two or three thousand. There were at the time no troops at Wexford ; all that could be gathered up did not number more than one hundred or one hundred and fifty soldiers, who marched to meet the country folk.

On their way to the town the White Boys arrested an officer who happened to be on the road, and sent a messenger to the Major that this officer would answer with his head for the surety of their comrades in jail. This caused much uneasiness in Wexford, where it was feared that they would carry their threat to execution. The Major in charge imprudently advanced before his soldiers in order to speak with the White Boys, and after some lively discussions, he received a blow from a scythe which laid him dead. Immediately on seeing this the soldiers fired, and in two or three minutes the whole force of the White Boys was broken up and put

to flight, leaving behind them several hundreds dead.
A few of the unfortunates who were wounded, fearing
the punishment which would follow if they should be
taken, dragged themselves as well as they could into
the corn-fields and hedges, and there perished miserably.

After this battle nothing has been heard of the
rebellious peasants, and the country has been quiet.
This revolt appears to me to be in little, a perfect
parallel to the Revolution in France in its beginnings.
I imagine that if, on the approach of these 3000 men,
the Wexford authorities had given up their prisoners—
and that might have been expected, since they had
only 150 soldiers to oppose the countrymen—the pre-
tensions of the White Boys would have been greatly
augmented. They would have proceeded to impose
their wishes on the country, and perhaps to put the
magistrates in prison, and if only the Government
had left them alone for three weeks or a month, or
had temporised, or parleyed with them, instead of
3000 they would have numbered 30,000, and in all
probability they would have destroyed the Government
from which they had, at the beginning, asked favours.

I found here a French family who have been living
in Wexford for five or six years. It appears that a
vessel leaving Brittany in 1791 was obliged by force
of bad weather to disembark her cargo at Wexford.
There were twenty or thirty passengers on board, of
whom the greater part dispersed immediately. There
remained at Wexford only a lady and her three
daughters and her father, an aged man, with another
daughter. By the end of two years their resources were
entirely exhausted, and the inhabitants subscribed

a sum to help them ; this was enough to carry them on for three years longer, although miserably enough. Now, one of the daughters is married to a young man of the town, whose affairs seem to be fairly prosperous.

I would not mention this little detail if the old man I had mentioned had not been the occasion of a trait of gratitude which does honour to human nature. Some English prisoners were dying of hunger and misery in the reign of Robespierre in a little town in Brittany. An old lady, touched by compassion, succeeded at the peril of her own life in helping them, and later in giving them money to help them to make their escape. They asked her how they could show their gratitude for her goodness. Her reply was 'I have a relative at Wexford. He is an *émigré*. That will let you know what his situation must be. Will you please carry this letter to him or arrange that he shall get it, and if you can do anything for him, I shall be obliged.' They had no sooner left France when they made inquiries at Wexford whether such a person as their benefactor described were still in existence. Very soon after, the old man received, from Lisbon, a very honourable letter from a merchant named MacGibbon, who, in acknowledging his obligations to Mademoiselle —— in Brittany, begged him to accept a bank-draft for twenty guineas. The old man also received another letter, which I have seen. It was from an English officer named Yescombe, promising a pension of twenty-four pounds per annum until the exile could be restored to his estates, and paying the first quarter in advance. On hearing of such acts the heart dilates, and one is glad to .find gratitude and benevolence in man without the balderdash of fine language used by the common run of benefactors, who are often more affected by self-love and the desire for praise than by desire to help another.

I have so often met these amiable gentlemen, and I have been their dupe so often, that I am nearly always tempted to treat very haughtily a man who offers me his patronage or protection. One day an individual of this type made me certain offers of service, to which I responded politely but rather coldly. 'It seems to me,' said he, 'that you do not believe what I say.' After a few moments of tergiversation, as he insisted, I answered, 'No, certainly I do not believe you. If you do me the services of which you speak, I shall be very grateful; but if, as so many others, you forget me the moment I am out of your sight, then, pray, allow me to take my way without troubling you.'

While I was at Wexford, a republican corsair had the impudence to come to the entry of the bay and to lay the vessels departing under contribution, afterwards making its escape. I thought it well to make mine, and travelled a dozen miles to Golph-bridge to the house of a rich Quaker, at which I arrived wet and dirty. But these kind folks gave me an exceedingly hearty welcome. Among other things they lent me a riding coat in which I appeared at table. It would have covered three persons such as I, and I am quite sure its amplitude affected one of the Quakers of the house, for he cut fully half the roast beef and put it on my plate, saying, 'Friend, thou ought to fill thy belly.' I noticed that they said no grace before or after dinner, only that the good wife rested for a few minutes with her head bent over her plate, sighing a little. Afterwards she said to me that 'We believe it better to think without saying rather than say without thinking.' In the morning a pretty young girl of the house said to me with much charm and grace, 'Friend, hast thou slept well?' And I verily believe that if the damsel had said to me the night before, in the same gracious tone, 'Friend, sleep well,' I would have lain awake the whole night.

CHAPTER IV

In my travelling I came to a place called Passage.
It is a little town where one crosses the river Suir below
Waterford, and there I visited the new Geneva. It
is a large *caserne* which was built by the Genevese
to whom the Government had given shelter and protection. In one of the perpetual revolutions of their
country some artizans had been so disgusted with the
new administration that they quitted the Republic
and came to establish themselves near Waterford,
where they had obtained permission to build a town,
the Government assisting in the expense. Afterwards
they asked for privileges which would have placed
them in nearly the same position in which they were
on the Continent. They were perhaps rather turbulent
friends of their benefactors in Ireland, but, on the other
hand, their industry might have been of great use to
the country. While the question of these privileges
was being discussed, they learned that a new revolution
at Geneva had placed their friends in position of
power, and immediately they left their new town
and hurried back.

The Government endeavoured to make some use
of the buildings they had left behind them, and turned

these into a *caserne*, whose isolated situation must make it rather a disagreeable one for the officers.

Moving farther south I stopped at Tramore, which is one of the places in Ireland most frequented by the idle folk who assemble by the sea for bathing. There, at the time, was a very numerous company, and charming ease and abandon. The sand is excellent for bathing. To vessels, however, which have the misfortune to be thrown on it, it is very different—they are inevitably lost.

At a short distance, a little stream which flows into the sea opens a passage for the waves to the interior of estates where the salt water covers, at high tide, three or four thousand acres of good ground. I am convinced that £2000 sterling, well used, would be sufficient for the construction of a dyke or lock or water-trap, which would save for agriculture the whole of this vast area.

At last I arrived at Waterford, fairly tired with my long walk. I have already made some observations about this town, and I can only repeat what I have already said on the subject of ship-building yards and sheds on the quays ; and, what may seem singular, this is the only thing in connection with the municipal administration here about which it is possible to say anything by way of fault-finding, for the police seem to be, here, infinitely better than in most other towns in this country. There seems to be in this town a care for the public weal which I have not found elsewhere. The markets are well supplied, and beggars and tramps were not allowed to show themselves in the streets long before the arrival of Count Rumford, for whom I had the pleasure to be taken when I visited the

House of Industry. I was really astonished to find that everybody was alert to please me, running here and there, sweeping and polishing. I allowed them to go on and gave them great praise for their activity, but when, later, the care-taker, having conducted me into his private office, and submitted his accounts which I complacently examined, asked at what hour would I desire the Council of Administration to assemble to meet me, and when he told me that the Government had given orders that my directions were to be followed, it seemed to me desirable to ask to see this order, and when I saw it I found it was for Count Rumford.[1]

I am sure he would have been as satisfied as I was with the order which reigned in the hospital, which is maintained by subscription and, in part, by a small endowment. There are quarters for the weak-minded, and this is a matter of great importance, for one of the most painful spectacles to be seen in nearly

[1] Count Rumford is an Englishman and has been employed by the Elector Palatine for the maintenance of good order and the suppression of begging in his territory. He has shown much talent in the execution of these interesting projects, and in the short space of five or six years it seems he has succeeded in making the poor disgusted with a life of mendicancy, and has accustomed them so to work that there is no longer any need for compulsion in bringing them to the industrial establishments he has founded, and where they are clothed and lodged in return for their labour.

The spirit of economy there exhibited had apparently attracted the attention of the Irish Government, who consulted Count Rumford. The advice he gave has already produced happy effects, but, as I believe that begging in Ireland is not so much the product of indolence as of other more serious causes, his efforts will perhaps not succeed so completely as might be desired until these serious causes have been removed. Count Rumford has also invented a method by which the cost of heating is much diminished, and which does away with smoky chimneys. It consists principally in the contraction of the chimney close to the hearth, thereby augmenting the current of air.—*Note by Author.*

all the principal towns in Ireland is the number of weak-minded people in the streets. The famous Dean Swift was the first who built at his own charges a house in Dublin for these stricken ones. It would almost seem that his action indicated a sort of presentiment, for in his old age he was unfortunate enough to lose his reason, and came to be sheltered and cared for in the house which he himself had built.

The spirit of industry and commerce seems to me to be more active at Waterford than in any other Irish town, more active even than at Cork, although the size of the town is much less.

The Mayor of Waterford has the right to have carried before him a sword, even in presence of the Viceroy. The royal patents accorded to the town dispense with the necessity for laying it at the Viceroy's feet, and reserve this privilege to the Mayor alone.

I was introduced one day, by a lady of my acquaintance, to a rather grand assembly. The gentlemen were still at table drinking, and I was at first charmed, and afterwards much embarrassed, to find myself the only man in a circle of fifty pretty ladies, of whom I did not know a single one except the lady who introduced me. Up to that time I had always admired the rôle of Grand Seigneur, but that is all past and done with. True, if there had been a handkerchief to drop, I might have felt otherwise, but here not being able, unfortunately, to get a single response other than ' yes ' or ' no ' to a question, I was glad, at last, to be seated at a whist table, at which I was rather fortunate, for I won twelve or fifteen games. Next day another lady was kind enough to introduce me to another assembly, but this time they were the grandmamas of society, with rich mantles of black velvet, toothless, deaf, blind and grumbling. They made me play; I lost, and decamped as quickly as possible.

The same evening, during the act of a comedy in the theatre, I was a witness of one of those scenes which are exhibited too often in the towns of Great Britain. The public demanded the air of 'God save the King,' and, according to custom, obliged all the actors who had appeared in the piece to present themselves and sing in chorus. Shouts of 'Off with the hats' were directed with singular fury against those who had forgotten to uncover. A good creature who had been so much interested in the play that he had fallen asleep was unmoved by the cries until a soldier came and gave him a sound blow on the side of the head, at the same time pulling his hat off and throwing it into the pit. The poor devil, who was perhaps in the middle of a beautiful dream, was much surprised to be awakened in this fashion, and commenced to howl in a frightful manner to the inexpressible joy of the pit and stalls.

I must admit that this act of violence seemed to be too much like what I have seen on the Continent to allow me to laugh at it. Why should politics be mixed up with public amusements? And in this case, after having had, already, this favourite air, which I admire as much as anybody, why should the scenes be interrupted and the theatrical illusion entirely destroyed in forcing all the actors of a piece to appear at once and in the costumes proper to the rôles of the play? If this expression of opinion should displease anyone, I shall be sorry; it is far from my intention. I agree that, when one is in a public place, one must conform to the general taste or custom. I would indeed look upon it as an act of folly not to conform. All the same, if the public taste or custom was in favour of peace and quietness it would please me much better.

I had two letters from Mr. Burton Conyngham addressed to persons in the neighbourhood of this town. I thought it my duty to write to the Marquis of Waterford, telling him that I had a letter for him, given me by his late respected friend, and I desired to know when I could have the honour to present it. The Marquis replied, politely, that he would expect me two or three days later to breakfast. I thanked him for his politeness, and said that my manner of travelling did not permit me to make a journey of ten or twelve Irish miles before breakfast, and that I would do myself the pleasure of seeing him during the day. In the interval I presented my two letters to Mr. Cornelius Bolton and with him I passed some time very agreeably. It is only rarely that I make any mention of my experiences with the different persons to whom I have been introduced, and then only when I think the narration may be useful, and have the effect of encouraging the good. In this case I report the fact simply.

Mr. Cornelius Bolton lives a very retired life in the country, and has used a considerable part of his fortune to build a fairly large village, in which he has established weaving and other industries. The success which has attended his efforts makes it possible to predict that his charges will be repaid, and the industries will be, not only of public benefit, but a profit to him who established them from purely humane motives.

I returned to the town by the river, the banks of which are well cultivated and very romantic, and I started to walk to Curraghmore, where I arrived tired and breathless about four o'clock. I sent in my letter to the Marquis of Waterford, and, having been received by him very civilly, I asked permission after a few minutes' conversation to retire in order to dress. It was then explained to me that, while dinner would be willingly given, it would not be possible to give me a bed. That embarrassed me a little, as I had not the slightest notion where I could pass the night, but in the end I left the matter to the care of Providence, as is my usual custom.

The Marquis made me sit near him and treated me with singular politeness. He offered me his carriage, in order to conduct me to the inn ; his house, he said, was full ; he was very sorry, &c. &c. I thanked him for his offer, but declined it, and he then ordered a man to go with me and carry my parcel, which contained nothing other than the clothes which I carry with me. His son even offered me, in parting, another commodity which I absolutely refused, saying that I should be very sorry indeed to be a charge to the friends of the late Mr. Burton Conyngham. After having plunged through the mud in pumps and white silk stockings for two or three miles, I arrived at the inn at about half-past ten o'clock. I knocked and asked for a bed, and was told, rudely, by an ugly looking domestic that I could not have one. I snatched my package from the hands of my lord's servant, saying to report to his master that I had been refused a bed at his inn, and I started off at once at high speed. At the name of the Marquis everybody seemed to be turned upside down. They ran after me, begging me to return. ' I would rather pass the night in Hell,' I said, and promptly consigned them to the inhabitants of that place.

Behind a sheltered wall I put on my travelling clothes, with the intention of walking to Waterford, although it was already eleven o'clock at night. This stoppage gave me time to reflect, and to find that I was already fatigued. I thought it well, in the end, to return to the village and try to get lodging in some other house than the inn. On the way I met the priest of the parish, and explained to him my unfortunate position. My foreign accent determined him, charitably, to leave me to my own devices. This village resembles that to which, according to the fable, Jupiter and Mercury came seeking hospitality and finding their request refused at every door. Like them, in the end, I had to leave the village, and I perceived on the road, in the corner of a ditch, a miserable cabin, the horrible shelter of abjectest poverty. I knocked, and an old woman, another Baucis, clothed in rags, opened the door. I told her that I was a poor traveller who had lost his way, and was tired. She immediately asked me to come in and offered me all that her house afforded—a few potatoes, part of the alms she had received during the day.

Half a dozen nearly naked children were lying on heaps of straw, pell-mell with a pig, a dog, a cat, two hens, and a duck. Never in my life had I seen such a hideous spectacle. The poor woman told me that her husband was a sailor, that he had gone to sea three years ago, and that she had not heard a word from him since.

She spread a mat on a box, the only piece of furniture in the house, and invited me to rest on it. The rain was falling in torrents, I knew not where to go, and I accepted the offer and placed myself on this hard bed of misfortune. The animals saluted, with loud cries, the first rays of the sun, and immediately began to hunt through the apartment for something to satisfy their devouring hunger.

The novelty of the situation was so singular as to amuse me for a moment, and after I felt as if transported to the ark, and believed myself to be Noah.

I must have appeared as extraordinary to the poor beasts as they appeared to me. The dog came and smelt me all over, showing his teeth ; the pig examined me, grumbling the while ; the hens and the duck devoured my powder puff ; the children laughed ; and I made haste to decamp before I should be myself devoured. I should add that I had a great deal of trouble to get my poor hostess to accept a miserable shilling.

My intention was at first to go to Carrick-on-Suir and Clonmel, and even to push on to Mallow, these three towns being situated in a most beautiful and fertile country. The last is especially favoured, for, in addition to other attractions, there are mineral waters which are esteemed, and which draw numerous visitors. I intended to return from there to Lismore, but, disgusted with the world, I preferred to bury myself in a wild and rarely visited country. After two hours' walk I felt that I needed breakfast, and without much ceremony I entered the house of some peasants who appeared to be fairly well off. I said simply that I wished to have something to eat, and would pay whatever was proper. These good folk, I am assured, took me for an escaped French prisoner. They con-

ducted me to a rather dark room and brought me what
I wanted with the appearance of mystery. When
I had finished, I asked what I owed, but I could not
get them to mention any sum, and therefore I left
some silver on the table. I had hardly proceeded
a hundred yards when I heard one of the daughters
running, and calling to me. She brought the money
which I had left on the table, saying that her mother
was 'quite affronted.' 'I am very sorry indeed,' I
replied, 'it was far from my intention. I am much
obliged to your mother, but I hope you will allow me the
pleasure of presenting the money to yourself. It will
buy a ribbon.' She made a little grimace, dropped a
curtsey, put the money in her pocket, and wished me
a good journey. After many turns and circuits of a
winding way through this poor country I arrived at
Kilmacthomas, which is a rather large town, where I
dined. And here, too, I discovered that I had left the
cabin which sheltered me in the night with some rather
unpleasant companions. There was no remedy at
hand, and so I made an effort and completed twenty-two
Irish miles in the day, and arrived in the evening, very
tired, at Dungarvan, where the first thing I did was to
go and drown in the sea the good friends of Curraghmore who had become attached to my person, and
then retiring, I slept until noon the next day, by
which time my strength had returned, and with it my
ordinary good humour.

Dungarvan is a little town rather well situated on
a large bay, which unfortunately is filled with sand. It
is hardly anything beyond a place for sea-bathers.
Although I was hardly quite recovered from my long
walk of the day before, and the bad night which had

preceded it, I thought it better, as I knew no one in
the place, to leave in the afternoon. I was able to
cover eight or nine miles and reached Caperquin,[1] which
is very prettily situated on the river called the Blackwater. This river crosses the island nearly the whole
way from east to west, and in part of its course waters
a most beautiful country.

In the morning I was surprised to see the host of the
inn in which I had passed the night, seated tranquilly
in an apothecary's shop, which was on the ground
floor of the same building.

'You are an apothecary,' I said.

'Yes, sir, at your service.'

'D——n your service. I am not surprised if you
have poisoned me. If I had known yesterday I would
rather have been d——d than enter your house.'

I give this as an example among a thousand. What
an appetising idea to find an innkeeper an apothecary!
The cuisine of an apothecary! . . .

I came to Lismore on the Blackwater. Its old
castle covered with ivy, and situated on an eminence
upon the river, is a very striking sight. This is one of
the most agreeably situated towns in Ireland ; it is
surrounded by woods and charming walks, but it is
almost entirely in a state of ruin at present. It seems
that there were here before the Reformation various
colleges and seminaries. These no longer exist, only
the great Cathedral Church remains. The Bishop, who
is also Bishop of Waterford, the Dean, and two or
three other ecclesiastics of the English Church have
nothing else to do than lift the income from the estates
which are set aside for their maintenance.

[1] Cappoquin.

71

The Duke of Devonshire, to whom the castle belongs, and who has, in this neighbourhood, an estate which may be worth twelve to fifteen thousand pounds sterling per annum, has just built at his own charges a large inn and a superb bridge of a single arch, in order to make the inhabitants accept, patiently, his absenteeism, and keep them from grumbling too much about sending their rents. The arch is really magnificent. It rises about twenty feet above the level of the river and is about one hundred feet wide. At the risk of tumbling into the water I went below, and crept along a string course giving a foothold only of two or three inches. I wanted to hear the echo which will, very distinctly, repeat a word of one syllable seven times, and for a good quarter of an hour I tested it with 'What, What, What' to my great satisfaction. There was a man standing near who examined me with as much attention as I had given to the scrutiny of the bridge, and doubtless I appeared to him as a very strange being. To put him out of doubt I addressed him in broad Scotch. 'That's a muckle braw brig, mon,' I said. 'Yes, Mr. Scot,' he replied. 'Have you got such a one in your country?'

Here I was received by Dr. Power, at whose house I was very glad to rest. On Sunday morning I attended the Catholic Church and could hardly find room to stand, both church and cemetery round it being full of people. When the service was over I went to the Protestant Church, where I was able to seat myself at my ease in one of the Canon stalls. They have preserved in the Irish cathedrals the stalls of the Canons, with the titles of their benefices, although there are no dignitaries other than the Dean. I directed my course now to Castle Lyons, and in the middle of the way, finding myself thirsty and seeing no inn, I asked my way of an old man—an old soldier—who was standing on a terrace near his house, and at the same time I told him my needs. 'Come in, young man,' he said, 'you shall have a good drink,' and a good drink I had. The castle of Castle Lyons was a large square building which was burnt about thirty years ago. It had 365 windows, and was then the principal residence of Lord Barrymore. There does not seem to be the least industry or manufacture in the little town—everything languishes and has a miserable air. Rathcormick is a little better, because it is on the main road from Dublin to Cork. The nearer one approaches to the latter town, the more the country takes on a neglected look. I was able to see it at my ease rather more than usual, having been offered a seat on a carriage by the conductor, who wanted to have the pleasure of talking to someone. I arrived at Cork, the dullest and dirtiest town which can be imagined. The people met with are yawning, and one is stopped every minute by funerals, or hideous troops of beggars, or pigs which run the streets in hundreds, and yet this town is one of the richest and most commercial of Europe. The principal merchants are nearly all foreigners, Scotch for the most part, and in the short period of ten years are able sometimes to make large fortunes.

There is no town where there is so much needful to do to make the place agreeable to a great number of the poor inhabitants. The spirit of commerce and self-interest has laid hold of all branches of the administration. For example, it would be very easy to furnish the town with a public fountain, but the person or company which has the privilege of bringing water in pipes to the houses thinks that by the building of such a fountain there would be lost a number of guinea subscriptions. Therefore, in order that the avidity of an obscure individual should be satisfied, thirty thousand inhabitants must suffer the punishment of Tantalus. I have seen poor people obliged to collect the water falling from the roofs on a rainy day, or to take it even from the stream in the streets. All the time there is perhaps hardly a place which it would be so easy to supply with water as Cork, by reason of the heights which surround it. There is even a spring or fountain about a mile away, which is called Sunday's Well, which appears to me to have sufficient water for the supply of a public fountain in the centre of the town. The water supply for private houses is drawn from the bed of the river a mile above the town. Why should it be so difficult to do for the public what interest has done for the richer classes ?

The dirt of the streets in the middle of the town is shameful, and as if that were not enough, it would seem as if it were wished to hinder the wind and the sun from drying the filth, for the two ends of the street are terminated by prisons, which close the way entirely and prevent the air from circulating.

The grain market in a town of such considerable size ought naturally to be much frequented. Actually it has been placed on the first floor of a building, and the crowd can only reach it by a stairway two or three feet wide, exposed to all weathers; and to make matters worse, the steps are so much worn that they are slippery and dangerous. One would imagine that there should be nobody allowed on this stairway excepting those who come to or go from the market ; but the most disgusting beggars have taken possession of the wall-side and assail the passers-by with their cries, while presenting a porringer or bag in which they are nearly obliged to throw a handful of meal. I have seen a poor woman fall the whole length of the stairs, upsetting nearly everyone on them, and breaking her own arm.

The meat market is the only one which is as it ought to be. It is new, and it is to be hoped that the magistrates will, in the end, think of the other places where the public must congregate.

Although the people are very poor, nothing or no one can persuade the mothers to send their children to the poorhouse or almshouse. They are afraid that they would be sent away to other places—a thing which formerly did happen, but a less cruel system is observed now. The mothers wish that their children should not be brought up in the Protestant religion, which is professed in these establishments. A frequent sight is one of these poor unfortunates with two children on her back and another in her apron, holding another by the hand, and beseeching for the cold charity of the passers-by, who being accustomed to such sights generally turn away their eyes. The poor woman, however, also accustomed to such indifference, consoles herself by smoking a black pipe, so short that the fire almost seems to be in her mouth.

The rich people accuse the poor of being content to live in dirt and to sleep with their cattle. They like it no better than their rich brethren and sisters ; necessity, cruel necessity, is the reason for their manner of life. Their misery is such that they become indifferent to decencies. Let them be furnished with the means of changing this life. Let them be put in a position to cultivate the decencies, and know some of the comforts of life, and it will be seen how unjust are the accusations which have been made.

The peasant is idle here; but of what use would activity be to him? The price of his day's work hardly suffices to maintain him and his family. Costs of various food commodities have been multiplied by three, and yet the price of labour remains the same. Over nearly the whole of Ireland the labourer earns only sixpence a day; his wife and his children are hopeless about doing anything in a country where there are no manufactures. What can, then, such an unfortunate family do? The sixpence suffices only to furnish potatoes and water. Should the father fall sick or die, the poor mother is obliged to quit the country with her children and wander, begging a horrible subsistence. Cursed be the cruel man who first dared to make game of the misery of his fellow. It is one of the shocking artifices of the avaricious, for immediately when we have come to laugh at the ills of others, we feel ourselves freed from any necessity to help them.

I visited the Cove which is the port of Cork, ten or twelve miles lower down at the mouth of the river—it is one of the prettiest bays and one of the safest in Europe. There I was well and kindly received by the brave General Vallencey, to whom I presented the last letter I possessed of Mr. Burton Conyngham. The researches of the General in Irish antiquities are known through the whole literary world; perhaps he has pushed a little too far his enthusiasm for the Irish language, in which (although an Englishman) he has made surprising progress. He asserts, or pretends to believe, that it is as old as the world, and is perhaps the same which Adam and Eve made use of in the Garden of Eden, the general mother of all languages of the universe from the Huron to the Chinese. He quotes in his grammar singular examples of its agreement with about thirty living languages in all parts of the world.

It is certain that all the nations of Europe, the greater part of those of Asia and even of Africa, have had origin in the country from whence came the Irish. It may be that the isolated situation of these people has facilitated the preservation in its purity of the ancient language of their country of origin.[1]

General Vallencey has travelled over Ireland for fifteen years, and has made surveys for maps of the different counties. The Government in the end, as a reward for his labours, has given him the post which he occupies at the moment, that of Commandant of the Port of Cove, which is now so strongly fortified that there is no danger that any hostile vessel can enter. It cannot be denied that he is a man of value to the State in more than one way, seeing that he has twelve children of a first marriage, ten of a second, and twenty-one of a third. There are very few men who have done their duty so well.

I presented my respects to Lady Colthurst, an amiable widow, and much too pretty to remain one for long. The General, to whom I showed the letters in my possession, planned my course towards the north,

---

[1] At this point are omitted various notes connected with General Vallencey's speculations about the language of Carthage and its affinity to Irish.—Tr.

making it unnecessary for me to return immediately to Cork.

I walked the whole length of the island of Cove, and, fatigued, I sat myself down to rest in a graveyard, amusing myself by reading the epitaphs. I had often heard of Irish ' bulls,' but had not been fortunate in finding one, and there I found on a tomb, on which, after the names of the family, I read with pleasure, ' Lord, have mercy on the souls *here* interred.' And so, I said to myself, these good folk have buried under this stone both soul and body. Over nearly the whole of Ireland, but more particularly in the south, I find a peculiar manner of expression which, as far as I can judge, comes from a mixture of the two languages, and this manner accounts for the ' bull ' or stupidity. The mistakes are not any greater than those made by a person speaking a language which is not his own. Here they commonly call the fosse *dyke*, the name which is given to the wall in England ; and here they call the wall *ditch*, which is the name there given to the fosse.

Passing Inchiquin, the spot from which one has the finest view of the bay, I came to Castle Mary, belonging to Lord Longueville, and saw in his park a Druid's altar. This was a large one, twenty or thirty feet long by about fifteen wide, supported on three large stones. One is astonished in reflecting on the power or apparatus that was necessary to lift such weights. These great stones prove that the people who placed them knew something of mechanical science, and consequently must have attained a high degree of civilisation. As to the use to which they put these stones there are doubts. Some say that the Druids offered on them human

78

sacrifices, which may be true, but it is perhaps enough to say that they would serve on all occasions when the priests judged it necessary to expose any object to the view of the people. From here I went to Cloyne, and there attended a service of benediction which the Bishop bestowed on his clergy on the Sunday after the service. Near the cathedral is one of those round towers of which I have spoken. It is higher and bigger than the ordinary type. The peasants of the neighbourhood are persuaded that it was built by the devil in a single night, and that he brought the stones for it from a far country. I saw no difference between the stones of the tower and those at hand. All I can say is that if the devil built it, the devil is a good mason.

Cloyne is one of the principal bishoprics in Ireland in point of income. The episcopal town, however, is a little place, but rather larger than that of Ferns. Following the crowd of peasants going to mass, I took the road to Castle Martyr, and, at some distance from this pretty little town, I met a man of very respectable appearance riding on horseback and accompanied by a lady. I had a shrewd guess as to who this should be, and, by inquiring from a servant, I found that I was correct in supposing the gentleman to be Lord Shannon. I asked the domestic to say that a foreigner who had a letter for his lordship desired to speak with him. My letter was delivered on the king's highway, and, after it was read, his lordship asked me to continue my road to his house, where he would join me soon.

Castle Martyr is one of the most beautiful and one of the best cared-for places, not merely in Ireland, but, perhaps, in Europe. The garden, which Lady

Shannon finds pleasure in cultivating, is a charming retreat where flowers of every species are arranged with singular skill. I spent five or six days here, and, on leaving, Lord Shannon was good enough to give me an extremely flattering general letter of recommendation. It was addressed only to his friends, but I have since shown it, practically, to everybody, and the manner in which it has been received is a testimony to the esteem in which his lordship is held by the public. Returning towards Cork I stopped at Middleton to see a large cloth manufactory. It is an entirely new manufacture in this part of Ireland, and has had a great many difficulties to surmount before attaining its present success. It is, however, not altogether as great as might be desired. Several persons in Cork have assured me that if this company could borrow £20,000 sterling for ten years, without interest, it would certainly become a very flourishing industry; but who is going to lend £20,000 without interest? Only the Government could do it, and there is a simple way of doing it. This would be to put a heavy tax on whisky, and to put the resulting revenue in the hands of manufacturers. This would produce two desirable effects at once : it would encourage industry, and arrest the progress of drunkenness.

I spent some time in the island of Foaty with a spoiled child of fortune, Mr. Smith Barry. He has travelled much, is very courteous and reasonable, appears to be well educated, is good natured, and would be happy if he had only £500 a year instead of £25,000 ; but his riches have so surfeited him and disgusted him with the world that he has almost totally retired from society, and lives a rather melancholy life

in his island, which is not the island of Calypso.
Calling at the little island of Cove, I introduced myself
to Mr. Silver Oliver, a gentleman who has given hospitality for a long time to an old, exiled French officer,
who is treated as one of the house, and with much
kindness. Mr. Oliver asserts that he has fulfilled all
the duties that society can reasonably require from a
man. He has been Member of Parliament two or
three times, he has been Privy Councillor, he has been
married, he has several children, &c., &c., and consequently he has a right to live according to his fancies,
and these are sometimes rather original. I returned
to Cork by the river, and had opportunity to observe
that the boatmen here are very much of the bantering
type we know on the great rivers of France. Necessity
obliged me to return to this City of Yawns. This
time, however, the people appeared to be animated,
and bands of workers marched through the streets
shouting. I asked what was the reason for the row,
and was told that the apprentice-shoemakers had,
by common accord, struck work, in order to force their
masters to increase their wages. I followed them and
saw them stop at different times before the houses of
master-shoemakers, and have some warm exchanges
of words with them. At last the magistrates inter-
fered, and one of them at the head of some soldiers
promenaded the streets, endeavouring to disperse the
discontented apprentices ; but these only made fun
of him, and arranged matters so cleverly that he was
always in the place where they were not. Night,
as in England, made the tumult cease and sent everyone home to bed.

I had a recommendation to the Bishop, who received

me very kindly, and this gave me great pleasure, for I think it proves that all animosities between the two religions are at an end. He sent me to the Catholic Bishop, Dr. Moylan, who is an educated man, and much respected in the country.

On the occasion of I know not what fête the children made a fire of bones (which is a common practice all over Ireland on days of rejoicing), and they amuse themselves by dancing around the fire and even by running over it with their bare feet. This gave me occasion to make some reflections on the etymology of *bone fire* in England, which term seems to me to come from this fire of bones, rather than from the forced French of *bon feu* or *feu de joie*.

The climate of Cork is rainy in the extreme. It rains every day in life, and the temperature of the air has perhaps influenced the character of the inhabitants. It would not be incorrect to call this country ' The Land of Whim and Spleen.' There are a great number of people here who are called ' characters,' and who have all sorts of strange whims and crotchets. One will never sit down to table for fear of being suffocated by the odour of the viands, and takes his meals alone in the vestibule ; another spends his income on favourite animals, or ' pets,' as they are called ; a third, after having enchanted you by a beautiful voice and charming music, finishes up by boxing you. There is one with a red cap who gallops through the streets and enters shops on horseback, when he wants to buy anything. There is one who plays the bagpipes and who is willing to be disinherited from nearly two thousand pounds sterling per annum, rather than give up his pipes, which are at present his sole source of income. There is a man who believes that everybody wishes to poison him. He watches for the entry of any person into a baker's shop, follows him, and when the stranger has bought a loaf he seizes it and runs off with it, believing that the bakers are not anxious to poison anybody but himself. He acts the same way in butchers' shops. Another has constituted himself children's nurse, and washes, rubs, combs, and wipes them. I could mention many other examples of these ' characters,' but have said enough.

There is no place of shelter for the weak-minded of Cork—it is a hideous spectacle to see them in the streets. For the greater part, it is true, they are quiet, but it is so cruel and humiliating to see human nature degraded that an effort should be made to separate them from society.

Yet it must be admitted that the city of Cork has recently made great progress in commerce, in increase of houses, and of inhabitants, and, to some degree, in their amelioration. The city stands on several little marshy islands in the middle of the river, and it is from this circumstance that it takes its name, for Cork means ' muddy ' in Irish, and it is passably well named. The narrow canals which separate the islands are only filled with water at high tide, and so destroy considerably the salubrity of the air.

It would seem to be absolutely necessary for the prosperity of the town that the principal magistrates, for a dozen years, should be strong and prudent men, whose judgment would not be narrowed to the dust of their offices, and who would not be so much accustomed to count halfpennies and farthings, or to think of interest at four, five or six per cent. In the whole of Great Britain, the Mayor or Provost is always elected from amongst the merchants and general traders, the inhabitants justly confiding their interests to one who has a commercial career. This arrangement works very well in towns that are much frequented, where the opinion of the merchant is enlightened by that of a large public, and of strangers who may visit the place ; but in towns where the merchant can have no ideas other than his own, or where, being a foreigner, his sole aim is to gather as much money as possible, and quit the country afterwards, it must be evident that the embellishments and amelioration of the city, of which he is a principal magistrate for a year, will not interest him very much.

I believe that what I have said may explain the little progress which Cork has made in the arts and in matters of public welfare and interest. I imagine that if a man of character generally esteemed (Lord Shannon, for instance) would consent, during several years, to clean this Augean stable, he would be actuated by a desire for the public good, instead of by self-interest, and he would not be found to retard the construction of establishments required by the mass of the inhabitants because the revenues of the city might diminish by a few shillings or pounds.

Since I have extended my remarks on this subject so much, the reader will perhaps want to know what are the ameliorations of which I speak, and what I think the public-spirited Mayor might do. I shall mention a few of the principal, and in a manner most concise. First of all, demolish the two hideous prisons which are at the end of the bridges joining this muddy island with the banks of the river and build new, outside the town, in an airy position. Clean the streets—don't permit the inhabitants to allow their pigs to roam wherever they may seek pasture, and don't let these pigs be seen after their throats have been cut. Build a grain market in a suitable position. Establish public schools and hospitals where the people may be sure that their children are instructed in the religion they wish to follow, and not in that which others wish them to follow. Build an asylum for the insane. Furnish the city with public fountains. Clear the quays of the sheds which disfigure them. Encourage, as far as possible, manufactures of all kinds, and establish a House of Industry, so as to get rid of the beggars which dishonour the streets. Have public works in which every man wanting bread may find the means to earn it, &c.

I am convinced that if these plans could be carried out during fifty years, Cork would become more important than Dublin itself, on account of the safety and fine situation of its port. The principal exportation is at present of salted meat; beasts are killed in the season by thousands, and the season over, there is nothing to do. I have known a merchant who, from what I am told, kills every year between twenty and twenty-five thousand pigs, which statement gave me occasion to say to him that he was the greatest murderer of hogs I ever knew. This digression is a little long, and may perhaps appear fastidious to some who do not take much interest in Cork, but it is more for the Irish than the foreigner that I write, and I hope that the purity of my motive will be taken as excuse.

I quitted Cork at last, and took my way to Bandon,

where, unfortunately, the Lord of the soil was not at home. Formerly, this town had a reputation for revolutionary zeal. It was said that the inhabitants had decreed that no Catholic could spend a night there. All I can say about the subject is that the nine-tenths of the inhabitants must have been great cowards.

Lord Bandon is amusing himself by making a *pas de côté* to the house ; that is to say, he has built a new one beside the old. It will not be as good as the first, but it is no matter ; the rich should build and demolish, it is good for the country. On leaving the town I was very happy to fall in with a young man who wished to be my travelling companion, since the inhabitants did not speak English, and my knowledge of Irish did nor enable me to do more than express the equivalents of ' How do you do ? ' and ' Give me.'

My travelling companion seemed to be a good sort of creature, and after we had tramped ten miles together, he said, ' I am very sorry, Mister, I am very sorry.' ' And what, my good fellow,' said I, ' is the reason for your sorrow ? ' ' Ah, Sir, I am very sorry that I have no money so that I could offer you a drink of whisky.' I found this manner of making a request rather original, and replied that he need not trouble himself, as I would offer the whisky to him.

When he had taken with me a little drop of ' the creature' (which is an amiable name they have given to whisky), he said to me, ' To show my gratitude and do you a good turn, I will show you a well that heals all diseases.' He led me to the cemetery, and showed me there a stone vessel attached to a tomb. 'This stone,' he said, ' is always full of water, and yet no one ever puts any into it ; the water is good for nearly all diseases. I came here from Bandon three weeks ago to get a bottle of it for my mother, who has dropsy, but she is not much better.' 'Don't you see why that is so ? ' I said to him. 'The water is dirty, and the holy water basin full of filth ; clean it out, and the water will be good.' Together we took handfuls of grass and scraped out the hollow in the stone, and so effectively that we took out, with the dirt, all the water. My friend was very much surprised to see that the vessel did not refill. He thought he saw in this a sign of some great misfortune. ' Let us hurry away,' he said, ' for if the people here knew what we have done they would be ready to kill us.'

The huts of the poor in this district are really pitiable to see. Sometimes they lay two pieces of wood across the corner of a ditch, build up the third side with earth, and make a sort of roof over all with turf. Such dwellings make it possible to understand the story of a horseman falling from his horse into the middle of a frightened family.

At last I came to Macroom. At Cork I had got an umbrella addition made to my sword-stick. The form of the shelter was perhaps unusual, as about six or seven inches of the stick projected beyond the open umbrella. It was raining as I entered Macroom, and I noticed that the girls and women were giggling and chuckling as they looked at me, and soon I had such a troop of children at my heels that I could hardly walk. When I saw that I closed my umbrella and immediately they cried, ' Oh, it is nothing, it is an umbrella stick,' and they left me.

I inquired for the residence of Mr. Henry Hedges, and it was pointed out to me, far away, on a height at the end of a long avenue. On my way up this avenue I was met by Mr. Hedges, and after putting one or two questions to me, he said, ' You are a stranger'; and then, taking my hand, and before he had read the letter which I carried addressed to him, he said, ' All that is in my house is at your service.' This is the real, good, ancient hospitality of Ireland. How pleasant it is when one meets with such cordiality in this perverse world !

From Mont-Hedges there is to be had a most agreeable view over a rich valley, and the river on the banks of which the town of Macroom is situated. One object in the landscape is an old castle, formerly the residence of the rulers of the country. It serves at present as *caserne* for the troops in garrison in this town.

The life of Wandering Jew agreed with me so well that, although I was wet to the skin nearly every day, and often much fatigued, I grew visibly fairer and fatter. If I met with good or ill, I knew how to enjoy the one without becoming desperate over the other. Allowing myself to be guided by a good Providence, I put the whole of the cares and anxieties of this world aside. My whole baggage slung over my shoulder, or in my pocket, I walked, I ran, I searched ; nature appeared to me in many guises, new scenes occupied my attention and gave me instruction. Before the Revolution I was the inhabitant of a little corner of the earth ; emigration had made me a citizen of

the universe ; the whole world seemed to belong to
me—

> All places that the eye of heaven visits
> Are to a wise man ports and happy havens.
> . . . Now, no way can I stray
> Save back to France, all the world is my way.

After all it was not difficult to understand why my
travels brought me more vigorous health, for the
fatigues of the way was not more than moderate.
Thanks to the great number of letters of recommendation which had been given to me, I was nearly always
certain to find good quarters in the evening. I went,
literally, from house to house ; from some it was difficult
to escape even on the third or fourth day, and if I could
have believed some of the things said to me, I might
have finished my walk at some of my resting-places.
Although to many that would seem to be preferable
to tramping the country, I was not a Breton for nothing,
and I was determined to pursue, with perseverance,
the plan of my journey.

I came to Dunmanway by the mountains, which
are of the wildest, and crossed a large marsh which has
been formed in this beautiful valley because the river
has no fixed bed. Here and there little islands of
fertile earth proved that nothing would be easier than
to drain the valley ; if they had here a few *Dutch
frogs* it would be soon done.

I heard loud cries, and soon I perceived a crowd of
people assembling on the road. I could not imagine
the cause of the noise and the assembly, but drawing
nearer I found that it was a funeral. This was the
first time I had been witness of that singular custom,

the Irish *keen*. The women cried in chorus one after the other—*hu lu lu*. They wept freely and tore their hair, throwing themselves down on the bier. They had all the air of being in exteme sorrow, but this was not the case ; they believe they owe the duty to every corpse which passes their house to express sorrow in this violent way. When these good women have done what they think enough to satisfy the *manes* of the dead, they retire and become immediately as happy as they were before. If a neighbour or acquaintance neglected to appear at a funeral without giving good reasons for his absence, his action would be the cause of interminable hatreds in the family.

This *pille-lu* or *hu lu lu* seems to have some connection with the *ululatus* of the Romans and the funeral cries of ancient peoples. The manner in which it is pronounced has also given me the idea that it may be a representation of the *de profundis* which the priests in Catholic countries chant while following the dead to the grave, a ceremony of which the people in Ireland are deprived, but of which, perhaps, they have an unconscious recollection. I imagine it would not be possible, in the middle of the funeral ceremonies of the Catholic religion, to emit such cries without spoiling the pomp and hindering the priests from doing their duty.

I passed near to one of the ruined forts which are so common in Ireland, and which are commonly attributed to the work of the Danes. I think it possible that the Danes did construct some, but that the greater part were simply the dwellings of chiefs or kings of the country. They are called here *gragun re* (meaning, I believe, the palace of the king). The inhabitants

speaking of them call them *rath* or *lis*—I am not versed
enough in the language of the country to indicate the
difference between these, which may be one simply
arising out of position. Thus one may be quite sure
that all the towns of which the names begin with
Rath or *Lis*, like Rathdrum or Lismore, had such forti-
fication ; or, to put it better, these towns had their
beginnings in the enclosure. These forts were all constructed on the same plan—perfectly round with a
double fosse, and in all those of any size, when trouble
has been taken to excavate, there has been discovered a
souterrain of four or five feet high, the roof being formed
by long stones. I have gone into several of these and
I have always found them perfectly dry, with, commonly, a little spring in the centre. They are all made
Z fashion, and have two openings : the one is inside the
enclosure, and the other is in the first ditch or fosse.
The use of these *souterrains* has much troubled the
antiquarians, who think that they cannot have been
used for living spaces, seeing that they are too low and
too narrow. It has been supposed that they were
shelters for the cattle, and although I have seen one big
enough to allow of cows and sheep taking refuge in it
from the heat of the day, it is hardly likely that this
was their proper use. The dryness of these chambers
makes me think that the inhabitants used them as
chambers in which to store food, and if the fort were
surprised by an enemy they had by the *souterrain* the
means of escape unperceived. I saw by the roadway
one of those schools of which the English make such
fun, and which are called hedge-schools. Among a
peasantry so poor, it is not to be expected to find a fine
house used as a school ; consequently when it is a house

it has usually a miserable roof, the chamber being not more than five feet high. Children and the master will certainly not feel comfortable in such a hut, and, when the weather permits, they establish themselves under a tree, or under a hedge, and the master gives his lesson in the open air. To my mind it is very much pleasanter to give or receive a lesson in the fresh air than in an overcrowded and ill-smelling school; but it is not the custom in England.

I arrived at last at Dunmanway, where I was welcomed by Mr. Cox. There are few men who have done so much as he for the amelioration of their country, and his work was very necessary in this remote corner of the world. In his village he has encouraged manufactures of all kinds, giving long leases to his workers at a very low rent, and furnishing them with the means of carrying on their work. He has drained bogs, cultivated fields, and planted woods; also, he has almost entirely rebuilt the little town. In time, doubtless, these things, from being expenses, will become sources of profit. Why do so few proprietors understand that it is for their own interest to place their money in the manner indicated here? The manufactures of calico are here the most numerous. They make also certain kinds of linen, and, in spite of Mr. Arthur Young, I am far from believing that one might as well introduce the plague in the south of Ireland as the cultivation of flax.

There were in this little town two hundred French republican officers, prisoners on parole, and I was glad to have the opportunity to know what kind of people these men might be. At Mr. Cox's house I dined with two or three of them, and found them polite enough.

With pleasure I perceived that that ferocious enthusiasm which distinguished the partisans of the Revolution at its commencement no longer possessed them. But I noticed among them a sort of blind and unreasoning fury against the *émigrés*; they accused them of many things of which I had never thought, and reproached them with having borne arms against France, as if the greater number of *émigrés*, with the first campaign, had not been obliged to submit themselves to a requisition more despotic than that of Robespierre, the requisition of need, which they could not avoid, like that of France, by hiding themselves in caves. But at last peace . . . peace. . . . One day misfortune will unite us all and leave to all parties only the power of weeping over past ills, and the task of repairing in common what division and wrath have destroyed. God grant it! My sole wish is, one day, to see this accomplished. In the meantime the greater part of officers and republican soldiers fight for the republic because they have already done so, and the republic is victorious, and they hate the *émigrés* without knowing why.

One who spoke to me about the finances of the republic told me that they were certainly in a bad way; but, he added, Holland, Spain, Italy, Our Holy Father, the Pope, and part of Germany have already been good enough to come to our aid, and we hope that before long England herself will take pity on us and accord us the same grace. These gentlemen joke.

Mr. Cox is a gentleman greatly respected in the country; his good nature makes him to be beloved by all. I have noticed a rather original trait of this good nature. The minister of the parish came to him and complained that turnips were stolen from his fields every day. 'And from mine also,' said Mr. Cox. 'Then,' said the minister, 'let us join forces and prosecute the ill-doers.' 'Oh,' said Mr. Cox, 'that would be too severe; but I will tell you what we might do. Let us sow arsenic among the turnips and we shall soon know who is the thief.' 'But,' said the minister, 'we would be the first to suffer ourselves.' 'In that case,' said Mr. Cox, 'it is perhaps better for you to let things alone as I do, and leave these poor folk to the eating of a few miserable turnips without making a noise about it.' The anger of the saintly man at this was small in comparison to the amusement of the servants who heard the discussion.

The Lords Lieutenant of Ireland, as I believe I have already said, have the right to confer the honour of knighthood on any person; they have done this indeed sometimes as a joke, and not a very good joke in my opinion. The Duke of Rutland, after having well drunk, was so charmed by the music of a certain player of bagpipes that he ordered him to kneel down, and then and there he created him knight by sword and accolade. This man has been called, ever since, Sir Denis. . . . He continues, however, the practice of his profession of player of bagpipes, and in this capacity accepts engagements to play in houses while a dinner is proceeding. He is really a clever man with his instrument, but I must admit that I am not a lover of bagpipes.

I have also been told that Lord Townshend, in one of his journeys through Ireland, stopped a night at an inn, where he was surprised and charmed to find an extremely good claret, of which he drank copiously;

then he asked his host to drink with him, and finished up by making the innkeeper knight under the name of Sir Thomas. In the morning, according to the story, remembering his folly of the evening before, he called his host and said to him, 'We have been acting the fool after supper last night ; you will say no more about it.' ' My lord,' said the good man, ' as far as I am concerned, that is all right, but I must consult my wife.' The wife's answer was ' I never did hope to be a lady, but since Fortune has made me one, I shall be a lady all the days of my life,' and, as a matter of fact, she is called My Lady and her husband is called Sir.

Crossing a rather wild bit of country I came to Bantry, where I was received by Mr. White in a most hospitable manner. Bantry is a poor little town, situated at the end of a superb bay of the same name, which has been much on the tongue lately on account of the appearance there of the French fleet. The Bay of Bantry must be about forty English miles in length by fifteen or twenty wide ; it is at all parts very deep, except in the neighbourhood of the little town, and is everywhere surrounded by a sterile mountainous and rocky country, in which, nevertheless, one may find from time to time some charming little spots. Mr. White was good enough to take me in his boat to the Port of Glengariff, between Bantry and the island of Bear. This is a most ancient little spot. The way is literally sown with rocks, which are covered with plants and shrubs of every species. I went with my host a little way into the country to a small house belonging to him, and found to my surprise a well-wooded and romantic little valley in the middle of these rocky and arid hills. Plant life is here very vigorous. I have seen pretty large oaks and other trees growing in crevasses of rocks hardly large enough to admit a finger ; surely they must draw their subsistence from the moisture of the air.

Between Glengariff and Bear Haven is seen a very high cascade, of nearly perpendicular fall from a mountain which has got the name of the ' Hungry Hill,' and not without reason. The island of Bear, where the French stopped for a few days, is at the mouth of the bay and, although pretty large, has very few inhabitants—it is a mere mass of mountains and rocks. Whiddy is another island not nearly so large but very productive, with some of the best land in the country. At different places I saw the walls of buildings which had been erected in connection with the sardine industry, this little fish having formerly frequented this bay ; but it has been said that they ceased to appear after the naval battle here between the French and the English in the time of King William III. At present the fish is never seen here, and it is almost entirely unknown in England or in Ireland, even under its English name of pilchard.

Cape Clear, the most southern point in Ireland, is only about twenty miles distant from Bantry, but as a visit to it would have necessitated a return over the same ground, I dispensed with the journey. I have never been so near the country of my birth since the day of the fatal emigration. The thought came to me that in one or two days, with a favouring wind, I might go from here, and land on my own property and calm the anguish of my relatives. Could I have believed years ago that ever my compatriots should one day look upon me as their enemy . . . their enemy ! No, never. I could blame them, detest their atrocities, suffer by their follies and blind rage ; I shall be a wanderer, miserable, without a stone on which to rest my head, and France will always be France for me. Always to my native land shall my thoughts return until the last day of my life, always my most ardent wishes shall be for her welfare.

I quitted with great regret the hospitable roof which sheltered me here. It was a sorrow for me to turn my back now on the south and set my face northward, but I had reached the end of the land. I climbed to the top of the high mountain by which is the only approach to Bantry from the west, and which is called ' The Priest's Leap.' The tradition of the good women of the country on this subject is, that a holy priest, coming from Co. Kerry to Bantry to visit a sick person, learnt on the summit of this mountain that the sick one was dying. Fearing to arrive too late to give him his passport for the other world, he knelt down and prayed, and immediately leaped from the summit of the mountain to his destination, a distance of five miles.

They will show you, near the town, the rock on which he alighted, and on which you will see the print of his knees, of his fingers, and of his nose. Assuredly this is proof positive. Nevertheless, I fear that there are hardened unbelievers in the world who will not believe the story—so perverse is the human heart.

CHAPTER V

KILLARNEY—ARDFERT—THE SHANNON

AFTER having travelled about a dozen miles among these wild and absolutely deserted hills, the eye is suddenly gratified by the appearance of a little cultivated valley round the village of Needen. The guide who came with me to take back my horse had never passed this way before, and on the lonely way he seemed sad and troubled. But when his eye caught sight of this little corner of the world, he cried out suddenly, ' Oh, at last, here is a place with a natural look !'

Lately the name of Kenmare has been given to the village situated in this valley, out of compliment to Lord Kenmare, for in this country, as well as in Great Britain, more than elsewhere do riches attract admiration and respect. One or two miles before arriving at this place there is to be seen in a peat moss, a hundred feet or so from the road, an isolated rock ; it may measure about thirty feet in height by fifteen or twenty on each face. It has a circumference of about sixty feet, and it is a stone absolutely different from any found in the country on this side of the river.[1]

[1] It is singular that nearly everywhere in Ireland stones on one side of a river are of a different nature from those on the other. Limestone, for example, is found on one side of the Suir and not on the other. The same thing is also to be noticed at Cork and in the case of the rivers Kenmare, Shannon, and Galway.—*Note by Author.*

It is an enormous block of limestone which by some natural convulsion must have been thrown about four miles from the place from which it was torn. I went over to see it, and went round it ; I even climbed with trouble to the top of it and found that formerly there had been on it a little tower, of which the ruins remained. It is covered with plants of various kinds— little shrubs, hollies, ivies, &c.—while the peat which surrounds it produces nothing but heath.

The inhabitants of the country pretend that a certain giant, whose name I have forgotten, amused himself by carrying this piece of limestone to a granite country and a smaller block of granite to the other side of the river, where he placed it in limestone territory. There is, really, a similar sized block of granite on the other side. This phenomenon could only be explained by supposing a great convulsion of the earth ; but how terrific must have been the explosion which was capable of throwing a stone weighing more than one million pounds a distance of five or six miles !

The large bay, which is called Kenmare River, looks very imposing from this point. Two peninsulas approach in the middle and form a safe harbour for vessels. There is no country so well provided with deep and safe bays as the south of Ireland.

Hardly has one quitted the miserable village of Kenmare than he finds himself again in the mountains—a little less wild, perhaps, than those I had just quitted —and just when the traveller is most oppressed by this depressing continuity of wild scenery in the midst of arid mountains, he is greeted on coming out of a narrow passage at the foot of Mangerton with a delightful view of the charming lake of Killarney. The impression which the ravishing view of its numerous islands and cultivated banks made on me can only be compared to the sensation experienced by an unfortunate who quits a prison to see again the glorious light of day. I continued my journey very slowly, not knowing what to admire the most—the high mountains covered with wood, the beautiful piece of water shaded by them, the islands, the peninsula which divides the lake into two, or the beautiful country which borders it on the north.

I presented myself at the house of Lord Kenmare and passed there eight most agreeable days, during which I enjoyed several excursions on the lake. The soul most indifferent to beauty cannot but be charmed by this delightful spot.

Generally the visitor is taken about two miles from Killarney to the island of Ross, which is the largest island of the lake, and is only separated from the shore by a narrow stream crossed by a bridge. On this island is the castle of Prince O'Donoghue, to whom this country belonged in old times, and the inhabitants believe that they can still see him, on horseback, crossing the water on a certain day of the year. Following the coast to the east, the peninsula of Muckross is reached, and here is one of the most beautiful places I have ever seen in its singular *mélange* of wood and plain.

The venerable ruins of the Abbey inspire a sentiment of religious melancholy which is almost agreeable. The yew which is planted in the middle of a cloister covers it entirely with its branches and allows only a few rays of light to fall on the tombs at its feet. The natives here are persuaded that the mortal who would

have the temerity to cut its branches, or even to pierce
it, would inevitably perish during the year. They
have a most extreme feeling of devotion to the saint of
the place, and they make long pilgrimages to this spot,
and perform here penitences which, as elsewhere in
Ireland, consist in making the tour of the buildings
a certain number of times while reciting prayers. They
bury their dead here also, bringing them often from
great distances. Interments are only made on the
southern and eastern sides of the church. The north is
commonly reputed to be the devil's side, and the west
is reserved for children dying without baptism, and
for soldiers and strangers. They look upon it as
scandalous impiety to carry away any remains of
coffins. In the Abbey are two large vaults entirely
filled with them, while they allow bones to be scattered
here and there where the spade of the gravedigger has
placed them; but nothing in the world would induce
them to touch one of these. In a corner outside the
church they appear in a hideous pile. Although, at
the time of the Reformation, the rich divided the Abbey
spoils, they have never attempted to displace the
burying-place. It is always round the ruins of an
old church that the peasants wish to be buried, and
nothing can be done to make them accept any other
situation. Here attempts have been made often to
find another burying-place, but such attempts have
never succeeded. Nevertheless, it is a very necessary
thing, for, beside the fact that over the rock there is
hardly earth enough to cover the dead, the cemetery
is so full that it should be closed, at any rate for some
time. This crowding does not trouble the peasantry;
they are content that the dead of a year or two should

give place to those of to-day, and I have seen in this horrible vault more than one skull still covered with hair.

A few years ago a man of rather good appearance made his home in one of the ruined chambers of this Abbey. He made his bed out of boards which had formed part of coffins, and placed them in the embrasure of the window, which was the only covered part of the chamber. Soon he acquired a reputation for singular holiness, and the peasants carried food to him, while the rich invited him sometimes to their table, where he comported himself with the manner of a man accustomed to the best society. When he was asked for a reason for his penitence, he replied that he could never do enough to expiate his crimes. He was a fine-looking man, and it is reported that when a lady regarded him with some attention he said, ' Take care of those eyes, they have done a great deal of harm.' He lived about two years in this melancholy solitude, and then disappeared. Many conjectures had been formed as to who this singular personage could be, and many stories have been made to account for his conduct during his stay at Muckross, but they were only stories and doubtless with little foundation.

The peninsula of Muckross divides the lake of Killarney into two parts. The smaller one is very beautiful in its disposition and diversity. There is a spot on the mountain called the Eagle's Nest, where in reality eagles are to be found, and where the curious are amused by the extraordinary repercussion of an echo which does not repeat itself as others, but pauses for some time, and afterwards repeats the sound of a cannon shot like a roll of thunder. The banks of the little river which is followed for four or five miles on the way to the larger lake are very interesting, and this lake contrasts, by the wild and savage mountains which surround it, with the smaller lake, of which the banks are well cultivated.

The visitor is carried down the river to the lower lake, and brought to the O'Sullivan waterfall in the middle of the wood, afterwards being taken to Innisfallen, a charming island, on which at one time was an abbey. This island belongs to Lord Kenmare, and when one is fortunate enough to be numbered in the parties which he and My Lady arrange for visitors, after having admired the beauties of nature, homage should be rendered here to the hosts' politeness and their friendly hospitality.

There are some deer in the woods, and sometimes one of them is hunted in the mountains, and after many winds and turns, finishes by jumping into the lake, where the boats and dogs follow it and force it to land on one of the islands.

Numerous companies of people come here from all parts of Ireland, drawn by the beauty of the spot, but they only stay as long as is necessary to see this beauty. An effort ought to be made to keep them in the country by arranging some amusements, or finding mineral waters ; these last established would greatly increase the wealth of the country, and I do not know of any place more agreeable and more fit for re-establishing broken health. There is a fountain of excellent mineral water in Lord Kenmare's park. Unfortunately, it has not yet attracted the fancy or attention of the disciples of Hippocrates, but that will come with time. The town is agreeable enough—it seems to be new, and is built nearly in the formation of the letter T.

Walking early one morning I heard dreadful cries, the sound coming from a house. Led by natural instinct and by curiosity I entered, and found myself immediately in a room among a crowd of fifty or more women, who cried and wept over an uncovered bier, on which lay the pale figure of an old man, dead two days earlier. Four of these women, in particular, cried louder than others, tearing their hair and often embracing the corpse. I remarked that at the end of a quarter of an hour, as they became fatigued, they passed into a neighbouring chamber, and were replaced by four others, who immediately commenced to cry and weep in desperate fashion, and this they continued until the first four, restored by a good glass of whisky, were able to return and take up their wailing.

This sort of an assembly is called ' a wake,' and every peasant who dies is sure of having it every night up to the moment of his interment—all his friends and his acquaintances round him, crying, weeping, singing his praises in impromptu Irish verse, and drinking to his health. It is a rather costly custom, but the poor do not feel that they can, with decency, dispense with it. It was different formerly, for, according to the ancient Brehon laws, the quantity of drink and meat consumed were regulated according to the rank of the dead person, in order to prevent families from ruining themselves in trying to surpass the doings of others. This explains perfectly the answer of a good woman who had just lost her husband, and who was reproached with having allowed him to die without sending for the doctor. ' Oh,' said she, ' I thought 'twas plenty for a poor woman like me to pay the cost of the burying.'

I think, perhaps, the poor woman was right. The doctor is for the rich, a sort of moralist who urges his patient to moderate his pangs, and repair by attention to diet the effects of his excess ; but for the poor peasant who has never in his life done anything to excess, and whose best remedy would be, perhaps, nourishing food, of what use could the doctor's advice be to him ? If he cure him of his malady, he would kill him with hunger through the charges he would make for his services. His wife then would have double expense.

I was witness here, a few days after, of a somewhat strange scene. Hearing the funeral bell, I went out to observe the procedure. It was the funeral of a poor woman who was being carried to her last resting-place, the coffin surrounded by a prodigious number of females who wept and chanted their ' *hu lu lu* ' in chorus, the men looking on rather indifferently. When the funeral arrived at the head of the ' T,' that is at the end of the principal street of the town, a singular dispute occurred between the husband and the brother of the deceased. One of the parting ways led to the Abbey of Muckross, where it was the custom for the family of the husband to bury their dead ; the other led to Aghadoe, where were buried the family of the brother. The latter assumed the right to direct the funeral towards Aghadoe, while the husband wished to go in the other direction to Muckross. The friends of the two parties took hold in turn of the remains of the poor woman, each wishing them to be carried to the side they favoured ; but each finding themselves unable

to succeed, by common accord they deposited the bier
on the street and commenced a vigorous fight to determine by blows of sticks to which side the remains
should be carried.   I was at the time with the minister
of the parish, Mr. Herbert, who was also a Justice of
the Peace.   With great courage he threw himself
into the middle of the fight, seized the collars of the
two principal combatants, and, after some explanation,
he decided that the husband had the right to decide
where his wife should be buried. He allowed the
husband then to go without letting go hold of the
brother-in-law, and the funeral moved in the direction
of Muckross. I remarked that neither fight nor
controversy which followed arrested the cries of the
wailing women, who continued to beat their breasts,
tear their hair, and cry ' *hu lu lu* ' as if neither fight nor
controversy proceeded. When I saw the Justice of
the Peace throw himself into the middle of the crowd,
I must say I imagined that the combatants would
unite to tear him to pieces, as a stranger meddling
with things which did not belong to him.   I mounted
on a little wall more conveniently to see the punishment, but I was soon disabused ; the peasants showed
the greatest respect to the magistrate, and submitted
promptly to his decision.   This was no doubt the best
thing that could happen, and the magistrate did his
duty, but it was so amusing to me to find the people
fighting over a dead woman, that I rather regretted
that the business was so soon terminated.

I went one day to the summit of Mangerton, from
which there is a view over a great extent of country,
although that is far from being a sight of all the
kingdoms of the earth. The eye wanders over arid

mountains and parts of little lakes. That of Killarney appeared beautiful, with the serpentine peninsula of Muckross cutting it in two. Nearly at the summit of the mountain was a little round pool called 'The Devil's Punch-Bowl,' where I drank to the health of the patron, and to the health of his children ; that is to say the bulk of humanity, pretty girls particularly.

As this town is much frequented in summer, beggars come from all parts. They build miserable huts along the road and importune the passers-by. I have often thought that this annoyance could easily be abolished by the establishment of a small House of Industry, in which the beggars should be forced to work.

It would not be very difficult to join the lake with the sea by a canal which could be brought to the Bay of Kenmare, or by taking the bed of the river to that of Dingle. If it were taken to Kenmare this would be better, as the bay is much safer and deeper than that of Dingle, which is sandy. To one or other there would be not more than seven or eight miles of cutting to do, and the connection would add much to the importance of the town and neighbouring country by encouraging commerce.

On the road to Tralee I was accosted by a man who pointed out to me three old castles which had belonged to three brothers who were the masters of this country, and had been chased from it by the English. I asked why they had been chased, and his answer was ' It was because they were not the stronger.' This is what may be called the argument *ad hominem*.

Tralee is rather a nice place, and is not wanting in trade. These coasts, as far as Limerick, were formerly the principal residence of the Danes, who seemed to have scattered, nearly at every step, their round forts, which the inhabitants call by the name of *rath* or *lis*. There are four of them, not more than two hundred feet from each other, near the mouth of the river in the Bay of Tralee. This town is well frequented by bathers, and the people who come to drink the mineral waters found a mile or two away.

I came to Ardfert, where I presented myself to the Dean, Mr. Grave, and was received as usual with that charming hospitality which always makes me forget, immediately, the fatigues of the road. Ardfert was formerly a bishopric ; at present it is united to that of Limerick. In old times there were here many ecclesiastical establishments ; the ruins of the old cathedral are the most remarkable remains, although nothing very great. The air of the place is said to be extraordinarily healthy. This has induced a celebrated surgeon to choose it for his place of burying ; his tomb is constructed, and his epitaph engraved on it while he is still alive.

In ancient times there stood, in the cemetery of this cathedral, a high round tower with not more than the ordinary appearance of wear. It crushed itself, if the expression may be used, some twelve or fifteen years ago. I say ' crushed ' because one would expect that such a building would naturally fall to one side or other, but in this case the stones appeared to tumble straight down, forming a large mass on the spot where the tower had stood. I went a little distance to see the venerable ruins of a Franciscan abbey, and, passing through the scattered debris of remains, I found myself in the presence of the two most beautiful and amiable ladies of Ireland, Lady Glandore and Mrs.

108

Woodcock, who had resolved to be cruel enough to society to absent themselves from it for more than a year. I do not know whether it was their good example which affected me so much at the moment. Certain it is that never in my life did I feel such a desire to become a hermit.

At a little distance there is to be found one of those holy wells round which the inhabitants perform their devotions. This well is very famous, and the people come from afar. They pretend or assert that it can cure all evils, and the devotion consists in going round the well, bare-footed, seven times while reciting prayers, kneeling for a moment at each turn before a black stone, which seems to have been a tombstone, and, while kneeling, they rub the hand over three heads which are cut in the stone, and which are much worn by reason of this hand-rubbing and kissing. Afterwards they pass the hand which has touched the stone over the part of the body which is afflicted, drink a large glass of the water, and wash their feet in the current. Children are sometimes plunged seven times into the cold water, and I have seen people, well clad and having the appearance of being in comfortable circumstances, perform these ceremonies just like the others. I have also seen a very pretty young girl kissing these ugly stones, and I could not help thinking that I would have been a much better restorer if she had paid the reverence to me.

This well is widely renowned in the country, and even the Protestants, who are not very numerous here, when they have tried other remedies in vain, will make up their minds to try the well and go through the usual performances like their Catholic friends.

The greater part of these peasants, however, come in a rather careless spirit, seemingly more with a desire to meet their friends than to perform penitences. Speaking to one of the visitors I asked him what was the benefit to be derived from this water. His reply was that he could not tell, and when I asked him why he went through the usual performances, all he could say was ' to do what the others do and to see the women.' In effect, it is at these wells that a great number of marriages are arranged. It is in vain that the priest of the parish has often forbidden his people to go to such places; they have followed this custom so long before the establishment of Christianity that they cannot be broken off it.

In reality, there can hardly be anything more innocent than to go round one of these wells a number of times reciting prayers, and afterwards drinking a glass of water. I will go so far to say that it must be very good for the health of the poor women, since it forces them to take some exercise and to clean themselves. The only thing left to the priest is to see that order is observed in these gatherings, and by his exhortations to warn his people against any impropriety or indecency, and in this the priest of this parish has perfectly succeeded. The good folk come here on Saturday morning and finish their devotions by two o'clock. Then the young fellows make up to their girls and see them safe home to their mothers, chatting the while.

Nearly all the people in this part of the country are Catholics, but Catholic and Protestant agree here very well. The priest performs mass, and the minister preaches, and the two flocks seem not to trouble themselves about each other's religion for the rest of the week. I went on Sunday to the Catholic chapel. The women are always separated from the men here. I suppose this to be to avoid distraction. In the middle of the service the priest made a long discourse in Irish, afterwards translating the principal part into English. He consigned to all the devils (although in highly proper terms) all those infamous enough not to pay his dues.

The priests have great power over their people. They are, in fact, the judges of the country and settle everything connected with morals and manners. They excommunicate a peasant and oblige him to leave a parish. Great care, then, must be taken not to displease them, and especially care must be taken that they get their dues. The Government knows perfectly well that the priests have their people in the hollow of their hand, and, nevertheless, they make enemies of them and treat them badly. Can they make the peasants go whatever way they wish? Well, make them your friends and you have gained the people. I am convinced that a dozen benefices in favour of Catholic priests, at the disposition of the Viceroy, would make them all as flexible and courteous and as desirous to please as their dear brethren in God, the ministers and bishops of the Protestant Church.

The churches are all placed east and west—when the priest is at the altar he always looks towards the east. It is singular that this should be such a common practice over the whole of Europe, even in the case of the Lutheran churches, and perhaps there is not one person in a thousand who has noticed it. I remember perfectly that, in France, all the old churches are built in this manner, and I had not noticed it. It is true that the new were often placed indifferently, but even in the new the great number will have the door at the west and the altar at the east. It is a custom introduced into the world long before the establishment of Christianity, and which is yet followed by nearly all the people of the earth. The usual reason given is that the Christian religion took birth to the east of Europe, and that it is a mark of respect for the holy places where were manifested the first mysteries of religion. If that is so, Christians in Persia should look to the west, but I believe that this reason has been used simply to sanctify ancient custom, as Mohammedans look also to the east out of respect for the town of Mecca. Although I am not in a position to give the real reason, I cannot take the one mentioned as the true one. I would rather believe that the custom is simply a universal homage which men in old time rendered to the rising sun as the symbol of divinity.

The neighbourhood of the flat and sandy bay of Ballyheigh brings some visitors to Ardfert for sea-bathing. Following the line of the coast, and crossing a tongue of land infrequently visited, I arrived at last at Kerryhead, at the mouth of the Shannon. This river is the largest in Ireland; the inhabitants have for it a singular veneration of which it seems to be worthy. He is not truly an Irishman who has not yet plunged into it, and as I desired to do always in Rome as the Romans do, a plunge into the Shannon was my first operation here. The river is seven or eight miles wide at its mouth. Its shores are lined with high rocks, in which are deep caves, the waves breaking at their mouths with astonishing fury. At a little distance, on an isolated rock, are to be seen the remains of fortifications, and at another place the traces of a little town, among which can be distinguished lines of streets and the foundations of houses. These seem to have been no larger than ordinary cabins, although the fortified enclosure is very considerable.

Following the coast I passed the Cushin, which throws itself into the Shannon. It takes its source at the foot of some rising ground from the other side of which the Blackwater flows. There is no country in the world better situated than this for commerce, and there is none where with so little trouble communications with the interior could be made easy.

Whenever the Royal Canal is finished and the Liffey and the Shannon joined, I believe it will be found to be a matter of great public usefulness to deepen the bed of these two rivers, the Cushin and the Blackwater, and to join them by means of canals. After that it will not be difficult to find means to join the Blackwater to the Suir and even to the Lee. Ireland would then have interior and circular navigation of more than five hundred miles in length, which would pass by the four principal cities of the south—Dublin, Limerick, Cork, and Waterford. Drogheda might even be joined, since it would be possible to make the Boyne navigable as far as the end of the canal.

CHAPTER VI

LIMERICK—KILLALOE—THE HOLY MOUNTAIN

AT some distance from the ferry by which the Cushin
is crossed there is to be seen in the middle of a court-
yard a tree of extraordinary size and entirely covered
with foliage. Its singularity made me approach to
examine it, and when I reached it I found that it was
one of the so often mentioned round towers covered
with ivy from top to bottom. Probably there were
some churches here. At present there is not the
slightest trace of them. At three miles from Tarbot
I saw very considerable ruins of an abbey, and fell in
with several men, pilgrims, walking barefooted round
the walls. From this spot can be seen the Holy Island
in the middle of the Shannon, where formerly were
eleven churches. These are now in ruins, and near them
is one of the round towers which have such a charming
effect when seen from afar. There are at Tarbot
two batteries of cannon, well situated at the narrowest
part of the Shannon. These are all the more effective,
since at the other side of the river there is scarcely any
depth of water, and vessels are obliged to pass within
five hundred feet of the cannon, which are well placed
and in perfect order. Fatigued by the long walk of
the day before, and by the great heat, I thought it well
to stop at the village of Glin, which gives the title of

Knight to its proprietor. There are but four places
in the whole of Ireland which have this privilege, and
all are in this part of the country. It is not a title of
English origin. It was given by the sovereign to four
brave men of the country before or at the time of the
conquest, and those who bear the titles at present are
their descendants.

I asked a big priest whom I met where I could find
lodging, and he led me to a miserable eating-house,
assuring me that it was the only inn in the place and
that it was very good. I passed the night defending
myself from the monsters who regarded me as their
lawful prey, and when the sun rose it was on a bloody
scene. I had the appearance of having taken part in
a battle, as really I had. Happily the sea was not far
off ; to it I fled quickly to drown unwelcome guests,
and that operation finished, I saw my friend the priest
going, himself, to the water. I told him of my miserable
hap, but this he took to be merely an everyday matter
and made light of it—in fact, he laughed very heartily.
I felt inclined to wish him in a warm place, but calmed
myself and only wished him, for the good of his soul,
several nights such as the one I had just passed. I
went on my way, and finding at the entry of the village
a beautiful inn, the sight made me so angry with the
priest that I could hardly resist returning to seek him
and administer to him some well-deserved chastisement. However, I resisted the impulse and proceeded
on my way. I saw on a height the ruins of an old
castle, which sustained a siege by the forces of Queen
Elizabeth. It is still surrounded by its ancient fortifications and outworks ; there are also in the neighbourhood some ancient *raths*. I had already walked

ten miles, and I had been on foot since three o'clock in the morning, and began to hear the wailings of my stomach ; there was no inn to be seen, but I saw on the heights a pleasant-looking house, and made inquiry as to the name of the owner. The answer was John Evan.

I had observed several times that while the poor are very hospitable and offer to the tired stranger according to his needs, yet if this same traveller presented himself at the house of well-to-do people he could get nothing more than a glass of water. The occasion seemed to me fit for making an experiment, and I presented myself at the door.

The owner, Mr. John Evan, appeared. ' Monsieur,' I said, ' I have not the honour of your acquaintance, and I have no letter of recommendation to you, but I declare to you that I am extremely hungry, and if you will give me something to eat, I shall be extremely obliged.' ' Faith,' said he, ' you could not have come at a better time, for breakfast is ready.' He brought me into his house, where I found everything I could desire. I was charmed to find myself wrong in my conjecture, but promised to myself that I would not try such an experiment again, lest I should find my first opinion to be justified.

Making a little zigzag of ten or twelve miles I came to Newcastle, where I was received by Mr. Locke and his brother, who is the minister of the place. This town is situated in a long, fertile valley, which is only separated from that of the Blackwater by a little range of heights. This castle formerly belonged to the Templars, and must have been at one time of very considerable size. It is now in the possession of Lord Courtenay.

If the great English proprietors had the wit to place on their estates men of the type found here, the country would have no occasion to complain about their absence. Mr. Locke has founded, at his own charges, a manufactory of linen, in which children can be employed from a very early age. There is no doubt that such establishments cannot make a profit at present, but they are useful for the country, and cannot be too much encouraged. The proprietor will find himself amply rewarded for his trouble and cost by the new spirit of industry which will be fostered among the peasants.

The price of labour in this country is very low, not more than twopence halfpenny or threepence.[1] The observation is commonly made that the price of provisions is, in consequence, very low, but this is false, and very false, for, if potatoes are excepted, everything is just as dear as in England. True, the people live entirely on potatoes and water or buttermilk ; but why can the English not live in the same manner ? If anyone tried to get the English peasantry to work on such food, he would soon find that he had no labourers. A great number of the peasantry in Ireland know perfectly well that for the same work they would receive in England two shillings, and in Ireland only sixpence. And further, they would be much more sure of getting their two shillings in the one country than their sixpence in the other. Many of them have made the journey, and these same people who are accused of indolence at home are, in England, very active. There they practise the same sobriety of life to which they are

---

[1] The author says ' cinq à six sous.' Possibly he meant ' five to six pence.'—Tr.

accustomed in their own country, and they are always
eager to return home as soon as their work has procured
them a little sum of money.

I know that, with all the good-will possible, the
proprietor cannot increase the price of labour without
exposing himself to the just reproaches of his neighbours, but, in encouraging manufactures, hands would
become more scarce and the price of labour would
necessarily advance.

From Newcastle to Limerick the country is superb.
This is, without contradiction, the most fertile stretch
of land in Ireland. Near Rathkeale I had occasion to
visit three or four villages inhabited by the descendants
of a German colony from the Palatinate, established
by the owner of the soil nearly eighty years ago.
Until now they have always married among themselves,
and have preserved the customs of their country. At
the time of my visit there was only one man living of
the original members of the colony. There is no doubt
that they were received on very advantageous conditions, each family receiving, in perpetuity, ground for
house and garden, as well as several acres of farm land
at a very moderate rate. The rich and fertile country
on which they were established was uncultivated before
their arrival. Their industry is still very remarkable.
Their farms are certainly better cultivated than others
near, and their houses, built after the fashion of their
former country, are of a comfortable character, and
so clean that they look like palaces in comparison with
the poor cabins of the Irish. The women still wear the
large straw hat and short petticoat as worn in the
Palatinate. The natives hated them cordially at the
beginning, and do not love them much better now, as

they are very jealous of their successes, and such feelings do not tend to make them attempt to imitate the foreigners with intention to equal or even surpass them in results. Naturally, I suppose, the Palatines will finish by becoming Irish like their neighbours.

Passing through the long town of Rathkeale I directed my steps to Adare, where I was received by Sir Richard Quin. This town was formerly full of colleges and ecclesiastical establishments. The ruins of several well-preserved buildings are still to be seen, and four or five miles away, at Skelton, are ruins of abbeys, which are perhaps the largest I have seen in this country.

The ruins in the west of Ireland are of a style of architecture absolutely different from that in the east, where they are commonly rather small, while here they are somewhat of the grandeur and style of the Gothic churches of the Continent.

In reflecting on the prodigious number of ruins of churches and abbeys, and on the immense riches which still remain in the hands of the clergy of the established religion, one is tempted to believe that at one time the whole island belonged to priests, for if the Anglican clergyman could make the most of his estates himself, I imagine that his part would still be not very far away from the half of it. The manner in which these lands are let or farmed out is a hindrance. No beneficiary can let his land for longer than twenty-one years, but this time is pretty long for a man who is advanced in years, and who is pressed to make some provision for his family. To rectify the trouble as much as possible, the Bishop or other beneficiary renews his leases every year with his tenant, on condition that he will be given what we call *un pot de vin*, which puts a certain sum into his pocket and makes him patient. Every clergy-man who takes possession of a benefice is sure by this custom to find a tenancy renewed from the year before, and is obliged himself in some fashion to follow the same practice. I am convinced that there are certain bishoprics which are not let at the tenth part of their value, and which would produce in case of renewal of holding, sums of fifty, sixty, or even one hundred thousand pounds sterling per annum, instead of five, eight, or ten thousand. The Lord is mindful of his own.

I took the road to Limerick, and saw on the way a ' wake ' in the house of a dead man. It was Sunday, and the women do not cry so loudly on that day, but the scene was, nevertheless, a rather singular one. The dead lay on a table, and the house was so full of women sitting on their heels that a bullet dropped among them would not have touched ground. The men were outside on the road, to the number of about two hundred, on foot or on horseback, and a great number prudently waiting at a neighbouring inn until it would please the dead to move.

It was the time of the horse races at Limerick, and also it was the duelling season. The confusion every-where was extreme. The town was full of people coming and going. The workers were doing nothing. Everything had given way to the desire to see some breakneck performances on horseback ; there were on the course more than twenty thousand persons. What made the people anxious to see was that three of the jockeys were peers ; or was it that three of the peers were jockeys ? You can take it whichever way you wish. The one is as bad as the other.

There came to the races some bullies from Cork and

Youghal, with the laudable intention of putting lead into the brains of the Limerick folk. They went about saying to anyone they met, ' Do you want powder and ball ? for we can give it.' During the eight days of the races there were ten or twelve duels—an officer of the Irish brigade was killed. Then it occurred to the Chancellor to put an end to these quarrels by proceedings for criminal acts, and the warlike gentlemen took their departure.

The races finished at last, and happily for the country, for had they lasted three weeks longer, the inhabitants were so given over to sport that the harvest would have lain in the fields ungathered.

The city of Limerick is famous in history as having sustained a long siege by the troops of King William, holding out for the cause of his unfortunate father-in-law ; famous also for the capitulation which the besieged troops made in the name of all Ireland. The terms of this capitulation were most scrupulously observed during the lifetime of King William, but, without assignment of reason other than the desire to discourage the religion of the inhabitants, and force these to adopt the established form, they were most cruelly violated in the reign of Queen Anne. Priests were condemned to be hung for saying mass, and any person convicted of hearing it said, suffered severe penalties. I must add that the excessive severity of these laws was its own antidote, for judges often sought pretexts for acquitting the accused.[1] These laws were

[1] I have been told that a witness in one of such actions, having sworn that he had seen So-and-so at mass, the judge asked him if he knew what mass was. Not being able to answer, the judge said, ' Wretch, how can you swear to what you do not know ? ' and acquitted the prisoner.—*Note by Author.*

rarely or, indeed, it may be said, never put into execution ; but the son, the brother, or even the distant relation of a Catholic could make himself possessor of his friend's property by becoming a Protestant. These cruel laws existed for nearly eighty years, and it is only about fourteen or fifteen years since they were abrogated, and that necessity was felt to make the laws supportable to the inhabitants. In this short space of time Ireland has attained to an extraordinary degree of prosperity, giving occasion to hope that, with a continuance of the present system of moderation and kindness, Ireland will soon rival the country that held her in bondage, and this will mean good fortune for both.

The new city of Limerick is very pretty and very regular, but just to as great degree is the old disgusting. One can hardly believe that there are here fifty thousand inhabitants.

I had here the unspeakable pleasure of receiving the visit of two bankers, who were kind enough to give me an invitation for four or five days ahead. As I have no money which can bring profit to these gentlemen, and as they on their side rarely think of anything but gain, I am not often the subject of their favours, and so when I receive such civilities I am more than ordinarily grateful for them. In a certain Scotch Society to which I was introduced I met a Mr. A——, an Edinburgh banker, who, hearing that I was to pass the winter after my travels in his city, did me the favour, publicly, to give me his card and bind me in a promise to visit him. I kept that card very carefully—I am sure I carried it twelve hundred miles—and at the end of my journey I went to present it to its owner. The reader, I take it, will not be astonished, I am sure, to learn that my reception was of the coolest.

I met in this town a certain reverend doctor, inventor of a new method of growing potatoes. This consists in cutting out, in spring, the shoots or eyes and planting them. It appears that the result is just as good as if the potatoes were cut up and planted, and with this benefit, that the tubers furnishing the shoots are still available as food—for pigs at any rate. This good man, knowing that my intention was to write the story of my travels, did me the favour to give me, in writing, the details of his method, in order that I should translate the notice and convey it to the public. Thinking that, possibly, it may be useful, I print the document exactly as he wrote it out himself :—

' In Limerick the Rev. Doctor Mansell, about three years ago, made the most useful discovery in agriculture that ever was made, and reduced the culture to a certain system, and that is the producing potatoes from the shoots that heretofore had been thrown away as of no kind of value. This discovery promises fair for feeding the lower orders of the people with food at a very cheap rate, when the culture comes to be in general practice. This gentleman, I am informed, has taken very great pains to disseminate the culture, and deserves great credit from the public for the very disinterested manner in which he has conveyed his discoveries to the world.'

Since I have enlarged so much on potatoes, it is perhaps right that I should mention very delicate roots called ' pig-nuts,' which I have seen here for the first time. Possibly the pigs are as clever in finding them as they are in scenting truffles in Languedoc, hence the name. This root is never larger than a filbert and has a flavour as delicate as that of the nut. Children amuse themselves by digging them up in the fields and eating them raw. I have an idea that these might be so improved by cultivation as to become a very nourishing and agreeable food, and this is my reason for mentioning this product of nature.

The Shannon is not navigable, properly speaking, above Limerick; its course is thereafter often interrupted by rocks and cascades through which a plank could hardly pass in safety. To make navigation possible there have been cut, lately, certain canals making connection between those parts of the river which are deep enough for boats. One of these canals, a mile long, ends at Limerick, and in its short course there is a fall of not less than thirty feet. Boats can only ascend, by the locks, at a suitable time of tide, which here rises or falls from twelve to fifteen feet, although the town is sixty miles from the mouth of the river. One or two miles higher up, there is another canal, newly-finished, joining the river seven or eight miles from Castle Connell, which place I reached after, perhaps, a needless roundabout, and where I was received by Mr. George Bruce, to whom the estate belongs.

My travels have always been delightful in the country. Were I able to jump over the towns on my way, I would do it with all my heart. Hospitality in them is too ceremonious, and although in the course of life a little ceremony is sometimes not disagreeable, in my quality of pilgrim I found it very irksome. It would be very unjust, however, not to acknowledge the kindness shown me by Dean Crosbie, and by General Walsh, who, finding me embarrassed in procuring lodging at the time of the races, had the goodness to receive me in his own house.

At Limerick I was obliged entirely to renew my wardrobe, which at the time of my departure from Dublin consisted only of my clothes and what could be contained in two silk stockings from which I had cut the feet. Although my baggage was inconsiderable, I wanted for nothing, and had the means of appearing in society as well dressed as others.

For the information of future travellers on foot, it is my pleasure here to give details of my complete equipment.

A powder bag made out of a woman's glove.
A razor.
Thread.
Needles.
Scissors.
A comb, carried in one of a pair of dress shoes.
A pair of silk stockings.
Breeches, fine enough to be, when folded, not bigger than a fist.
Two very fine shirts.
Three cravats.
Three handkerchiefs.
The clothes in which I travelled.

The sundries I divided in three, two lots going into the silk stockings which served as bags, the third packet contained my shoes. I had six pockets: in three of them were stowed the packets, as described, when I was about to enter a house of consequence; but as this packing would be very inconvenient while walking, I was accustomed, on the road, to tie my three packets in a handkerchief and carry the load over my shoulder at the end of my sword-stick, on which I had grafted an umbrella which excited, everywhere, curiosity, and made the girls laugh—I can't tell why. The remaining pockets were reserved for letters, my pocket-book, and ordinary uses.

The persons who received me, and whose offers of linen I always refused, were much astonished to see me reappear in the drawing-room in silk stockings and powder, as if I had travelled with considerable baggage at my ease, and in a fine carriage. Hey! Mr. Sterne, what do you think of the wardrobe with which I travelled for six solid months?—putting up at the very best houses. My portmanteau was as good as yours, I trow.

Castle Connell is a charming spot situated on the bank of the Shannon, which here flows like a torrent through stones and rocks. The beauty of the place and the mineral waters draw here a great number of Limerick's idlers, who pass the summer in the village and drink, every morning of their stay, a glass of the water. The rich strangers attract beggars from afar, and there are already more here than elsewhere in Ireland. It may seem a strange remark, but it is true, that the richer the country in Ireland, the poorer are the people and the lower the labourer's daily wage.

The misery of the people is generally attributed in Ireland to the manner in which estates are let. A rich man who does not wish to trouble himself with details will let a large extent of ground to a single man, whose intention is not to work, but to underlet to three or four others. These in their turn, having still very large areas, underlet perhaps to twenty persons; they, again, will let to perhaps a hundred peasants moderately well off; and these, once again, will let at an exorbitant rent to perhaps a thousand poor labourers. Necessity obliges these last to take their little corner of land at a rent enormously over real value. They cultivate the greater part of it in potatoes, which serve to nourish a family, and to fatten a great pig and a few fowls, by the sale of which they commonly find the money to pay their rents. It can easily be understood that, with all these ' cascades,' it is probable that the proprietor receives not more than one-third of the money which the lowest under-tenants are obliged to pay, and the remainder goes to the profit of the rent-farmers. I ought to say that such abuses have been apparent to many proprietors, and that to my knowledge several of them in the north combined and resolved to let their estates themselves directly to the working farmers; but with what result? These latter, finding themselves no longer harassed by the small rent-farming class from whom they held, have not paid the rents, and proprietors have been obliged to revert to the old method. I know little or nothing of cultivation, but I believe that it should be possible to find a means of arranging matters so as to avoid the dangers of the two extremes.

Several persons near Castle Connell· (among others the Lord Chancellor and Mr. Bruce) in multiplying industries have increased the rate of wages—there can be no better way for the rich man to employ his money. Often I have heard the peasant reproached for his idleness and drunkenness, but when one is reduced to danger of dying from hunger, is it not a better thing to do nothing, since the most assiduous work will not hinder the evil from arriving ? In such a situation also, is it not natural to drink when one can, a drop from the waters of Lethe, in order to forget one's misery ? If the poor man could really feel that work would ameliorate his situation, he would quickly abandon that apathy and indifference which are born of despair.

Mr. Bruce has built, at his own charges, a great number of comfortable houses for the peasantry, and these people, so often accused with injustice of defects which really do not belong to them, have proved very careful. When he has needed workers he can always find them, even in times when his neighbours cannot get a sufficiency I have been assured that his labourers do not wish to take from him the price which they are willing to receive from others.

The inhabitants of Castle Connell were assessed with a rate to provide means to build a Catholic chapel. I do not know what fault had been committed by the priest of the parish, but the Catholic bishop of Killaloe interdicted the work, and the church remained half built, and without a roof. Mass, however, was celebrated in a corner covered by a few planks, and the people continued to come as before, but resolutely resolved not to finish the church unless or until the favourite priest should be recalled.

Crossing the mosses which surround this village, I came by O'Brien's Bridge to Glanamore to Mr. Thomas Arthur, with whom I spent several days. His house is at the end of a fertile, little valley, surrounded by mountains covered with peat. I saw with him bones representing almost an entire skeleton of that monstrous animal which is called in this country ' moss ' or

' moose deer,' and the name of which I do not know in French.

The race has been so long extinct in Ireland that history, and even tradition, have nothing to say about it. It was a species of deer which, from the size of the horns and bones which are found in the peat moss, must have been at least three times as large as any we know now. These horns are generally seven or eight feet high—they have been found indeed to be ten feet. The bones of the legs are at least double the thickness and three times the length of those of an ox.

It is extremely strange that no tradition whatever makes mention of this animal in Ireland. It is no less strange that trace of it has never been found on the continent. What was Nature thinking of to lodge in an island an animal which must have felt itself imprisoned?

In my quality of traveller it is permitted to me to dream dreams, and in that of writer of travels to make these, in some fashion, known to the public. When I have travelled a few hundred miles more, I shall have arrived at a place where it may be possible for me to propound some beautiful, conjectural matter about the singular traditions of this country.

I returned to O'Brien's Bridge, and after having taken a plunge into the Shannon in order to put him in a good temper with me, I ascended the river with Mr. Waller in a little boat, for which my umbrella served as sail. The river was charming, beautiful, calm, and it seemed to be deep, but soon we came to a waterfall and were obliged to land. They are here digging a little canal of about one hundred paces long, to join the two navigable parts of the river. Returning in the boat we travelled about ten miles and were again obliged to land and even to leave the boat. Here they are making a canal which shall be about a mile long, and which will terminate near the beautiful palace of the bishop of Killaloe. The fall of water here is very considerable, and in a distance of about fifty feet it falls fourteen or fifteen through large, round stones. This is the kind of obstruction in the rivers which forms the lakes. This one makes an immense lake of thirty miles long by twelve or fifteen wide, and although it offers, at different parts, interesting and pleasing views, like the greater part of the lakes of Ireland, it has rather the look of a great inundation, and the islands through it give *vraisemblance* to the appearance. A company offered to drain nearly the whole of this lake, provided that the riverside proprietors would give them half the new-formed land. Difficulties arose, and the matter has not been carried through. This company had calculated that, in lowering the bed of the river at Killaloe by twelve feet, they would drain fourteen thousand acres. The cost of the works would have amounted to over twenty thousand pounds sterling. It would not have been a great deal to pay for seven thousand acres of land, but it is to be presumed that this would not produce very much in the early years, and perhaps one-third of it would be sandy or unfit for cultivation.

The proprietors are usually very jealous about companies executing such works. Often they oppose the designs and prefer to have their land under water than divide with the interfering company; but it should be possible to find a way of arranging the matter to the satisfaction of both parties. A proprietor might be persuaded to pay four or five pounds sterling for every acre of land, good or bad, that the company should drain for him at its risk and expense.

The little town of Killaloe is very ugly ; the cathedral is large and appears to be fairly well built. The stone bridge which crosses the Shannon here has eighteen arches, but they are very small, and the bridge will have to be rebuilt—a modern one need not have more than nine or ten arches. I paid a visit to the minister of the parish, who has a superb house at a little distance from the town, on a height dominating Lough Derg. From there is to be had a really magnificent view of this vast sheet of water, whose banks are almost everywhere high, and cultivated with care. There is a bay of seven or eight miles, which cannot be seen without climbing to the summit of a fairly high mountain in the neighbourhood. From this height the Shannon can be seen winding through the plain as far as Limerick, with all the little towns which are on its banks, the principal of these being Nenagh.

It is disappointing that there is nowhere to be seen any appearance of industry. There are no manufactures. Beyond the labouring of the soil there is nothing to do, but patience !—a certain time must be allowed to a nation to come out of its stupor of seven hundred years. It is only fourteen years since its genius made effort to fly, and already thought is being taken to find means to surmount the immense difficulties which the navigation of the Shannon presents. A certain measure of success has followed through the use of communicating canals. The Grand Canal is proceeding very slowly, but it will be finished in a few years, when interior communication will be opened across Ireland from Dublin to Limerick, and industry will grow in proportion as the means are provided for the disposal of its product.

The new movement has not stopped here. · I have seen several maps of the Shannon, on which are indicated communication canals between the larger lakes, from that of Derg to Lough Allen beyond Leitrim, a distance of more than two hundred miles Irish. I do not see why the effort should not be made to do better still, and join Lough Clean, the last, or rather the first, lake of the Shannon with the river and Lough Gill and the river which flows into the sea at Sligo. The distance between the two rivers is not really more than five or six miles. They are certainly separated by heights, but not nearly so considerable as one would imagine for the head of such a river which rises fifteen or sixteen miles from the sea, and has a course of about two hundred and fifty miles in the same way and same direction as the Severn in England.

It must be admitted, however, that the navigation of the great lakes found in its course would be very difficult for canal or river boats. These lakes are subject, like the waters of the Mediterranean, to sudden tempests, which may overturn even the strongest boats. The only remedy I can see is to drain the lakes, and with money and good-will this should not be a very difficult thing, and it would give Ireland two hundred thousand more acres of earth.

The first step in the civilisation of a country is to cut the woods, drain the marshes, lower the beds of rivers, and allow stagnant waters to flow away. The people of this country have succeeded perfectly well in the matter first mentioned, seeing that they have not left wood enough to make a toothpick in many places, but they have hardly yet commenced to think about the remaining works.

Near Killaloe is to be seen one of those round forts which are so numerous in Ireland. This one is called ' O'Brien's Palace.' Tradition reports that Brian Boru, who defeated the Danes at Clontarf, and perished in the battle, lived here. It is well situated for defence at the point where the river leaves the lake. The fort is not as large as several that I have seen, but the parapets seem higher and the fosses deeper. I cannot conceive the sort of palace or, indeed, dwelling of any kind which could be erected inside such an enclosure, unless it were simply an arrangement of plank shelters or tents.

I followed the western course of Lough Derg, and on the way met an honest attorney going gaily to put the surrounding country under contribution. He pointed out to me, at some distance from the shore, a square tower situated on a rock. Some determined contrabandists had there established a distillery, with intention to pay no duties. They barricaded the place, and being provided with firearms, no customs officer dare hazard his life in approaching these friends of the ' creature.' To dislodge them, it was necessary to send troops with cannon, but the distance from the bank being considerable, and there being also a wish not to proceed to extremes, they proceeded to starve out the illicit distillers, who did not surrender until the fifteenth day, and then only after having effected an honourable capitulation.

I paid a visit to Mr. H. Brady at Tomgrany, which is a rather pretty village situated at the end of the bay of which I have already spoken. From it can be seen many of the islands in the lake, among others one which is called Holy Island, which has a high round tower, and where formerly were seven churches, the inhabitants still going, with great devotion, to make their pilgrimages round the ruins. The Catholics of the country have taken exclusive possession of the cemetery, and will not permit that the bones of a Protestant should there be deposited. A rich man of the parish threatened to send a labourer out of it. 'All right,' said the other, 'but I have more right in the parish than you, for you can't take from me my six feet of earth in Holy Island, and with all your riches you will never have that.'

Walking through the ruined town of Mount Shannon, I came to Mellick to Mr. Thomas Burke. Near his house was formerly an abbey, and its ruins are still regarded with veneration. Near the chapel is a species of cell which is of singular form. There is just room for a person standing in it to turn round—it would seem to have been a confessional. Above a tomb there is a stone, squarely hollowed and full of the *water of heaven*, which water is said to have the virtue of curing corns. How charming it is to travel in Ireland ! I hope by the time my promenade is finished that I shall be cured of every ill.

The borders of the lake in this district were some time ago covered with wood, but this has all been cut down, and the whole country is naked and arid. Near Woodfort the landscape begins to improve, and is rather pretty near a village called Abbey, on the confines of the provinces of Munster and Connaught. Formerly there was a considerable abbey here, with a church dedicated to the Virgin. It was a *fête* day on which I saw it, and the place was crowded. This ruin is one of the few of which the inhabitants have had the good sense to make use, so as to avoid the trouble and expense of building a new church. Catholics have lately obtained permission to use two of the lateral chapels, of which the vault remained intact; it is hardly possible to exaggerate the miserable look of these chapels and of the poor folk who frequent them. In the cemetery two or three priests were occupied in confessing the penitents. They sat on stones, and each held a little flag, which was used to separate the penitent from the crowd. The priests, as I am told, receive something for their trouble, according to a fixed tariff; this is said to be their principal source of income. After all, they must live, and it is only through the little charges they exact from the faithful that their kitchen can be kept going. I have, however, seen some, to my great surprise, who are by no means badly off, having between one and two hundred pounds sterling per annum of income, besides a passable house, and, according to custom, dinners without end with their parishioners who are in easy circumstances.

The law allows to every Catholic priest who will turn Protestant the sum of forty pounds sterling per annum, to be paid by the county in which he lives; he has also the promise of the first curacy vacant. The insults which the people heap on the few who profit by these advantages are sufficient to disgust those whose conscience would allow them to place their temporal interests before all other considerations. However, the law is on the side of these, and yet I do not believe that there are a dozen of them in the whole of Ireland. I went to visit near this abbey a holy well of the place. It is not, like most of them, in open country ; it is surrounded by houses, and although I was prepared for what I was to find there, I confess it was very difficult for me to retain a serious countenance before a score of women with their clothes tucked up, moving in single file round the enclosure on their bare knees. One had to think of the serious intention to avoid bursting into laughter on seeing the contortions of the devotees occasioned by the pebbles underneath, and in noticing the devices adopted to prevent the soiling of fine red petticoats. . . . Oh, Monsieur Twiss ! what an occasion this would have been for you, and what remarks you would have made ! . . . But I shall be more discreet than you were.

A decent man was standing at a little distance and, seeing that I was a stranger, approached. I asked for what was the water of this well good. ' Oh, Sir,' said he, ' it is good for everything,—the blind return walking, the lame speaking, and the deaf seeing. If you have any infirmities, just go round on your knees seven times and see what happens.'

I did not need to make the experience myself in order to learn what would happen, for after the pilgrimage was over, and the poor folk were washing at the well, I saw many a scarred and bloody knee. I wonder if this severe penitence can prevent faults through fear of the pain and hurt of the stones ! What matter ! I am of those who think it preferable to prevent faults by folly rather than that they should be punished, after committal, by the sword of justice.

CHAPTER VII

LA CONACIE OR CONNAUGHT.—THE ROAD OF THE DISHES—GALWAY—EYRE CONNAUGHT

WHEN I crossed the stream separating Conacie from Momonie or Munster from Connaught, it really seemed to me that I was no longer in the same country! The features of the people were not the same, their dwellings were not arranged in the same manner. Here were long villages with fields through them, on the other side they were compactly ordered. Following a road carried along the crest of a long hill which seemed artificially to be set in the middle of a plain, I reached Pallace, the residence of Lord Riverston.

The tithes here are not nearly so onerous as in Munster, being collected only on grain and sheep, while in Munster the milk of the cows, the hens and their eggs, and the vegetables of the garden are liable, if the minister likes to exact his dues.

At Portumna they have begun to build a bridge over the Shannon. The type is that of Wexford, Ross, and Waterford, a type beginning to be common, but losing nothing of its beauty thereby. Here, where the Shannon flows into Lough Derg, there is an old and fine castle, the property of the Marquis of Clanricard.

Twelve miles to the west there is a charming sheet of water called Lough Rea. It gives its name to a pretty little town situated on its banks, which seems even more prosperous than Galway, although the latter is a seaport. It is a pity that the inhabitants do not pay some attention to the shore of the lake ; a quay should be constructed, which, leaving improvement aside, would make a very agreeable promenade.

I heard of a proposal to effect a junction of this lake, on the one side with the bay of Galway, on the other with the Shannon. The work should not offer any great difficulty, the country not being very mountainous, and the lake situated at the highest level.

I had two letters of recommendation for places at nearly equal distance from the town, and I had to determine which should be presented. Meeting a wayfarer, I asked him if he knew Mr. So-and-so, mentioning the name on one of my introductions. ' Oh yes,' he replied, ' he is a very rich man.' ' And what sort of a man is he ? ' I asked, but asked in vain, for all the countryman would say was that he was ' a very fine gentleman.' ' Well, do you know Mr. So-and-so ? ' said I, mentioning the name of my second letter. And immediately I had the response that he was ' a good, honest, hospitable, well-informed man.' This settled the doubt for me, and I made my way to Castle Taylor.

On the way I fell in with several Irish-speaking peasants who wished to hold conversation with me, but my very small acquaintance with their language made exchange of ideas difficult. They managed to make me understand, however, that they wished to relieve me of the trouble of carrying my packet, and they really did carry it for me until I reached Castle

Taylor, where I met with one of those flattering recep-
tions which banish all thoughts of sorrow and fatigue.

There are more curious things to be seen on this
estate than are to be found in many a province, and
Mr. Taylor was good enough to show them to me. At
a little distance is a great round fort, called the palace
of Dondorlass, once the seat of Goora, King of Connaught. Unlike similar forts elsewhere, there is not on
this the smallest vestige of vegetation. This palace
was close to a once-famous town called Ardrahan.
This is at present only a village, but tradition rather
than history affirms it to have been, at one time,
immense, and from traces along the road leading to it
now, it really does appear that it, the road, had formerly
double the width it has at present. Unless the space
included a planting on each side, it is difficult to say
what was the need for such a broad highway. This
road is called in Irish *Bothar lean da nae mias*—
the road over which they followed the dishes, and this
curious name is accounted for by the following story :

A certain Saint Macduagh, brother of the king, had
retired with a monk to a lonely mountain, there to
offer up prayers. After two days the monk, who was
not sufficiently interested in devotions to neglect the
calls of his interior, commenced to grumble, and said to
the saint, ' Saving your holiness, you have brought me
to this desert mountain to die of hunger. I know that,
to-day, your brother Goora gives a great feast to his
nobles, I would rather be at it than here.' ' O man of
little faith,' said the saint, ' do you really think that I
have brought you here to die of hunger ? ' And, forth-
with, he began to pray with greater ardour than ever.
All at once the delighted monk saw an excellent dinner

arrive, and its various dishes range themselves round him.

Meanwhile King Goora and his nobles, returning famished from the chase and various combats, had the misfortune to see the dishes prepared for them leave the table and fly off. In the surprising circumstances they did at once what was eminently reasonable, for, seeing their dinner in flight, the cook with his spit, domestics and grooms, dogs and cats fell in behind the king and his court ; and the whole party, on foot or on horse, joined at full speed in the hunt of the flying dishes.

The dinner arrived a full quarter-hour earlier than the court ; and the monk, who had commenced to do himself well with the delicacies, saw approach, with horror, a crowd which threatened to take the food from his mouth. He made a new complaint to the saint, protesting that it had been better not to bring the food than to bring it and with it the hungry court of Goora to kill and perhaps devour him. 'O man of little faith,' said the saint, ' let them all come.'

They did come, and when they were within thirty feet of the provisions, the saint placed them in a situation as disagreeable as can be conceived. He fastened their feet to the rock, and obliged them to be unwilling witnesses of the monk's junketing with their dinner. There can be seen yet, in the rock, the marks of the feet of men and horses and dogs, and even of the ends of the lances, which were secured lest their owners should have taken the notion to throw them at the monk. As must be admitted, this is proof positive of the truth of the story, and justification of the name of the road.

O great Saint Macduagh ! how thankful should I be if only you would repeat this little miracle from time to time in favour of your humble servant !

The good saint is still much respected in these parts ; —there was a very considerable abbey which bore his name, and, indeed, a bishopric which is at present united to that of Killaloe. I have seen the ruins of it, very fine they are and very extensive,—seven or eight little churches, and a cathedral which must have been rather imposing. Near it is a round tower which is very high and in perfect state of preservation. Cromwell's soldiers, passing through the country, were base enough to attempt its destruction, firing at it cannon balls, the marks of which are still visible. Here are also the ruins of several colleges and seminaries for the education of priests.

The penitences round these churches are very rigorous. First the circle is made on bare feet, and afterwards on the knees, and, as the course is rather long, the penitent is allowed the comfort and support of two bones of the dead. There is a tree in the cemetery specially dedicated to the saint—the devout wear scraps of it as protection against fire. I have seen Protestants who, half mocking, half believing, carried these scraps about with them, and there are tales told of the virtue of the wood proving effective in the extinguishing of fires on several occasions. What a pity that I neglected to secure a supply ! It would have been of value to a London Fire Insurance Company.

Mr. Taylor conducted me to one of his estates called Capavarna, where he showed me several large hollows which were full of water when I passed five hours earlier and were now dry ; also he showed me a little lake which in the morning had a circumference measuring a mile, and which later in the day had shrunk to the dimensions of a cattle drinking-pond.

This country appears to be supported on vaults in limestone ; there is no running water on the surface, but I have seen subterranean rivers in caverns. Sometimes the roof of the vault has fallen in, and in the hollows thus produced is seen the phenomenon of the disappearing ponds and lake ; the rising tide drives or holds back the subterranean river water, which falls or disappears from sight at low tide. In winter, when the rivers are full, wide lakes are formed where in summer was meadowland.

It would seem that this country has been swept by the ocean in some great convulsion of the globe, and that the covering earth has been in this way removed. Here are to be seen plains of seven or eight miles long without the least vestige of soil, and without verdure other than that of a few hazel-nut bushes which grow in odd corners among the stones. Such wild and desolate places were commonly chosen by the Druids for the practice of their rites. Two of their altars are here, enormous stones twenty to thirty feet long, and nearly as wide, supported on three stones seven or eight feet in height. I climbed on both ; it is really inconceivable how these ancient people were able to place such rocks so high, and so solidly set that I imagine it impossible to dislodge them unless by breaking the supporting stones.

It has been concluded that, since these altars are commonly supported by three stones, the Druids held this number in reverence, and associated with it some idea of the Trinity, as do the Brahmins of India. I am inclined to believe that they attached no importance to the number, and that they placed their altars on three stones simply because that number was the best for their purpose. Eight miles from Dublin, in Bannan's Glen, on the road to Bray, I have seen one of these slabs supported on four stones, and General Vallencey figures a representation of one sustained by two stones, and of another supported by six. To give an idea of the size of these great slabs of stone, I may say that, under that which I saw near the village of Cabinteely, a father, a mother, a family, of ten children, with their dog, cat, goat, pig, and fowls lived for years, and only quitted their dwelling when the proprietor, wishing to allow the public to inspect this ancient monument, built for the family a cabin in the neighbourhood.

The little valley of Capavarna presents a very striking contrast to the desert which surrounds it. The land in it is very fertile, and the view is agreeably diversified by a mixture of wood and cultivated fields through which, by easy paths, the different extraordinary things I have mentioned are reached. I noticed there a large stone commemorative of the restoration of her just rights to Ireland in 1782.

This corner of the earth, so little known, so seldom visited, seems to me to have more claims on a traveller's curiosity than many of the places made famous by fashion. Returning by way of the Road of the Flying Dishes to the famous town of Ardrahan, I passed near to a *cromliah*, or great circle of stones. The learned are much exercised in deciding what this is or was, some holding that these circles were formed round the burying-place of a chief, others that the origin is religious.

For my part I think the reason for their construction to have been the same as for the raths, that is, defence. On a little eminence, the only one in this plain of stones, in digging in what has the appearance of burnt earth, there has been found a hideous statue which is supposed to be that of Beal.

Tradition records that Beal (which is a word signifying the sun or a quality of the sun) was worshipped at this spot. A bishop's cross and keys are carved on the stone ; but we know that Christianity was obliged to make terms with the ancient cult and to observe some of its practices. In other countries of Europe the traces of the ancient religion are not so marked as they are in this island. What appears to me most markedly Druidic in present day Irish devotions is the attachment to holy wells. Their use is the same all over Ireland, though with variation in the religious sentiment to fit the degree of veneration of the saint who has displaced the god or nymph adored of old time.

This country is covered with old castles to which the new proprietors have commonly given their names ; but if you wish to ask the way to any, it is better to learn what it was called in Irish, for the peasants have not taken the trouble to learn the new names, perhaps do not want to learn them, unless they happen to wish well to the owners. There is not a particle of peat in these parts, and the inhabitants are obliged to bring it from the other side of Galway Bay. For wood there is none but what is found in the valley of Capavarna, and it is not surprising that the proprietor there finds considerable difficulty in preventing the peasants from cutting down his trees.

LA CONACIE OR CONNAUGHT

The nakedness of the poor near Galway is most unpleasant—is it not possible to organise industries which would enable these people to lead a less painful existence ? Their huts are not like the houses of men, and yet out of them troop flocks of children healthy and fresh as roses. Their state can be observed all the easier, since they are often as naked as the hand, and play in front of the cabins with no clothing but what Nature has given them.

These poor folk, however, reduced to such misery as cannot be imagined by a man of better fortune, are humane, good, patient, and, notwithstanding what avarice may advance, would be industrious and hard-working if they could believe that work would ameliorate their lot. They live on potatoes, and they have for that edible (which is all in all to them) a singular respect, attributing to it all that happens to them. I asked a peasant, who had a dozen pretty children, ' How is it that your countrymen have so many and so healthy children ? ' ' It's the praties, Sir,' he replied.

One finds numerous schools in the hedges—always for the reason I have indicated already. It is a mistake to think the peasant of this country so ignorant or so stupid. Misery, it is true, does stupefy him and make him indifferent. Yet, I declare that it is among these people that I find indications of disposition to do everything that could render society happy and prosperous, where it has been possible to inspire them with interest in their country.

I called at Ardfrey, the home of Mr. Blake. From his house can be seen a most beautiful view of the bay of Galway. Inside his house was a view still more interesting, but the gentle A—— was far too pretty to allow of any hope of seeing her again. Nearly all the inhabitants in this district are Catholics, rich as well as poor ; only the rich submitted, formerly, to the Anglican form, in order that they might possess their goods in peace, and, now, in order that they may be eligible for election to Parliament. Thirty years ago the proprietor of a very fine estate called Oranmore, fearing that some cousin might turn Protestant in order to filch it away from him, sought the bishop and offered to renounce the superstitions of the Church of Rome. 'What motives, my son,' said the pastor, 'urge you to enter the fold of the faithful, and to abandon the Babylonish Woman ? ' ' Oranmore,' said the convert, and to all the customary questions he had but the single word—' Oranmore '—for answer. The bishop was not inclined to admit him to communion on such exhibition of worldly motive, but the convert had offered to submit to the law, and nothing more could be demanded.

Crossing the beautiful bay of Galway I came to the town of same name. It is situated between a great lake and the sea without deriving much advantage from one or other. The river leaving the lake a quarter mile from the sea flows like a torrent, no effort has been made to construct a canal, and the port is outside the town.

One is surprised, on entering Galway, to see the disposition of the streets, and especially the placing of the houses, which is different from that in other Irish towns. Almost every one has the gable turned to the street, and has a *porte cochère*, such as is found in old towns on the Continent. Galway was built, they say, by the Spanish, to whom it belonged.[1] It is still possible to follow the regularity of the plan, although disfigured at present. It is said also that thirteen families, whose names are still common, laid the city's foundations, and tradition avers that, while a good lady of the name of Joyce watched the masons who built Galway Bridge at her expense, an eagle dropped a chain of gold in her lap, and placed a crown on her head. The gold chain is still preserved by the Joyce family—according to the story told to me. The people have always loved fables—had Galway become a Rome this one would certainly have been believed.

This city had formerly an extensive commerce, but it is much decayed in recent times. Efforts are needed for the encouragement of industry, and it is desirable that some means should be adopted to make beggars work, and prevent lunatics from running about the streets.

A wine merchant gave me, in good faith, an explanation of the decay of commerce. ' Before France knew how to make wine,' said he, ' we made it here.' ' What,' said I, ' I never heard that you grew grapes at Galway.' ' Oh, we never did,' he replied, ' but in France the wine was simply juice of the grape, and we brought it to Galway to make it drinkable. Unfortunately, the Bordeaux merchants can prepare it now as well as we did, and that has cut the feet from under us.'

---

[1] I report this as it was stated to me. The period during which the Spaniards were masters of a part of Ireland is not well defined in history. All places on the western coast, however, from Galway to Bantry, have the tradition of their occupation, and some place-names are Spanish, such as Valentia, &c.—*Note by Author.*

The natives are not accustomed to see much of foreigners, and they paid me the compliment of assuming me to be a Crœsus. People were so fond of making me pay the *costs of the war* that I should have been hard put to for boarding charges had not Mr. Anthony Lynch, to whom I had been recommended, done me the kindness to offer me a bed at his house.

Lough Corrib, which discharges its waters at Galway, may be thirty miles in length, and I am convinced that, with one or two locks, it would be possible to bring boats from the port into the river. The existence of this lake is due to an accumulation of enormous stones near the mouth of the river, and to the peat mosses where the river begins its course. It appears that, formerly, there was a canal which circled the old walls and discharged into the bay, but it was long ago filled up and built over, and since there is no desire at present to incur the cost of a similar waterway, the Galway people might, at least, utilise the waters of the river above the town to provide a stream in each of the streets. There are few places where such a precaution is more necessary. I would suggest, too, that the old walls, which are ruinous and no longer of any use, should be pulled down, and if they would build quays along the sea and river fronts, these would be a great embellishment to the city.

The shops here are open on Sunday nearly as on other days—perhaps the whisky-shops more than others. However, everybody goes to church, one set after another. The merchants have a custom of keeping a few shutters on a shop window, but the door is open just as usual. There are various clubs to which people resort to read the newspapers. To have entry to one—The Amicable Society—one must be a subscriber, but anyone can go to the Mercantile Coffee House.

The principal church dignitary here is called ' The Warden,' that is to say ' The Guardian.' He has as much authority as have bishops elsewhere—it is a privilege which the Pope granted at one time to the Chapter, permitting them to make election from among the canons. The Protestants have adopted the same procedure since the Reformation. Here the people are all Catholic, and it is fortunate that there are plenty of Anglican ministers, for, otherwise, there would not be anyone to represent the dominant religion.

Young Irishmen travel far to seek their fortunes, and have a trick of hooking on to rich old widows, by whom, with great address, they manage to make themselves beloved, spite of brothers, sisters, children, and even grandchildren. Those who have not the means to travel the world seem to make of Galway general rendezvous. They come here from all parts of the province under pretence of sea-bathing, but I venture to say that the attraction is quite other, and more important. There are few countries which can show prettier brunettes, or such a number of them, and all things here seem to conspire to further their *humane* projects. The milliners furnish them, on credit, with ribbons and finery to any extent, refraining from any request for payment until after the wedding, when the poor man finds himself in much the same situation as vanquished nations, forced by their conquerors to pay for the bombs and bullets by which they have been brought into subjection.

There are *Assemblies*, with very moderate price of

entry, nearly every day, sometimes full-dress, sometimes half-dress, sometimes undress, and called as
they are one or other—*Assembly*, *Drum*, or *Promenade*.
The price of entry varies with the name, but the thing
itself is always the same. There is an air of merriment
and good-humour about these gatherings, and the
Galway belles frequenting them could certainly teach
their French sisters something in *coquetterie*. It is
to be expected that such concourses of pretty women
should attract a great number of young men, who,
for the most part, go at first for simple amusement, but
finish, often, by returning to their homes with one rib
more. There is in the city a certain clergyman,
formerly a Catholic priest, who, having nothing to
live on but the £40 sterling per annum which the
law allows to Catholic priests embracing the Anglican
religion, augments his meagre income by solemnising
marriages according to the Scotch manner.

In the morning the young damsels, packed five or
six on a car, legs dangling, go to refresh their charms in
the sea about two miles from the city. In the evening
—if there is no assembly—they wander from shop to
shop, buying, laughing, chatting with the friends they
meet. The stay at Galway for three summer months is,
for the young folks, a veritable Land of Cockaigne.

All, however, do not marry. There are maids who
grow old in this city without knowing it, and who
continue to shop, dance, and bathe until they have
reached the mature age of fifty or more years. Sure
I am that nowhere else in any country could they pass
the ageing years more agreeably or happily.

The neighbourhood of Galway is the most arid and
stony in Ireland, but the rock to the east of the river

being limestone, it has been possible to cultivate some patches with success. It is a singular thing that I have often had occasion to note that the uglier the country the prettier are the women—they are charming here. Connemara is said to be the most abominably ugly place in nature, and therefore ought to be inhabited by angels. I had thought of visiting it, and this sweet reflection confirmed me in my resolution.

It is most extraordinary that this country, forming part of the County of Galway, and not more than fifteen miles from the city of that name, should be less known than the islands of the Pacific Ocean. Of the persons from whom I asked information some replied vaguely, others begged me not to visit such a barbarous country, where I should not find a dry stone to sit down on, and where the few inhabitants were as barbarous as the Iroquois. But the more I was dissuaded the stronger became the desire to see a country so dreadful. The Galway men in former times held it in such dread that, over the city gate leading to it, they engraved the words 'Lord deliver us from the ferocious O'Flahertys,' and they made a law that any man of the name of O'Flaherty who should spend a night in their town should be put to death.

Arming myself with all my courage I crossed the spot where once stood the gate of prayer, and, after a walk of fourteen or fifteen miles, I came to Lemon Field, the seat of Sir John O'Flaherty, where, so far from meeting with ferocity, I received a most charming welcome. The country between this place and Galway I found to be called Eyre Connaught. I was not yet in Connemara. In many parts it was fairly well cultivated, and although seldom visited, had nothing frightful about it. The view of Lough Corrib had in it something of the majestic, compelling the spectator's admiration. The lake is full of little islands, most of them cultivated. If you should ask the number of them, the answer is certain to be 365, one for every day in the year. I have seen three lakes in Ireland which have exactly the same number ; perhaps it would be more correct to say that the peasantry have adopted this number to save themselves the trouble of actual count.

Although this mixture of land and water is pleasing to the view, it suggests to the stranger the idea of floods of great rivers, and this association somewhat diminishes the pleasure of the scene. Nothing in the world will make me believe that these lakes exist of necessity, and I am convinced that when industry has progressed, these water spaces will disappear one after the other.

Certain curiosities are to be seen in the neighbour-hood. The rock is of the same character as that near the Abbey of Killmacduagh, and, as in that place, there are here subterranean rivers which appear and disappear often. Advantage has been taken at one place of a natural vault to carry the road through it ; at another place this honeycombed rock has been used, in old times, in the construction of a castle which offered a strong resistance to the soldiers of Cromwell. This resistance was so strong that the besiegers commenced to retreat, but the poor governor, overjoyed at the baffling of his enemies, was imprudent enough to show himself at a window, when a gunshot put an end to his life, and the castle surrendered immediately afterwards.

These countries of Connemara and Eyre Connaught

are almost quite separated from the rest of Ireland by the two great lakes, Lough Corrib and Lough Mask, between them sixty miles long. A patch of mountainous land and the bridge of Galway are the only means of reaching the territory by land. Armies have never been able to penetrate to the interior of the country, which has been of old time the refuge of deserters and contrabandists. Even at present there are poor peasants who descend from their mountains and hire themselves on the other side of the lakes. Then when they have been clothed and paid, one fine morning they recross the water, and are heard of no more.

Lough Corrib is about nine or ten miles wide. There is a public boat which crosses to a little town called Cong, where is a deep cavern into which some of the waters of the lake are poured. The only trading which seems to require the use of boats here is not very important. It is that in turf, which is used often to hide hogsheads of brandy and French wines which the boatmen bring from Connemara, where never customs official dare appear.

Many Irish peers take their titles from these expanses of water, and from rivers ; I am told that in Ireland there are Lords Corrib, Neagh, Erne, &c. One of the most respected among those who had received me takes his title from the Shannon, another is named from the bay of Kenmare, a third from the bay of Glandore ; sometimes a title has been taken from a high mountain, a striking object in the landscape. I have heard of a man who wished to take the title of Lord Peloponnesus, Earl of Greece. Since great things flatter self-love, why has nobody thought of calling himself Lord Atlantic? The sound of Lady Ocean seems to me to be very delightful.

I remarked, at several places in the country, great piles of stones, and could not imagine what the use of these could be. I was told later that these were erected as a sort of homage to the dead. When a funeral cortege reaches one of these places, it is stopped, and does not proceed until a pile has been erected to the honour of the deceased. I suppose that this respect is only accorded in the case of those who have been much loved and are greatly regretted.

The word for one of these piles is, in Irish, *carn*, and the higher the erection the more honourable or celebrated has been the deceased. ' I shall throw no stone on your cairn ' is a phrase used by inhabitants of this country to express anger at, or dissatisfaction with, the person to whom the words are addressed. It is very much as if a wife should tell her husband that she hoped to dance on his grave.

Here is a holy well of character somewhat different from the ordinary. The water appears at two places. At one the water is used for the ordinary needs of life ; at the other only penitents may drink or take of the water to rub on their eyes. It is really a subterranean stream, similar to those I have already described, but much smaller in volume. When the good folk have said their prayers, they hang rags on the surrounding thorns, and for nothing in the world would they allow these to be removed. I do not know what idea attaches to the act ; the penitence is not performed on the knees, but simply barefooted. There may have been here, formerly, a chapel in which mass was said, or perhaps it was celebrated in the open, for an altar exists, and I could not see any remains of buildings.

Oughterard is the last village of Eyre Connaught. It possesses a mineral water spring and a waterfall which attract a good many Galway people. From this point the view of the lake and its numerous islands is very remarkable. There are here large barracks situated on an arm of one of the subterranean rivers of which I have spoken, and serving as hospital for the troops in garrison at Galway.

CHAPTER VIII

CONNEMARA—MANNER OF BAKING UNLEAVENED
BREAD—ANTI-DILUVIAN REVERIES

I RESOLVED at last to commence my travels in the
redoubtable Connemara. Hardly had I left the village
of Oughterard than the horses which Sir John had
been good enough to supply commenced to behave
badly. They did not seem to care for this excursion,
and jumped and sidled into the heath at the side of the
road, the one on which I was mounted expressing his
displeasure at last by lying down, and it was only with
great difficulty that I could get him to rise and walk.
Balaam's ass was not more troublesome to his master
than was this beast to me. The only thing in which he
differed was in his lack of voice, but finding in the end
that I was resolute, he determined to proceed, and I
entered the territory of Connemara.

This is certainly a most extraordinary country,
almost entirely uncultivated, and covered with mountains or lakes. In some places, however, green grass
can be seen, which makes it possible to believe that the
ground is capable of culture. The district is about
sixty miles long by forty wide, and belongs almost
entirely to Colonel Martin. It is a very large estate,
and, in spite of its wild appearance, it brings him in
from ten to twelve thousand pounds sterling per annum,

which, after all, is hardly more than twopence an acre. Some years ago he gave to an intelligent French *valet-de-chambre* some ground to cultivate, and built a house for him. This man really did succeed in cultivating a pretty large space near his house, which space is yet to be seen as a little oasis in the desert, but finding himself alone and too far from society, he tired of his situation and disappeared.

I quickly arrived at Ballinahinch, the home of Colonel Martin, who, for a man of such fortune, has chosen a strange retreat in this wild country. The house was built by his father for an inn, and the nearest town is Galway, which is thirty miles away, and it is necessary to send to it for all provisions needed ; even for the bread, which often they cannot bake at home for lack of barm or yeast of beer, which is used as leaven. It is very singular that in Great Britain and Ireland they do not know how to make bread as it is made in France or Germany, and that they have always to send to a brewer for this barm, a very difficult thing to get in remote districts. I never could have imagined that the making of bread was such a difficult thing. Our good women on the Continent make it with the greatest ease. The whole operation consists in allowing a certain amount of fermented dough to sour, then mixing it with the flour from which the bread is to be made, but taking, of course, care to put only the exact quantity needful, otherwise the bread will be sour. I am quite sure that a very short experience would teach anyone how this operation should be conducted, but people in this country are but little disposed to change their customs.

As it is my intention in writing this book to try to

157

make it as useful as possible, I have taken some pains in this connection, and I have written out with most minute detail the procedure of people on the Continent in making leaven and using it. The instructions which I give below were sent to me from London by one of my friends who, at my request, had procured the information from Germany, and it describes accurately how our peasants make bread. He sent me the matter in French, but in the effort to make it more generally available I have translated it into English, perhaps English in French guise; but provided I am understood, that is all I ask. Those who know how to make bread, or those who don't wish to know, will do well to skip this bit of English, although I am persuaded that it is in a somewhat unusual style.

Manner of Baking with Leaven [1]

They give the name of leaven to a quantity of dough put into fermentation, occasioned by the addition of some of the old dough preserved from the precedent kneading.

The manner of getting it good, is to mix (the day before one intends to bake, and before going to bed) a little of the old dough before mentioned, with a third of the flour intended to make bread : the whole is to be mixed and diluted with cold water : this forms a firm and compact dough, which ought to be left all night in a corner of the trough, covered with a proportion of flour, raised in rolls and pressed hard to give it more solidity and to prevent the leaven from extending itself out of its limits. The day after, at about six in the

[1] In the English of the author.

morning, it is fit to be used ; with cold water it takes commonly seven or eight hours to be ready, with warm water about three, but the dough is always soft.

If found that on the following day, the leaven was passed, that is, already turned sour, as may happen in the great heat of summer, or when a storm has taken place during the night ; it is sufficient then to renew and to refresh it, by adding to it half its weight in new flour and cold water : three hours after, it is fit to be used.

When the leaven is thus prepared, they begin by putting it entire without breaking it, with a proportion of water, and it ought to be diluted very quickly and very exactly, to prevent any lumps from remaining ; when it is sufficiently diluted, they add to it the remainder of the water, which ought to be cold in summer, and tepid or warm on the contrary in winter, to counteract the effects of the hands in the two seasons, and to produce an opposite one. They then mix all the flour destined to be employed with the leaven, and assemble the whole in a lump which they work with the hands, carrying it from left to right, heaving it up, cutting and dividing it with the open hands, nipping and pulling the dough with the fingers folded and the thumbs stretched out ; that is what is called thrilling ; they work it up several times in the same manner, scraping the trough every time ; they introduce afterwards in the lump the dough that has been detached from it with a little water and carrys it, in the same manner on the other side ; that is what is called ' *contre fraser*,' or thrilling in the opposite way. The kneading is ended by making a hollow place in the dough and pouring water in it ; this labour serves to confound and divide the coarsest part of the flour, and by the continued, quick and speedy motion, forms new air, which renders the dough more viscous, more equal, longer, and lighter, and it produces a bread better tasted and whiter ; this third labour is called ' *bassinage* ' or fomentation. To add yet to the perfection which the fomentation gives to the dough, they strike it with the hands, pressing it by the sides and folding it up on itself, extending and cutting it with the hands closed, and letting it fall with effort.

The dough being thus sufficiently worked out, is taken from the trough and divided into such parts as are judged proper, cutting and striking it still, and placing it in a lump near the oven, where it must remain half an hour in winter, to enable it to preserve its warmth and to ferment ; it must be turned and divided on the contrary, when the weather is hot.

The effect of fermentation is to divide and to attenuate the new dough, to introduce in it a good deal of air, which as it cannot disengage itself entirely, being prevented by its viscosity and consistency, forms in it eyes, or little concavities, raises it up, widens and swells it ; it is for that reason, that this portion of flour kneaded with the old dough, which determines all its effects, has obtained the name of *leaven* or ' *levain* ' from the French *lever*, to raise.

This operation requires a certain degree of heat to be made slowly and gradually : it is essential to accelerate or to stop the fermentation, according to the season of the year, to make it produce its effects about in the same time summer or winter ; for that purpose the dough ought to be put in baskets covered, with linen or flannel, in a warm or cold place, according to the season ; fire must be put in the oven, as the necessary time to heat it is much about that required for the fermentation to come to its point, or for the bread to have taken what is called, its due preparation.

I am sure, this is an eloquent piece, filled with fine hard words, which I have got with hard labour in the dictionary. I could have delivered this fine method, as a physician does his pills, perhaps also some people will think me a fool not to have done it ; everybody has his way of seeing things : as for me, had I discovered a marvellous receipt to cure the plague, the ague, and even the Ministerial or Antiministerial fever, I would think it my duty, to give it to the public as generously.

I perceive after all, that I have no great difficulty in writing English. I regret now, that my promenade is in French, but since I have begun I must continue, and come back to the wild Connemara, where I think, this dissertation is placed with more propriety than at London, where likely ' John Bull ' would have scorned and d——d my labour.

I have never in my life been in the house of a rich man who appeared to care so little for the things of this world as Colonel Martin. He is a man of the best intentions, and thinks of nothing more than how to improve the country which belongs to him. Unfortunately some adventurers have abused his confidence, and have swindled him out of considerable sums under pretext of finding mines on his estate, or of clearing land for cultivation. The kind of clearing done was clearing out, after they got the money.

The fortune of any private individual could not possibly suffice to people or cultivate a territory as large as Connemara. If the Government would make an arrangement with the proprietor to build cabins for sixty thousand inhabitants, and to supply them with instruments of labour, ground for nothing, seed for sowing, and provisions for the first two years, I am convinced that they would be able to maintain themselves from the third year onward.

The only good plan which a proprietor can adopt is that which Colonel Martin has lately followed. He gives refuge to the unfortunate victims who have been obliged to leave the north of Ireland. I have seen quite a number of families who have been obliged to leave their country, and who have here formed new homes. Colonel Martin has given them ground for nothing for a certain number of years, and afterwards he lets the land to them at an extremely moderate rate.

The manner in which these unfortunate families have been chased from their country is cruel. They receive usually a card signed and conceived in these terms : ' Peter ——, James —— &c. &c., you have (so many) days to sell your things and go to Connaught or to Hell, for here you must not dwell.' I shall explain later, when I am at the various places, the character of these political and religious quarrels ; here I content myself with saying that those who have not obeyed the orders of their antagonists have often been massacred, or had their houses burned.

I have seen several of these new establishments, which seemed to be in a state of prosperity hardly to be expected on such soil. If a proprietor would put aside every year the wherewithal to build twelve or fifteen cabins, and would buy as many cows, it would be easy for him to attract cultivators. Attention has been given to the subject, but it is necessary that the labourer should be attracted by advantageous terms, in order to induce him to come and make his dwelling in a corner of the earth far removed from society, covered with peat mosses, and so drenched with water that, from the summit of Leitrig mountain which I climbed, it looks like a sea sown with mountains and tongues of earth, so numerous are the lakes and so near do they approach each other.

The Colonel had commenced to build a superb mansion on the borders of a pretty little lake at foot of this mountain, but when the foundations had reached the ground level, he saw that it was going to be so costly that he has abandoned the work, for the present at any rate. A palace would certainly seem an extraordinary thing in the middle of these mosses.

In some places near these lakes are to be found little woods, and some small patches of verdure which ameliorate the view. It is evident that, with a little care, it would be possible to increase these oases. It is not to be believed that the inhabitants of this country are more wicked or barbarous than elsewhere ; they seem indeed to be better clothed than those who live near the capital. It is very easy to call them savages and to make sport of their misery. Will you believe it, readers and good people, if I tell you where I have really found savage and barbarous men ? I tell you it was in Paris, in London, in Dublin, in Edinburgh— in fact in all the large cities. What animal in the universe is more ferocious and cruel than these men, who, proud of their riches, often badly acquired, treat with disdain all who are not like them covered with gold ; who insult indigent genius and merit ; who, far from attempting to help a friend more honest and honourable than they are themselves, will see him languish in prison for a debt, the repayment of which would not be of much advantage to them, a repayment which they know to be impossible.

I feel calmer. I get angry in writing as in speaking, but in both cases the anger soon passes. Yes, it is true, there are savage and barbarous members in every society of men, but there are also good souls who think of nothing more than the well-being of their fellows, and the pleasure of meeting one of these makes one forget entirely the detestable sight of these who, like the devils, are never happy except when they are doing evil. I have finished my reflections ; let us return to Connemara.

The safe and deep bays into which this coast is cut, as well as the freedom from fear of customs officials, accounts for the presence of a number of people who are here for what is called quite openly the ' smuggling business,' as if it were an ordinary trade. I have gone into different cabins and asked, straight away, for brandy or claret without finding any surprise to be expressed. One good woman, like many others, said to me, ' There is nothing at present in the house, but my husband is at sea, and if you come back in a month you can have all you want.'

Although the coasts are somewhat of the same character as the rest of the country, they are more populous by reason of the *commerce*; they are also drier and commonly covered with large stones, the little places between these being carefully cultivated.

In every country men are found willing to make profit out of the misfortunes of their fellows. The

CONNEMARA

shipwreck of vessels especially excites the avidity of
the ordinary man. It is only with infinite trouble that
the law is able to save vessels from being pillaged, and
it has even happened that the crew have been put to
death when they attempted to oppose the wreckers'
will. To prevent such wrong, the Government gives
to every proprietor who saves a vessel from pillage,
certain rights by way of recompense for his expenses,
this remuneration being called 'salvage.' While I
was in Connemara a vessel was unfortunate enough to
be wrecked on the estate of a proprietor who was absent :
the people of the country proceeded at once to board
and pillage the wreck. The captain of the vessel, who
was on board, sent to Colonel Martin begging for aid,
which was readily given, the Colonel sending some of
his tenants with fire-arms, who restored order and
dispersed the pillagers.

This country may be called the boundary of the
ocean on the eastern side ; there is only one small single
island between these coasts and those of America.
Below the sea, however, is traced a wide bank, or rather
chain of mountains, in the same direction as those of
this country, and this bank or range reaches to Newfoundland, and forms the cod-fishing grounds.

The ancient Greek authors, Plato particularly,
record the old-world tradition of an immense island,
or rather vast continent, which was swallowed up in
the sea to the west of Europe. It is more than probable
that the inhabitants of Connemara never heard of
Plato, nor of the Greeks, nevertheless they also have
this tradition. 'Our country will one day reappear,'
say the old men to the young, leading them on a certain
day of the year up a mountain and pointing to the sea.

The fishers of the coasts also believe in this vanished land, and pretend that they have seen towns and villages at the bottom of the sea. The descriptions which they give of this imaginary country are as bombastic and exaggerated as those of the Promised Land ; milk flows in some streams and wine in others. This appears to indicate that the tradition was not invented here, for, otherwise, they certainly would have made some of the streams to run with whisky or porter.

They cannot fix the time at which their country, as they call it, was engulfed in the waves, but they are convinced that this misfortune did happen in what they call the old times ; and they believe that the destruction was operated by wicked magicians, and that a time will come when the country shall come forth from the sea as flourishing as it was when submerged by the waves.

This singular opinion induces reflection on the situation of Ireland and the different things which are found in it, things of which there are no traces in the European Continent. Ireland seems to be a vast rock situated in the middle of the sea. Contrariwise to the state of other countries in which the ground rises gradually from the coast to the centre, the coasts here are, particularly to the west, always the highest point of the country. The great rivers do not take their sources in the interior of the island, but within a few miles from the sea ; thus the Shannon rises near Sligo, the river Derg near Ballyshannon, &c., &c. Everything seems to point to a vast territory on foundations less stable than those of the island, which has been detached and swallowed up in the sea.

This idea may appear to be ridiculous, but after the

description which I have made of the country near Galway, who would be surprised to hear one day that the whole of that part of the counties of Clare and Galway had disappeared suddenly, and that where there were wild rocks supported on vaults the waves of the sea now roll? I am indeed convinced that this misfortune would have happened to this territory long ago had it not been for the high mountains which rise on the coast side and defend it from the attacks of the sea. This chain of mountains which can be followed along the bottom of the sea to America, does it not make it appear that the island formed part of a large continent which may perhaps have been joined to the new world?

No tradition whatever has concerned itself with the monstrous animal with enormous horns which is to be found so often in the bogs. Certainly it would be considered remarkable that such an animal should originate in a confined country, the whole length of which it could run over in two or three days without fatigue. Could anyone suppose that this gigantic species of deer would be placed by Nature, always wise and always uniform, in an island so small as to become for it a prison, while the continents of Europe, Asia, Africa, and America show not the slightest remains of it, and even Great Britain, which in the north is separated from Ireland by only a dozen of miles, shows no trace of it?

This race, however, existed in the woods of North America, although it would seem to have been a much smaller beast than that of which the horns and bones are found in the bogs of Ireland. But it may have degenerated, as have done all the species of animals which have been found in the two worlds.

Anyone may propound a theory. Mine is that the globe has experienced, in its existence, many terrible revolutions and overturnings, that what was earth in many places is now water, that where the fishes once swam there are now flourishing towns, and that, according to observations I have actually made, Ireland was a rocky cape of an immense continent which has disappeared, and Ireland is the only part which has escaped, simply because the abyss which was under the continent did not extend below that part which is now the island.

Here, again, let me make another observation. The sudden submersion of such an extent of territory, which I would imagine joined Spitzbergen on the one side, and, forming a large gulf, to have joined Ireland, the Azores, and Newfoundland on the other, would naturally displace the waters of the abyss and cause them to mount suddenly over land which rested firmly on its foundations ; hence the Deluge, according exactly to the words of the Bible, which say ' les portes de l'abîme furent ouvertes et qu'elles se fermerent ensuite.'

In such a tremendous overturning all matter lighter than water would float on the surface at the mercy of the waves, and on the receding of the waters would be deposited in the valleys or against the sides of mountains opposed to the current. In the warm countries the heterogeneous matter by the constant alternations of drought and rain would soon be reduced to dust, which the wind would disperse and unite with the earth, so that it could not be distinguished from it, while matter of a more solid nature would keep its original form. In moist countries, on the contrary, the deposits of light matter would remain and would be increased in bulk by plants which could grow on them. Hence the morasses or bogs so frequent in Ireland, and which are also found in the north of Scotland, always to the east of mountains which have stopped them when the waters were retiring to the west, and deposited them on the eastern hill-sides. If their origin was entirely due to moisture they would be found more often on the western sides of hills, since that is the most exposed to rain, which comes from the west.

They say that bogs grow, and examples are given showing that where once were woods bogs are now found. This, however, is for the same reason which I have given. If these woods had been cut down or burned in a dry and warm climate, they would soon have been destroyed or made to disappear by the perpetual change from cold to heat, and from drought to humidity. But in a humid climate they are covered quickly by moss and other plants, forming a mass which becomes a bog on account of the continuity of condition which never changes from moist to dry. There can be no doubt that the plants which cover the top of these bogs increase its size in time, and it may even be that peat mosses which have been cut may grow again if the plants have not been entirely extirpated, and if the waters have not been drained away.

Oh what a noble thing is dreaming! I am not astonished that there are so many fools who practise it—it is so easy to go back nearly to the creation of the world, and arrange things according to one's ideas. Nothing is more amusing to me, the author, than such speculations; but it may be that they do not please you, the reader, so let us put an end to them and get back to Connemara.

I plunged into the mountains without other guide than my horse, who did not seem to trouble himself much about the road. It is a wolfish country, although there are no wolves. From time to time the view is beautified by the magnificent large bays which are so common, and which may be said to ' tooth ' the coast. They are all very deep, and their shores exhibit more verdure than the rest of the country. Here and there are seen one or two comfortable-looking houses and some villages.

I had to get down from my horse pretty often, in order to avoid quagmires—he had so much trouble in getting out of some of them by himself that I believe he never could have succeeded while carrying weight. Often I met women who, as they passed on their way, industriously knitted those thick woollen stockings by which alone, to so many people, and even to Irish people, it is known that Connemara exists. I found it very difficult to know my way—in some parts it dwindled to a mere track—and I saw very few cabins where I could go for direction. I met several men who, in passing, did me the honour to stop, take off their hats and make a lowly reverence, saying in their language, ' God bless you, Sir, may you arrive safe and sound at the end of your journey.' If I spoke to them they appeared very pleased ; one of them, for the sake of the pleasure of talking to a stranger, and in English, followed me for quite a mile, his hat under his arm, and nothing I could say could induce him to put it on his head.

At one of the places where the road seemed to

disappear altogether, I fell in with the guide of Colonel Martin, who, from the summit of a hill he was crossing, on seeing me in embarrassment, made the valley resound with the echo of his voice. He came to my aid, but just as he arrived my horse, putting his foot on a large round stone, fell on his nose and I on my side. While I lay in this position, my good friend, like his compatriots, cried out ' God bless you, Sir, God bless you ' ; and when he saw me rise he added, ' Please, your honour, you are hard to hurt.'

Following the line of a considerable bay which penetrates into the mountains, I arrived without further accident at the house of Mr. Anthony O'Flaherty of Renville, on the margin of the magnificent bay of Killery. This water stretches for quite nine miles into the interior of the country, but everywhere is very deep, and vessels, once entered, are in perfect shelter from every wind that blows. If this Connemara should ever become populous and industrial, these numerous, beautiful, and safe bays will be a great advantage for its commerce.

This country along the coast would seem to have been inhabited a long time ago. Often there are marks of furrows in places where the inhabitants have no recollection whatever of cultivation, and here, as elsewhere, where there is no knowledge or tradition, the work is attributed to the Danes. The ancient cultivation of this country has certainly been the work of an intelligent people ; whoever they were, they have drained peat mosses of considerable size and cultivated them, and it would seem that their method was, after having effected drainage, to cover the peat with coarse sea sand and pebbles. This operation alone, without the use of lime, has been sufficient to firm the ground and make it fit for working.

On this side of the mountains of Connemara there is no limestone whatever to be found, but formerly there was here a large deposit of oyster shells, out of which was manufactured an extremely hard lime. It has been used in the building of an old castle at the edge of the sea, and in this the stones are so excellently joined and laid that the whole appears as if cut from a rock. Mr. O'Flaherty himself used it for building his house. Unfortunately, the supply is now exhausted.

The inhabitants burn the seaweed on the coasts, and out of it form a greyish hard matter which they call *kelp*, a material which is used in glass making, and this is the most considerable industry of the neighbourhood. Hardly a tree is to be seen, but the country at one time must have been covered with them, for they are frequently found in the mosses, and the way of discovering them on the surface is very simple. The inhabitants go over the ground in the morning while the dew is on the ground, carrying with them long spits or rods of iron. They observe places where the dew has disappeared, and there they pierce the ground, nearly always finding wood, and being able immediately to say, pretty accurately, its length, size, and quality by renewing the operation at different places. When they have located the wood they proceed to dig. These trees are generally pretty sound, and furnish the only wood which the inhabitants can use in the building of their cabins.

CHAPTER IX

I CROSSED the beautiful bay of Killery, and following the shores of Clew Bay, I came easily to Westport House, to Lord Altamont. It was a real joy for me to offer my respects to the amiable daughter of the victorious Howe. The little town of Westport has been entirely built by the father and grandfather of the present lord, who, following the good examples set him, has commenced to lay the foundation of another town, to be called ' Louisburg.' Here he affords shelter to the unfortunates who are obliged to leave the north of Ireland.

Lady Altamont takes a great interest in the poor, who come to consult her about sickness. She listens to them, and afterwards gives them an order on an apothecary for any necessary medicines. Passing through the country I heard of a benevolent project of hers which may soon improve the state of affairs. This is to establish a manufacture in which children and women may be employed. I was also shown a hospital which she has founded, and which she maintains at her own charges.

Whenever, on my travels, I have had the good fortune to find virtues such as here exhibited, I felt it to be a duty to mention them, without the least

173

intention of flattery, but simply that I may incite others to follow such a good example.

The country in the neighbourhood of Westport is very well cultivated, and the view from the house and park of Lord Altamont seemed to me very pleasing and satisfying after my journeys through the wild and black mountains. In this neighbourhood is situated the famous mountain on the summit of which Saint Patrick assembled all the devils and venomous beasts, in order that he might cast them into the hole which is still to be found on the mountain top.

The mountain is called Croagh-Patrick, and is a very celebrated place for the penitences of the faithful, who come from all parts on certain days of the year. They climb the mountain partly on their knees, or barefooted—I do not know which—and I have been assured that on the *fête* day of the saint there may be as many as four or five thousand persons on the mountain. On the summit there is a little chapel at which mass is celebrated on this day, and in it is a black bell for which the inhabitants have a peculiar veneration. It is used as a thing to swear on in legal matters, and no one will dare to perjure himself on it. They have strange ideas on the subject of this bell, and believe that the devil will carry them off immediately if they dare to affirm on it anything that is not true.

Croagh-Patrick is cone-shaped, and looks as if it had been a volcano of which the hole, celebrated in St. Patrick's story, may possibly have been the crater. The country round about is covered with ruins of abbeys and buildings round holy wells. There has been specially pointed out to me a large stone on which there are two fairly deep holes, and the inhabitants

174

venerate it as having been used by St. Patrick, the holes having been worn by his knees while he prayed. Catholics and Protestants here made use of the same building for services while their churches were being built. King James established several cannon foundries in the valleys in the neighbourhood, and the ruins of these are also visible ; the intention was to profit by the neighbourhood of the sea and of the woods.

I had intended to make a tour in Erio,[1] a considerable country and almost as wild as Connemara, but the season was so advanced that I was obliged to give up the project, and to proceed to Castlebar, which I found to be a very pleasant little town. As I stayed there some time, I could not help noticing the form of the church tower, which is exactly shaped like a syringe. This will not appear surprising when I say that the architect was an apothecary. I was here well received by the Dean of Killala.

In the mountains I fell in with a man who had the air of being something of a *bon vivant*. He told me that his profession was that of inoculator, and that he was about to inoculate the children of the peasantry in this wild country. He assured me positively that of 361 children inoculated by him this year only one died. When it is understood that if he has been unfortunate enough to have a child die on his hands, not only is he not paid, but he must escape promptly in order to avoid a beating by the afflicted parents, it will be seen that the poor devil must take great pains with his patients. I have often thought that this

---

[1] I have been unable to find ' Erio ' on map or in gazetteer. The author cannot mean ' Eyre,' since he mentions his visit to Eyre— or Iar—Connaught (p. 155).—Tr.

practice of the peasantry would not be a bad one to introduce into towns, to encourage the doctors, to whom the death or cure of their patients is indifferent, for they are sure to be paid in either case, and are never beaten.

In travelling beside this decent creature, who appeared to be very light-hearted, he told me his whole story. He was born in this country, and had been brought up by his poor parents with the intention that he should enter the Church, the while depending for aid and protection on a rich man, who unfortunately died at Dublin. Finding himself then without friends, without promise of aid and without money, he thought for some time how he could employ himself. It was just the time when inoculation had begun to be put into practice, and the terrible effects often produced by smallpox on these mountain folk gave him the idea of visiting them and taking up the profession of inoculator, after he had taken some lessons in the hospitals. Now he has been practising with success for thirty or forty years, but all he makes by way of income is not more than thirty or forty pounds sterling per annum. It cannot be denied that this man is really useful to society, and I believe him to be worthy of the attention of the Government, who might give him a small pension by way of recompense for past efforts and for encouragement to continue them.

When he had told me his whole story he naturally wished to know mine. ' Pray, Sir,' said he, ' what do you follow yourself ? ' ' You perceive,' I answered, ' I follow the road.' Tapping me on the shoulder he said, ' You take me short.' It was a new idea for him, perhaps, that a stranger's affairs are his own affair.

After this little story, can people take for truth
the tales which represent the common folk of Ireland
as idle, stupid, and incapable of improvement, when
people reputed more clever have refused up to the
present to adopt the sanitary practice of inoculation?
On the Continent, not only would the peasants refuse
to allow their children to be inoculated, but even
people comfortably off would make a like refusal. In
England well-meaning proprietors are often obliged
to beg the parents to submit; in Scotland they have
not yet succeeded in securing adoption of the method,
and yet it is generally adopted in Ireland even in its
wildest parts. The children are not in any way
specially cared for; they run about and amuse themselves, nearly naked, after inoculation as before.
When the fever takes them, it is only then that the
inoculator is called to see them, when he administers a
few simple remedies, which, pardonably, he may make
somewhat mysterious in order to increase his credit,
and to prevent the parents from becoming accustomed
to apply these remedies themselves—a procedure
which would mean to him the loss of his daily bread.

Following the banks of Lough Conn, which is a very
large piece of water, and which should have been
drained and dried long ago, I came to Mr. Cuff's at
Castle Gore. I was told that he had gone to see his
uncle, but I was received with much kindness by his
young wife and by an aged man in the house, who had
been his tutor. I went to see the little town of Killala,
where there is one of those round towers of which I have
had so often occasion to speak. This one is situated
at a little distance from the church, and does not seem
to have been joined to it. It stands alone on an

elevated portion of ground ; it seems rather to have been built as a sort of signal tower for ships at sea than as a bell-tower or building in connection with a church. It is the only one I have seen in Ireland in such a situation. I went also to see the palace of the bishop, which in these provinces is the subject of a proverb used in connection with anything of rather poor quality, ' It is as bad as the palace of the bishop of Killala,' and this proverb seems to be in common use all through the province of Connaught. Unfortunately the present bishop has repaired it, and added to it a considerable wing, so that the proverb is no longer justified. This bishopric is reputed to be the poorest in Ireland, the bishop having only an income of £3000 sterling per annum. Poor man ! The deanery also is reputed to be very poor and not worth more than £500 sterling yearly.

As I rode through the streets, a man, who from his appearance I took to be the schoolmaster, stopped me, and with an air of importance said, ' Pray, Sir, what is your name ? ' ' Pray, Sir,' said I quite as gravely, ' what is yours ? ' He was a little surprised at my question and did not think fit to reply. I found this kind of curiosity to be very common, being questioned on the road as to my country, my name, my business, &c., &c.

I returned to Castle Gore by Ballina, which is a fairly well-built little town ; there is a salmon fishery in the river which flows out of Lough Conn and forms the bay of Killala. The situation of this bay shows at once that it is filled with sand. I stopped between Ballina and Killala to look at the considerable ruins of an abbey two miles from the latter town ; it seems

that formerly there was here a college, and some other
public establishments; the bell-tower is perfectly
preserved, and, like all others of the abbeys of this
island, it is placed in the middle of the church between
the nave and the choir. This building is still held in
reverence, and is one of the places to which the inhabitants come to perform their devotions. There is also a
holy well, but it is quite evident that it is not of nature's
making like so many others ; indeed, begging pardon of
the faithful, I would say that this is quite another thing.
It is a little chamber four or five feet wide behind the
buildings, and situated over a little stream. I have
seen many such cabinets in which people do not go
down on their knees. The banks of the river, which
flows out of Lough Conn, are very picturesque, and there
are many charming houses. On my way to Scuramore,
to Mr. Nisbet, I saw a large round fort such as I have
described. The *souterrain* (which I imagine is to be
found in all) was here large enough to admit cattle,
who took shelter in it from the heat of the day. Several
of them having broken their legs and given great trouble
to the peasantry in searching for them, the entry has
now been closed with stones and earth.

It had been devil's weather during the night, and
all the roads were watercourses. On one of them I
found a man riding a rather good horse. We talked
on various subjects for a while, and, knowing that the
horse which I had was not fit to carry me much farther,
he offered me another, and in the end, without other
recommendation than the passport of my face, he
took me to his house near Sligo and presented me to his
family. It is very pleasing to me to have this opportunity to offer my compliments to Mr. Holmes for the

fine Irish hospitality which he accorded to me. He called my attention, on the way, to a cavern in which the waves of the sea were sounding while it is yet a distance of two or three hundred feet from the shore. At the village of Ballyfedere I saw a waterfall of considerable height, falling directly into the sea, and near it was one of the thorn-covered holy wells to which the good folk go to say their prayers.

Sligo is an ancient city, and consequently a badly-built one and very irregular. The port, however, is not bad, although rather narrow. I only stayed in this town long enough to provide myself with a wrap against the bad weather now coming at the gallop, although I saw clearly that my walk could not be finished inside two months; in other words, I made an addition to my wardrobe of a spencer. I went also to visit a cattle-fair at the entrance to the town, and I found the farmers every bit as big as our Bas-Bretons, and finishing up their dealings exactly in the same way as at home, giving and receiving their guineas four or five times before coming to an end of the transaction by drinking a bottle. I presented myself immediately at Hazelwood, where Mr. Wynne lives. This is one of the most beautiful places I have seen in my travels, and it is also one of the places where I had the best of treatment and experienced every kindness. I have had a great many troubles in my long pilgrimage of exile. I have been often, very often, vexed by narrow souls who sought pretexts to wound me. One wrote me down as a democrat, another an aristocrat, a third as an atheist, and a fourth as Popish bigot; in fact there is no sort of ridiculous and cruel vexation which sordid interest has not made me feel, but the esteem of people of sense and the glad welcome of even one noble-minded family has made me glad to forget such annoyances.

I passed five or six charming days at Hazelwood. On the evening of my arrival here I was invited to a concert at Sligo It was given in the Hall of Sessions, and appeared like a complete revolution of the usual sittings. The big drum was on the Throne of Justice, the fifes and flutes in the barristers' quarters, and the audience in the place of the culprits.

Next day I committed the folly of going out in a boat on Lough Gill alone, a sudden tempest sprang up and proved nearly fatal to me and my poor boat. Like another Robinson Crusoe I was fortunate enough to find safety on an island, one of a number of others, all covered with wood, as are also the banks of the lough. There is not here the variety of foliage that one finds at Killarney, but there are, nevertheless, some very interesting and beautiful places. The lough is about eight miles in length, the river which flows into it passes through the mountains, from which, on the other side, the Shannon takes its source. I have been assured that a canal of seven or eight miles would very easily connect Lough Gill with a navigable part of the Shannon ; this would be a good work, and would open up valuable communications with the interior.

Setting out with Colonel Cole, I crossed the mountains to the house of his father, Lord Enniskillen at Florence Court. His lordship had to leave for Dublin, but I found shelter here for two days in a most beautiful castle. I passed here near two lakes of considerable size, which are joined by a little river ; their banks are wooded, and beautiful to the eyes of the traveller fatigued by the aridity of the mountain roads he had travelled.

I met here, on the way, a funeral, and I noted that the women did not cry as in the south or west of Ireland, from which it would seem that the south and north of this island are inhabited by people who have not the same origin. As a matter of fact, those of the north of Ireland are much more of a mixed race, their ancestors for the most part having been Scotch.

On the day I left Colonel Cole I brought into execution a project which I had formed some time previously, to go and visit the source of that venerable patriarch of Irish rivers, the Shannon, and offer to him my respects. I commenced my expedition by visiting that deep cavern which is called the Marble Arch. The stone is really of rather finely-veined marble. The caves are formed by a stream which sometimes is visible, and at other times runs like a torrent under enormous masses of rock. The whole mountain appears to be hollowed by the effect of this stream, and it would appear that at a former period it ran at a higher level—one indeed can see at several places the former bed of the river. On entering the Marble Cave my guides did not neglect to tell me all the horrible stories that ever were heard about the goblins, hobgoblins, witches, ghosts, &c., &c., who haunted these shades ; one of them certainly told his tales in a rather mocking manner, but the youngest seemed to believe in the stories. At the entrance to the cave the elder of the two stopped, saying that he knew all about the inside, and that the young man would be quite able to show me all that was to be seen. As it turned out, this was rather a fortunate arrangement, for, otherwise,

I should have been compelled to remain unwillingly for a time in this dwelling of fairies and ghosts.

After walking for nearly an hour among the rocks and precipices and waterfalls without end, I took the candle from the hands of my guide in order to look over a precipice, at the bottom of which I thought I could hear water running. How it came about I cannot tell, but the candle went out. 'Now,' said my guide, in a melancholy voice, 'we're done for ever, I would not move my foot from this place for a guinea.' After having, with a great deal of trouble and effort, made the man at the entrance to the cavern hear, I was certain that he would go for lights, and set myself down tranquilly to pass the time, being much amused at the fright of my companion. 'Have you ever seen him?' I said. 'Who?' he answered. 'The great devil who put out the candle with his cloven foot.' 'Oh no, Sir!' he said, 'it must have been the fairy. Oh, I am sure it was the fairy; she is jealous, and does not like anyone to come and bother her.' 'Oh,' said I, 'was it the fairy; then she is a d——d b——h to have played us such a trick.' 'Oh, Sir, Sir!' he cried, 'don't speak in that way about the good folk. You are on the edge of a precipice, and they could push you into it. I have never offended them, I respect them, and I am sure they will not harm me.' At this last statement I could not refrain from laughing, and I called his attention to a faint ray of light which appeared at the bottom of the precipice, and this seemed to reassure him a little. Patiently we waited for our guide with the lights, who came about an hour later, and released us from this disagreeable situation.

On leaving the cavern my guides tried to dissuade

me from attempting to visit the source of the Shannon, by representing the great number of difficulties I should encounter. It would be six miles there and six miles back, they said. Six Irish miles there and six back would be equal to fifteen English miles, and this distance over peat-bogs simply to see the source of a river was, they thought, a great labour for nothing. But Mr. Bruce, said I to myself, spent seven or eight years in searching for the source of another river (the Nile), why should I not spend four or five hours on a similar search ! and off I started across the mosses to find the source of the Shannon.

As with all great personages, the approach to this one was very difficult. As with them, too, access gained did not reveal anything very remarkable. However, there are few rivers which, having such a beginning—a stream of four or five feet wide by two or three deep, flowing out of a round basin about twenty feet in diameter, and, they say, without bottom—can show such result in such short space. Within a mile of westward course the Shannon forms Lough Clean, three miles long by one mile wide, and then, proceeding southward, it expands into an infinite number of lakes, of which the principal are Lough Allen, Lough Bofin, Lough Ree, and Lough Derg. The two last-mentioned are each about thirty miles long with a width of nine or ten, and are dotted with numerous islands.

The country near Lough Allen is full of coal and iron mines. Forges have been established, and will become very profitable enterprises when the river has been rendered navigable for the whole length of its course.

After satisfying my curiosity and drinking a

deep draught of the spring from the crown of my hat, I took my leave of the Shannon, and wished him, sincerely, the happiness of seeing prosperous the hospitable banks of the waters. ' It is very surprising,' said I to my conductor, ' that they have not made a holy well out of the source of the Shannon.' ' Only the saints can do that,' said he. But why have the saints not thought of it ?—that is what surprises me.

My conductor was evidently a lover of good living, for he reproached me, often, for neglect to bring with us something to eat. ' You are always talking of eating,' I said ; ' I am sure you must be an Englishman.' ' Don't call me names,' was his response. ' But,' said I, ' an Englishman is as good as an Irishman—is he not ? ' Thereupon my friend shook his head in a very significant way, and muttered a proper G—d d——n which gave me understanding of held opinion he cared not otherwise to express. It is very strange that, so many centuries after the conquest of Ireland, the two peoples should not be united—probably they never will be. In France a Provençal is as proud to be French as the Breton or inhabitant of Old Gaul. They have no prejudices against each other, except such unimportant ones as are born of distance.

With the wish to satisfy the needs of my conductor I entered a cabin, and the good folk dwelling in it counted it a pleasure to offer to us such as they had, refusing absolutely any payment in return.

Quitting the castle of Florence Court, I crossed a fine stretch of country and came to Enniskillen, where I was very warmly received by the Rev. Dr. Stock.

CHAPTER X

ENNISKILLEN is a pretty little town, situated on an
island formed by the great Lough Erne, in a place where
it narrows and forms a river of rapid current. This
lake is the longest in Ireland, if included with it is taken
the length of river which joins the upper to the lower
part. The lake is nearly forty miles long, and at
many places is from ten to twelve miles wide.

This town boasts of its attachment to King William ;
it sustained a siege against his father-in-law. I saw
on the gate this inscription, which had been placed
there recently : ' THE GLORIOUS MEMORY OF THE FIRST
OF JULY.' I do not like these memorials, they serve
but to humiliate and anger the vanquished—that is to
say, not those who are really wrong, but who happen to
be the weakest ; it would be more generous and more
politic to let the past be the past. This inscription
reminds me of one at Dublin, in Nassau Street, where
I have seen, cut on a stone, the words : ' MAY WE NEVER
WANT A WILLIAM TO KICK THE BREECH OF A JACOBITE.'
These inscriptions anger me, I admit ; they prove,
however, that there is still existing a great deal of
animosity between sections of the people, while not one

of the members of these sections had anything to do with the original quarrel, and consequently ought to forget all about it.

Lord Belmore has just built in this neighbourhood a superb palace, the masonry alone of the building costing him £80,000 sterling. The colonnade of the front elevation is of an architecture too fine, perhaps, for an individual and for a country house. The interior is full of rare marbles, and the walls of several rooms are covered with rare stucco work produced at great cost, and by workers brought from Italy. Comfort has been almost entirely sacrificed to beauty ; the rooms intended for visitors are like cellars, although at the top of the building. Light comes to them only through little windows eight feet below the level of the ceiling, and against these windows there is a stone balustrade, so that they may not be perceived in the design from the outside. My taste perhaps is odd, but I confess that a house that is comfortable appears to me to be preferable to a palace which is not. The temples should be left to the gods.

The whole of ͟this country seems, at one time, to have been covered by a prodigious number of little lakes or small branches of the principal one, which have now been drained ; the land is cut up entirely into little hills, and valleys without outlet. Lough Erne, they say, has still 365 islands, and this is said also about Lough Derg, Lough Ree, and Lough Allen. On one of these islands are the ruins of an ancient abbey and of several churches, which I went to see. The round tower is not so high as several I have seen in the province of Connaught. I was able to hoist myself up to the door, which is only about ten or twelve feet above the level of the ground. I have already mentioned that ingenious people have given themselves a great deal of trouble to find out how the summit of these towers was reached, but a simple inspection of the interior enables one to form a very good idea. There are always four or five projecting stones from story to story, and it is evident that they were intended to support beams on which floors were laid. There are several bell-towers on the Continent which have similar interior construction. That tells me—but I would be very sorry to take away the pleasure of dreaming from antiquaries. The ruins on this island are somewhat of the character of those on the east side of Ireland ; they are smaller than those of the provinces of Munster or Connaught, and have not been built with the same taste. There is here a vaulted chapel which resembles that at Glendalough which is called St. Kevin's Kitchen. In the cemetery is seen a stone coffin, and the folk of the neighbourhood are accustomed to lie down on it. I do not know of the evil it cures, the miracle is that it fits perfectly to all heights. I tried it myself, and certainly it fitted me very well. It is a sort of frock-coat of which the folds give no trouble, and which the tailor [1] is always sure to cut according to fashion.

The estates of the last Prince of Ulster were confiscated, and he himself hung at London, during the reign of Queen Elizabeth ; part of his lands were at that time assigned for the maintenance of a public school for the town. In consequence the place of the

---

[1] In the orginal there is a play ion the word *tailleur*, which the author prints in italics.—Tr.

schoolmaster at Enniskillen has become a sort of bishopric ; it brings in about two thousand pounds sterling per annum. One would think that the sure way of having no school would be to give the master two thousand pounds of annual income ; as a matter of fact, the result which I would anticipate is that which has arrived at Enniskillen. However, the person who occupies the situation at present, Dr. Stock (with whom I passed the two days I stayed in Enniskillen), is a very highly educated man, and besides having twelve or fifteen children of his own, has five or six nieces or nephews that he brings up himself, and seven or eight boarders at one hundred guineas per annum. I have seen very few houses in which there were so many children, where such order reigned ; but, on the other hand, I never saw such a schoolmaster.

I quitted the hospitable roof of Dr. Stock, and following the romantic and rocky borders of Lower Erne I came to Beleek, where is the first cataract on the river flowing from the lake. It is about three miles from the point of issue, and up to this point the river hardly seems to have any current, the level being almost exactly that of the lake. Here it falls suddenly, in the length of one hundred paces, more than sixty feet—the first fall may be twelve or fifteen feet.

I do not say anything here about the possibility of making this river navigable, because from here to the sea, which is only four miles off, it is simply a furious torrent. A canal had been commenced, half the cost was incurred, and then the whole thing was shamefully abandoned. Is it not evident that in removing the first cataract nearly the whole of the lower lake could be drained ? The operation would be so much easier here by reason of the fact that the river forms a large sheet of water just before the falls. This could be forced to take its course to one side of the waterfall, and so allow the work to proceed on the lower side protected by a dyke.

It may be objected that the lake is superb, and many other nice things may be said, but I should hardly imagine that the Irish are such lovers of water. They need not fear—they will always have plenty of this ; for my part I must say I would rather see fertile fields and meadows than the most beautiful sheet of water in the universe.

I was received at Ballyshannon by Mr. Gamble. This town is a small and little-used seaport on the bay of Donegal. It is situated at the last cascade of the river which flows from Lough Erne, and which falls fifteen or twenty feet perpendicularly into the sea. There is one side on which the flow is not so rapid, and it is curious here to watch the salmon in their efforts to proceed against the current. Enormous quantities are taken at this spot, so that I think very few manage to reach the lake.

Fifteen miles seawards, at the entry of the bay, is an island called Inismurray, famous for the ruins of its expiatory vaults or cellars, and for the Sun-stone or *Muidhr*, from which the island takes its name. General Vallencey assumes that this *Muidhr* is the *Mithra* of the Persians and the *Mahody* of the Gentous. He draws certain conclusions which seem to be well founded, and which are in agreement with ancient Irish tradition as to the origin of these stones. In his published work he gives a little engraving of the stone dedicated to *Mahody*, the supreme god, which Captain

Rike discovered in a Gentou temple in the island of Elephanta, India. He is sure it resembles very much the stone dedicated to *Muidhr* in Inismurray. The two stones are cut in cone shape, and both are surrounded by a circle to prevent profanation, and are placed in both islands with the same design. The first Christian missionaries, seeking to use the prejudices and customs of the people in order to make them adopt the new faith more easily, built two chapels in the enclosure of this temple, dedicated the one to St. Molaise and the other to St. Columba, and in this way appropriated to Christianity the rites and devotions which they were not strong enough to terminate.

Formerly the herrings frequented this bay on the south coast of Donegal. The late Mr. Burton Conyngham, who was always anxious to support enterprises which he believed to be of use to his country, spent £30,000 sterling of his fortune and £20,000 of Government money in establishing fisheries on these coasts. He even built a little town on an island for the fishers, but the herrings were, with reason, frightened by these immense preparations which seemed to menace their entire destruction, and took themselves off and have not reappeared since. The result is that all these warehouses, the town, and all its connections rest, uninhabited, in a desert country, where no one is ever seen. It looks very funny, but it must not be forgotten that the intention was praiseworthy, and that it could not have been foreseen that the herrings would desert the neighbourhood. It is, of course, just possible that they may return. I have often thought that they move from one coast to another for food reasons. When they have entirely eaten the grass on which they are nourished at one place, it is to be expected that they will go elsewhere. Why, then, not try to find out what is this marine grass or weed, and propagate it at the places to which it is desirable to attract the herrings ?

I went from here to Brown Hall, near Ballytra, to Mr. Hamilton, and there passed several days very agreeably. In the park enclosure there is a little lake, out of which flows a river which I look upon as one of the principal natural curiosities of this country. At times it flows slowly through subterranean caverns, filled with petrifactions, and along its side one can walk at ease ; at other times it is an impetuous torrent. It appears and disappears, and advantage has been taken of the natural vault, at several places, to carry the roads or paths over it. In one of the caverns pigeons have made a home and occupy it by themselves ; in another, bats have taken possession. At another cavern there is a sudden fall of twenty feet. In other hollows there are surprising echoes. Altogether it is the most singular piece of natural work I have seen, and as it is enclosed here in a well-kept pleasure ground or garden, it appears all the more remarkable. I take it that the river flows underground, in the different sections, altogether for about two miles.

I had heard of a peculiar practice of the inhabitants of this part of the country, and I desired to make some inquiries about it. I refer to what are called ' Sweating-Houses,' which are looked upon here as a remedy for all ills. Mr. Hamilton was good enough to take me to see one in the neighbourhood. I am sure it will trouble the reader to imagine what a sweating-house can be, and for his benefit I may say it is a species of oven five or six feet high by about three in width, with a hole for entrance of about one and a half feet high at the level of the earth, the whole construction being the shape of a thimble.

To use the sweating-house they heat it with turf, exactly in the way such a construction would be heated for the purpose of baking bread. When it is pretty hot, four or five men or women, entirely naked, creep in as best they can through the little opening, which is immediately closed with a piece of wood covered over with dung. The unfortunates stay in this for four or five hours without the possibility of getting out, and if one of them takes ill, he or she may sit down, but the plank will not be taken away before the proper time. As soon as the patients enter, an abundant perspiration starts, and, commonly, when they come out they are much thinner than when they went in. Wherever there are four or five cabins near each other there is sure to be a sweating-house, and no matter what may be the malady of the peasant, he uses this as a means of cure. The man who showed me the one I examined had been in it the day before for sore eyes.

To know exactly what it felt like to be in one I crept in myself, and although no fire had been in it for twenty-four hours, and although the hole through which I crept remained open, I must say that there are few maladies which I would not prefer to the sweating-house remedy. However, if breathing air can be provided for, a violent perspiration may be useful in many cases ; it is certain that many peasants here are cured by this means of rheumatism and other maladies caused by chills. On going out of the sweating-houses some are accustomed to lie in bed in the cabin and keep themselves warm for a little time, others do not trouble to do this, but simply put on their clothes and go back to their work as if nothing special had happened. The fowls seem to be fond of the sweating-house, it is always their shelter in time of bad weather —to be sure they only stand in the opening.

The *Tuatha da danaan*, who were, according to history, magicians and sorcerers, and who for the greater part dwelt in the north of Ireland in the county of Donegal, ' established,' says General Vallencey, ' an oracle on an island in a little lake named *Lough Gearg, Dearc*, or *Derg*. There is in it a cavern called *uamh Treibh-Oin*—the cave of the tribe of Oin, which was afterwards called St. Patrick's Purgatory.' This is the principal pilgrimage of Ireland, and here, in summer, come crowds of devotees from different parts of the island. The number of persons visiting the place is stated to be over thirty thousand. The ferry boat by which they cross is insured for £200 sterling, and sometimes the crowds crossing are so large that the passage is dangerous. Four or five years ago a boat, too heavily laden, was swamped in the passage and thirty persons were lost. In ancient times the devotees submitted to terrible trials; at present penitences are made on the belly, on the back, and on the knees. However, ' this famous and ancient cavern was broken open and filled up in the year 1497, on the day of the *fête* of St. Patrick, and condemned as a fabulous thing by the head of the Franciscans of Donegal, and other persons, by order of Pope Alexander the Sixth.' [1]

[1] Sir Richard Ware.

The mountains, and even the villages and territories in the neighbourhood of the lake, have all names which in Irish relate to sorcery of some form. *Rughd-Cruach, Cruach-Brioct, Sceir-gearg* or *gearog*, the mountain of charms, of the sorcerers, the last the Rock of Destiny, which has given the name to the lake *gearg*, or *dearg*.[1]

The approaches of the lake are by impregnable marshes and across mountains where one can scarcely get a safe or sound footing. The description given by Mathew Paris in a Latin work written in the twelfth century, and which I have read at Brown Hall, seems to be intended for the mysteries of Eleusis or for the grotto of Trophonius. The extraordinary things which the Irish captain declares he saw, require faith at least as great as that of a grain of mustard to be believed. He saw the devils and the damned stretched on burning wheels or stewing in cauldrons of sulphur; he himself was roasted and boiled for some time, and after many trials of this kind he arrived at last in the Champs Elysées, where he was received by bishops and monks, who showed him the Gate of Paradise, complimented him on his courage, fed him on celestial food, and then sent him back to Hell, that is to say back to this world for

Ce monde, hélas, est bien un autre enfer.

It will not be out of place to add that Mathew Paris explains that before entering into this cavern it is

---

[1] Here, in a lengthy note, the author quotes the theories of General Vallencey based on an assumed agreement in form and meaning of words belonging to the Irish and Arabic and Persian languages. The General's speculations are sometimes more curious than valuable, and some of the derivations he gives would not be accepted now as correct. The author's spelling of Irish words is retained.—Tr.

customary to confess the penitent, and make him fast, in order to prepare him for the surprising things he is about to see. We have an old French proverb which says ' A hungry belly has no ears,' and it may be said that the proverb is wrong, and that it is very easy to make a man so prepared hear and see everything that it is intended he should hear and see.

I come back to my travels. I came through the little town of Donegal, and, turning immediately westward, came to that singular opening in the mountains which seems to have been made by the wish of nature in order to allow of communication between one country and another ; it is the only pass in the mountains from the sea. I saw an old castle standing alone among the wild hills, and my conductor told me that formerly it was the home of troops placed there to keep the country free from Tories, who, he said, were highway robbers. At last, after a fatiguing day, I was able to present myself to the Bishop of Raphoe, who received me with great kindness, The county of Donegal, which I omitted from my tour by coming immediately to Raphoe by the mountain pass I have described, is a country almost as little known as Connemara. It is said, however, by people who know it to be much better. Ireland is very populous at parts, and if a dispersion could be effected so that the remote corners should be filled, it could contain and nourish at least double its present population. To keep them in the country would certainly be better than to allow them in crowds to emigrate to America, as they have been doing now for a long time.

After Sligo the Catholics appear to be less numerous ;

the inhabitants in this district appear to be divided as to religion almost equally, being Anglican, Catholics, and Presbyterians. On Sunday I went with the good bishop whose hospitality I enjoyed, and his church was full. From his house I went to that of the dean, and after staying with him for a day or two, I proceeded to Londonderry, passing near the arm of the sea which is called Lough Swilly. It is a bay of very considerable size, very deep and very safe almost everywhere, but the country round its shores is rather wild, and that was the reason why the English company making settlements here during the reign of Queen Elizabeth established themselves at Derry and not here. It was at that time that Derry had the addition of ' London ' made to its name.

CHAPTER XI

LONDONDERRY—THE GIANT'S CAUSEWAY—BALLY-CASTLE—FAIR HEAD

THE approaches to Londonderry are charming, and indicate the wealth of a great city. The borders of the pretty river Derg are cultivated and cared for like a garden, and dotted with country houses. The city itself, situated on an eminence, is seen from afar, and has a fine appearance, which is increased by the tall spire which Lord Bristol (Bishop of Derry) has had built by subscription.

The city enclosure, proper, is not very much, but the suburbs are very fine. The old walls exist and are used as an agreeable promenade, disfigured very little by an *arc de triomphe* which has only the look of a large door or gate ; on the keystone is cut the date, 1689, in large figures, being the year in which this city was besieged by King James. There should, at least, be a stairway made to allow of communication between the two ends of the promenade. As these ramparts are of no present utility, it seems to me that if they were put out of existence and used as material to extend the hill platform on which the city is situated, it would be infinitely better for the place, and would allow the air to circulate in the streets. However, the inhabitants are jealous of

198

attempts on their walls, and still recall the memorable siege the city sustained against King James. Certainly the walls would be of no use now in resisting an attack.

I went to visit the place of James' camp, as well as the different French posts. These latter seem to me to be cleverly chosen, but what astonished me was, how it was possible for the English frigate to force a passage in spite of the chain which barred the river, and the batteries which were on the banks. It was known that the city was almost on the point of surrendering, and that the English fleet had been obliged to retire to Lough Swilly, where it had waited nearly six weeks, without finding means of conveying succour to the besieged. Knowing, however, the extremity to which the inhabitants of the city were reduced, it was resolved to take the risk of forcing the passage by a frigate, accompanied by two or three transport vessels.

As the surrender of the place depended on the success or non-success of the enterprise, it can be imagined what interest this excited for both parties. The frigate, carried by a good breeze and by the tide current, struck the boom with violence, and by the rebound was thrown so far out of the channel as to be stranded; but, happily, the captain, profiting by the rising tide, freed his ship by the expedient of firing the whole of the cannons on the side on which the vessel had touched ground, and the tide carried the ship through the boom, which had been broken by the first shock. When the frigate had passed through, the captain and crew cried ' Huzza, huzza ! ' (called here ' three cheers '), and had the misfortune in commencing the third ' huzza ' to have his head carried off by a cannon ball.

Londonderry has not the air of an Irish town. There is there an activity and an industry which are not generally to be found in other parts of the country. The principal trade consists in linens, of which there is a market once or twice a week. It is surprising to note the speed with which the linen merchants examine the cloth. They stand on a sort of platform with a little desk before them, while the peasants carry their webs past and stop for just a moment. The merchant looks, and immediately mentions a price ; if it is accepted, he marks it on the cloth, and the peasant goes to the office for payment. There is one merchant who, on every market day, buys in a single hour cloth to the value of three or four hundred pounds sterling.

It is very strange that, although the flax from which this linen is made grows in the country, they have never been able to save seed, and are obliged to bring it from America. The first manufactures of linen were estab-lished in Ireland by the Protestants who quitted France under the reign of Louis XIV, and carried their industry to another country. The exportation of this linen is a source of immense profit to Ireland. According to the researches I have been able to make into the subject of the exportation of linen, salted beef, and grain, it would appear that in the last ten years (in spite of the great number of absentee rich who draw away enormous sums) Ireland has received annually about two hundred thousand pounds sterling more than she has paid out of the country. If such a state of affairs can be continued for some time, this country will soon reach a pitch of prosperity which few nations can hope to equal.[1]

When I was at Londonderry there was there, exhibiting himself, a Polish dwarf who called himself Count Boralosky. He may have been two and a half feet high. This is a most extraordinary little being. He speaks four or five languages, and has been very well brought up. His age is put down as between fifty and sixty years, and he has travelled much in Great Britain, where there are few towns which have not made his acquaintance. It is said that his wife, who is of ordinary stature, in a matrimonial quarrel, one day lifted him and set him on the mantelpiece. There was also in the same town a certain learned man, whose opposition to femininity was such that I have seen him throw his glass into the fire because, without his knowledge, it had been filled in order that he might drink to the health of the ladies.

The bishopric of Derry is one of the best of Ireland. They say it is worth £12,000 per annum. Oh, what a lovely thing it is to be an Anglican bishop or minister! These are the spoiled children of fortune, rich as bankers, enjoying good wine, good cheer, and pretty women, and all that for their benediction. God bless them! Oh, if I could one day wear the *philibeg* [2] of black satin—how much better than being exiled that would be! Lord Bristol, besides his bishopric, has a fortune of fifteen

[1] See the Journals of the Chamber of Commerce on Importation and Exportation, the Reports from the Customs, and the calculations of Arthur Young at the end of his book on Ireland.

[2] The Anglican bishops wear, as mark of their dignity, a small petticoat which descends only to the knees, and which is like what is worn by the Highlanders of Scotland, but with this exception, that in the case of the bishops, breeches are worn below.—*Note by Author.*

to twenty thousand pounds sterling per annum. He is a man of talent, a learned man, but of singular habits. He travels nearly all the time in foreign countries, and spends nearly his whole income in superb houses, which are of use to the country through the money they cost.

It is rather singular to remark how in Ireland there is so little ceremonious politeness in public, while there is a great deal of it in private houses. In the inn at which I stopped there was given a grand ball. When the supper was announced, it was not without interest for me to observe how the whole company ran to table, everybody hurrying for a place without regard to others. It happened one day that Lady ——, who was queen of the ball, by not hurrying enough, was left without a seat. The same thing happened to me on this occasion, for, while I was philosophically regarding the spectacle, all the places were filled, and it was only with some trouble that I found a seat at the end of a form. I do not cite this as peculiar to Londonderry, it is an amusing moment at the public balls in Ireland when supper is announced.

It was only at Londonderry that I began to observe the spirit of contention then reigning in this northern province. Leaving this pleasant town, and passing through Newton Limavady, I came to the house of Mr. M'Causland at Fruithill, and after a sojourn of a day or two there, he conducted me to the house of the Rev. Mr. Sampson, for whom I had a letter. This reverend gentleman is reputed to be a violent anti-ministerialist. Nevertheless, he is still esteemed by many who have political opinions differing from his. I found him a most agreeable and well-educated man. It is strange how I find it so easy to accommodate myself to persons whose opinions are totally different from mine, while it has often happened to me that I have had quarrels with people who were very much of my own way of thinking.

The shore began already to take on some of the character of the famous Giant's Causeway. The perpendicular rocks under which I passed are basaltic, and cover a stratum of limestone of singular whiteness.

The Bishop of Derry has built a superb palace in an unfrequented spot, or rather a place that was entirely desert before the erection of the building. It is with pleasure that one notices here a large number of houses for the peasants, built by the bishop at his own charges. They seem very fit and comfortable, and the peasants themselves, the tenants, seem to be greatly attached to their bishop, although they have never seen him. The house of Downhill is full of beautiful paintings, which Lord Bristol has brought with him from Italy. He has built a temple of fine architecture on the edge of a precipice, as if to brave the waves and winds. The sea furiously beats against the perpendicular rocks at its base, and rises at times to a height of 150 feet. The temple is, not without reason, dedicated to Eolus.

From here one can distinguish perfectly the coast of Scotland, and I looked at it, not without pleasure, having the intention to pass the winter in that country. Although my travels here, on the whole, have been agreeable, one tires towards the end, and I was now in my sixth month of a rather uncommon pilgrimage.

I was received here by the Rev. Mr. Burrowes, who is Archdeacon of the diocese, and it was just at this point that the public excitement showed itself most particularly. One of the domestics of the house, returning from Coleraine, reported that the house of one Captain O'Hara had been burned, and his family murdered. I thought at the time that it was an imposture of the lackey, in order to see what effect the news would produce on his master. The next day I went to Coleraine and found that nothing of the kind had happened. There had been a fight in the fair, in which blows of sticks had been received and given, but that was all.

I was received with much kindness in this town by Mr. Richardson, with whom I passed three or four days. The country women-folk at Coleraine are, on Sundays, very like the Scotch peasant women in the neighbourhood of Montrose. They are extremely well dressed, their shoulders usually covered by a red mantle. One can hardly believe that this is Ireland.

I walked one day along the river Bann, which flows out of Lough Neagh, a lake of which I shall speak later. Wishing to inform myself of the state of the country, I stopped Mr. Richardson's servant with the horse, and risked going into a cabin and talking with the family, as I was accustomed to do when moving on foot. I praised the country, and said that it was a cruel thing that any should say that the country people were not ready to defend the Constitution, &c., &c. The good folk were very reserved as long as I remained in the cabin, but as soon as I left, I was followed by a young man who had more confidence in me, and who commenced to retail to me the kind of trifling nonsense on which the people of France fed themselves before the Revolution. I was really surprised to hear all this talk about equality, fraternity, and oppression. After a little I asked him what was the oppression of which he complained. He named taxes on wine and beer, and when I asked him if he ever drank the one or the other, he said it was all the same ; it was very hard on those who had to pay, with more nonsense of this kind. He spoke also about the reform of Parliament, and complained much of abuses in elections, preached of tolerance, and indulged in philosophical discourse, such as was heard from our foppish talkers before the Revolution. To tell the truth, I returned from my excursion with a poor opinion of the United Irishman.

It is possible that there may be really some cause for complaint, for where is the country which has a government free from abuses ? But it is evident here that the murmurings of the peasants have been put into their heads by people of another feather. What difference to the peasants do plurality of votes, parliamentary elections, impediments of commerce, taxes on wine, and other goods, make ? He need not trouble himself about any of these things, provided he is allowed peaceably to enjoy the fruit of his labour, and that he is assured of personal liberty. Save in these matters ; what need he care whether it is Peter or James who occupies such and such a place, whether the Government under which he lives is republican or monarchical ; he need think of none of these things. To make him believe that he has cause for complaint, he must be led to believe that his ills come from things which have not the smallest relation to them. Thus it has always been in France ; thus it will be always.

The evening before my departure, Mr. Richardson asked me how I liked the horse which he had lent me for riding about the country, and on receiving my answer he said, ' The season is far advanced, the weather is

bad, he will be a good travelling companion for you.'
I refused the gift, but in the end he gave orders to a
servant to take the horse to a house which I was going
to. It *is* often agreeable to have a *Rosinante* with
whom to speak when travelling a bad road. This is
the second time that I had experienced such an act of
goodness in my travels, the first offer was made to me
by Mr. Peter Latouche. Then it was in the middle of
the summer, and the dread of being indiscreet joined
to the fear that I should not know what to do with the
poor horse made me, at that time, absolutely refuse.
Here the circumstances were quite different.

I paid my respects to the famous work of the
Giants, and stopped for a moment to see an old castle
belonging to the Marchioness of Antrim, to which alone
the goats have access. The only passage for man is
an arch one foot wide, without protection and over a
deep precipice. I observed, along the way, several
quarries in which the basalt is arranged in pillars of
five or six sides like those of the Causeway. The coasts
all along here are very high, and everywhere below the
basalt there is a thick stratum of limestone, white as
snow, and studded with flints. After a long circuit,
I arrived at last at the famous Giant's Causeway.
Persons who come here in the hope of seeing something
unnatural and extraordinary are commonly disappointed, and find it unlike the idea they had formed
of the place from description. The Causeway is not
any more astonishing than the quarries through the
country, where the basalt is found disposed in the same
manner. What is most striking is the perpendicular
rock face, four or five hundred feet high, springing
from the bosom of the sea. The different strata of

which it is composed are easily distinguished. Some-times there is a reddish tufa-like layer, at other points it is basalt in a confused contorted state, sometimes ranged in regular columns, and in one place having really some resemblance to the pipes of an organ. The Giant's Causeway, as they call it, is a part of the same matter detached from the mountain,—at low tides one can follow it pretty far. The waves break against it with singular fury. Here it forms a species of pavement about thirty or forty feet wide, the ends of the straight columns forming the pavement. There is no space between them, although their conformation is not very regular ; some have six, some seven, some eight, others only four sides, but the greatest number are pentagonal. The Causeway proceeds about two hundred paces by a gentle slope, finally disappearing under the water. The most remarkable thing about these pillars is that they are not of a single piece, but composed of detached stones, always convex at the upper end, and adjusting themselves perfectly to the concavity of the next stone above.

In the same direction, at ten or twelve leagues distance over the sea, on the coast of Scotland, is the island of Staffa, of which I have already made mention in the volume on Great Britain. It is composed of smaller stones and is not less curious.

Many people have examined this formation, and have formulated ingenious theories accounting for its origin. Some pretend that it is the product of a volcano, others that the basalt was at first soft, and according as it contained more or less mineral, its columns are more or less perfect.

I have seen, in many other places, stones of the

same character. The city of Edinburgh is situated on a rock of like material. Arthur's Seat, a mountain near Edinburgh, is entirely of this stone ; on the southern side, the basalt is even formed of pillars of five or six faces. Near the city there is exhibited a singular phenomenon : a line of basalt six or seven feet wide, which extends for an immense distance, and of which the end is really not known. It crosses stones of other species and coal, and it has been remarked that the coal which is found on its two sides has lost nearly all its quality, and resembles burnt coal. This observation has been the cause of many speculations, and of a theory which is perhaps not ill-founded. This assumes that the basalt is the product of remarkable convulsions, in which the earth has opened and vomited the basalt in a state of fusion. The columns which form at such places depend on the quantity of mineral contained in them. Examples are given of extraordinary effusion of basalt in the Isle of Arran at the mouth of the Clyde. There the principal mountain is of granite, and, in the middle, there is observable a line of basalt ten or twelve feet wide, right up to the summit. These theory-makers assert that this basalt in the interior of the rock at Arran and in the long line appearing at Edinburgh fill gigantic cracks, the result of some terrible earth convulsion, the basalt in a state of fusion rushing into openings made in the crust of the earth.

On going to the Causeway, to Mr. Moore, I saw a hill and some fields dotted over by a great number of peasants, or people of the small farmer class. I asked how they came to be there, and was told that they were occupied in raising the potatoes of a man for whom they had a friendly feeling; such action, it appears, is not uncommon. It is always somewhat disagreeable to be caught in a crowd, especially if one is a stranger, and I hesitated whether to advance or take another road. In the end, however, reflecting that I had no potatoes to unearth, and the people seeming to work very peaceably, I went on and passed through the crowd, no person taking any notice of me whatever.

I am told that it is an old custom with the peasantry here to assemble at the end of the autumn and to dig up the potatoes of persons for whom they have any sort of affection. What caused some uneasiness to the Government, on this occasion, was the fact that the potatoes which were raised were those of persons who had been arrested for high treason, or of persons who were known to be disaffected, although, to my knowledge, they had shown the same favour to persons who were attached to the Government. Mr. Moore, for example, whose hospitality I enjoyed that day, found that he could not refuse to allow the favour to be bestowed on him without attracting ill-will.

These gatherings are conducted with the greatest order. A man, with nothing special to distinguish him, exacted obedience and directed affairs by signs with the hand or by certain calls. The whole time the work went on men, women, and children sang, accompanied by one or other kind of instrument. No one is allowed at such gatherings to drink any strong liquor, and this certainly requires a great effort in this part of the country. I can say with truth that the regulation is observed most literally, for I have never seen a single person under the influence of drink near these potato gatherings. I do not say that there were not a few in the neighbouring villages, it would have been a miracle had it been otherwise. For the occasion the peasantry had put on their best clothes ; the air of gaiety and good-humour which showed itself among them would have made any spectator believe that he had arrived on a *fête* day. The road was covered with horses belonging to the farmers who assisted in the gathering. If a similar gathering took place in France, or even in England, I very much doubt if matters would proceed so peacefully. I believe that these gatherings, if allowed to continue, might have become dangerous, when the spirit of discontent which reigned at the time in the country is considered. The Government acted wisely in forbidding them some time afterwards, and it is to be reported in favour of the character of the people of this country, that they did not attempt to act against the wish of the authorities.

To me it is very strange to see that these Irish, with their mutinous dispositions, submit to rule so readily. I have already said, and I repeat with pleasure, that, guided by capable men who are actuated by motives of public welfare, there is no people I have known so easily led for good. These frequent seditions prove nothing more than the sensibility of the race, and if the Government would only give up at once and absolutely the attempt to Anglicise the Irish at any cost, and would lead them through their prejudices and customs, it would be possible to do with them anything that could be wished.

Following the coast along the summit of the hill, which is composed of the same materials as the Causeway, my attention was called to the different phenomena of the basalt, the different figures it takes, sometimes in the form of pillar, sometimes in matter confused and without order. The weather was magnificent; the sea beat against the foot of the rocks four or five hundred feet below; Scotland and the islands of the west showed on the horizon over a calm, blue sea. Even my horse seemed to joy in the beauty of the scene, approaching to the edge of the precipice and letting his eye range the horizon with a look of admiration. This need not be considered astonishing. Who has not read in travels and romances the affecting declarations of far more stupid beasts on some scene, sometimes only on the beauty of moonlight? I never come across these beautiful descriptions in books without turning over twenty or thirty pages, so as to come to the dawn if the author spoke of the moon, or to the night if he spoke of the sun.

I stopped at a little village where I saw numbers of people assembled, and I had the pleasure of being present at the baptism of an infant. In the north of Scotland in such cases they make the poor little creature swallow a spoonful of whisky, to keep it from crying; here, for the same reason, they put a little butter into an eggshell, and mix it with bread and sugar, and the nurse on the end of her finger puts a little of the mixture into the infant's mouth. I do not know if this is the custom in any other country, but I think the result must be very much as if they should put into the child's throat a little flax tow with cider mixed through it.

After a long walk I arrived at Ballycastle, where I was received with much kindness by Mr. Ezekiel Boyd. On the day of my arrival the company in garrison in this little town left, and was replaced by one of a Scotch regiment. These were very well received by the inhabitants, who, during the night, may it please you, stole the whole of the ammunition and the half of the arms of the soldiers ! Just imagine—stealing the arms and ammunition of soldiers. I'd rather that they would steal the shirts and breeches off my soldiers if they would leave them their arms and ammunition. All that was done here was to hale a few people before Mr. Boyd, who is a Justice of the Peace. They all swore on the Gospel, one after the other, that they had no knowledge whatever of the powder and guns stolen.

In one of my walks I came to Fair Head, a great cape pointing Scotlandwards and the extreme northerly point of Ireland. The rocks rise gradually from near Ballycastle, and the most northern portion is also the most elevated above the sea.

The singular disposition of the various strata in this mountain merits attention, especially at the part where the coal mine is worked, almost on the margin of the sea. I have marked the different layers as they appeared from the sea level, and measuring them, by look of eye only, the order and thickness appeared to be as I have marked down here.

Basalt	18	feet
Mixed coal	3	,,
Tufa, reddish stone	10	,,
Sulphurous coal	3	,,
Tufa, grey stone	10	,,
Mixed coal	6	,,
Tufa, red	8	,,
Mixed coal	1	,,
Tufa, red	8	,,
Coal, the true vein	7	,,
Tufa, red stone	...	

I had the fancy to enter this coal mine, and I went through it to the very end; it is a little amusement which, like marriage, one may try once, but I shall not indulge in it again. The mine stretches for about half a mile underground, in a horizontal direction, with sufficient elevation in the line to allow of water flowing away. There is another mine above, and the workers in the two sometimes approach near enough to hear each other working. Possibly the two workings will join soon. The proprietors should consider the question of digging a perpendicular shoot, or well, into the mine, in order to allow the air in it to be renewed, for when the wind is in the west the vapour is carried into the interior, and makes it suffocating. If this shaft were made, there would be a current, and no inconvenience would be felt. The coal which they take from this mine is the best I have seen in Ireland. It is exactly like Scotch coal, but does not burn so quickly, and the mine seems inexhaustible. The Irish Parliament, sensible of the immense advantage which may result to the country from the work of this mine, has spent enormous sums in the endeavour to make a port out of Ballycastle, but the tide is so strong and carries so much sand that the port is entirely filled up, so that there is no water in it even at high tide.

I followed the shore from the coal mine to the point of Fair Head, and, climbing the rocks by a goat path, I arrived with much trouble at the top, where the scene which lay before me amply recompensed me for my pains. The Causeway is praised with reason, the regularity of the columns is something surprising; but here the pillars of basalt are nearly six hundred feet high, and some of them stand out separate from the body of the mountain, at a distance of two, three, or four feet, clear from top to bottom, sustained only by a few stones in the middle. At a little distance from the edge of the precipice there are crevices, and from throwing a stone down any of these, it is made clear that they extend to the foot of the mountain.

From place to place hollows are observable, which seem at one time to have served as river or torrent beds ; the slope is always regular from the sea to two little lakes at some distance in the peninsula. From this I took it that formerly the cape or Head extended much farther out to sea, and that perhaps there was even a country beyond, and considerable mountains which supplied the water which filled these channels. This observation is justified by the frequent fall of these separate pillars, and even by the fall of portions of the principal mass. The young men of Ballycastle have assured me that they have ridden twelve or fifteen feet beyond what is now the face of the precipice. This agrees with my famous Connemara theory. It is so diverting to dream and theorise that I return to the task frequently. If I dare to continue, I would say that in the course of centuries this cape of Fair Head will entirely disappear, and the ocean will open for itself a wider passage into the Irish Sea.

The tidal current here is extremely rapid. It can be seen from the top of Fair Head, running like a torrent, sometimes from the ocean to the Irish Sea, and sometimes from the Irish Sea to the ocean. Scotland seems very near, but Fair Head does not exactly point to it. According to my Connemara theory, there must always have been a strait between the two, and afterwards an immense gulf extending westward to Greenland.

After having conceived, written, and even printed all the beautiful reflections, dreams, and theories presented to the reader when I was speaking of Connemara, I had the misfortune to read in the ' Vindication of the Ancient History of Ireland ' by General Vallencey, that others have amused themselves in exactly the same way, and have drawn conclusions almost similar to mine, among others Messrs. Whitehurst and Hamilton. The two are not exactly in agreement as to the rocks near the Giant's Causeway ; they do agree in saying that an immense territory must have been swallowed up by the sea, with the volcano which supplied the basalt of which the pillars are made.

' Add to this,' says General Vallencey, ' the tradition of the ancient Irish that a great part of the Island has been swallowed up by the sea. The peasants believe that at times portions of this rise above the waters to the north-west of Ireland. The inhabitants of these parts give to these appearing lands the name of *Tir Huddy,* or the country of Hudd. They say that they contained a city, formerly possessing immense riches, and that the key of this city was buried under a certain altar of the Druids.'

The General, always thinking of his theory of Ireland peopled by tribes from the Levant, adds :

' This city is evidently the lost city of the Arabs mentioned in the preface of the Alcoran and visited by their false prophet Hudd.'

What is still more cruel for a theory-spinner is that, in the comparison which the General makes between the Japanese, the Peruvians, and the Irish, I have found that a certain Varinius said exactly what I have thought out. A certain Bertius also asserts that the Deluge of Deucalion has been wrongly placed in Thessaly, and that it belongs to the coast of Scotland, or Caledonia, as it should be called, because *Dur* in Irish means water, and Deucalion is a corruption of Dur Caledonia—the Deluge of Caledonia

It is such a terrible thing to find one's pet theories appropriated in this way that I have determined never more to make any, or, at any rate, never again to read the books of those who have made theories like mine. It is some satisfaction, however, to find that the opinions of these gentlemen give weight to the theories of my invention.

CHAPTER XII

THE coast nearly everywhere is of the same boldness from Fair Head to Cushendun, ten or eleven miles further to the east. The strait here between Scotland and Ireland resembles a large river, and, in fact, the distance between the two countries is not more than eleven Irish miles or fourteen English. It happens often, in calm weather, that open boats can cross from one side to the other.

It would seem to be quite easy to establish a regular packet between Campbeltown, in the Mull of Cantyre, and Cushendun, or if not regular, at any rate when wind and bad weather do not allow of the crossings to Holyhead, or even to Portpatrick. The different sects are separated in districts in the Province of Ulster. The inhabitants of Cushendun, as well as those of the country in the neighbourhood, are Catholics, and they have this peculiarity, that they do not speak English as do the inhabitants in other parts of the province, who for the most part would not understand Irish. From here to Glenarm the coast is followed by a road of difficult construction between the rocks and the sea. The coast is always high, and often presents the most extraordinary appearance. The rock is nearly always crowned by basalt, but the

217

Causeway pillar formation is no longer found. The limestone which is beneath the basalt is not so white, being rather grey near Glenarm, a village which has nothing remarkable about it except the castle of the Marquis of Antrim. Quitting the coast, I had to cross the mountains to get to the interior, and I stopped at Brushin,[1] where most of the inhabitants are Presbyterians. One could hardly imagine that he is among the same people. The way of speaking, and even of dressing, is much more Scotch than Irish. Making a vigorous spurt, I reached the borders of Lough Neagh, or rather, I should say, Sea Neagh, and was received, with a kindness and politeness truly remarkable, at Shane's Castle by Lord O'Neill.

Lough Neagh is an immense sheet of water—they say forty to forty-five miles long by fifteen to twenty wide. It would appear that this lake did not always exist. It has very little depth, and at many places trees are found with their roots still in the bottom. Its greatest depth, at one place only, is seventy feet ; at no other place does it exceed forty-two; and, commonly, it is not more than six to twelve feet deep. At certain parts its waters seem to have a mineral quality, as in the neighbouring soil numerous pieces of petrified wood have been found. On one of the days I went to the point where the river Bann leaves the lake, in order to see for myself what sort of obstruction had caused the formation of this inland sea. This cause I found to be, principally, the bed of the river ; it is much too narrow for such a mass of water, and the river makes a curve of about two miles (although in a direct line the distance is not more than half a mile)

[1] Broughshane.

before throwing itself into another lake, five or six miles long by two or three wide, and called Lough Beg. At the point of departure from this lake, there is a pretty considerable waterfall. If an effort were made to drain a large part of Lough Neagh, and render the river Bann navigable to the sea, the first thing to do would be to cut a deep canal in the direct line from Lough Neagh to Lough Beg, taking care to commence above the sand bar which wind and the current have caused to form at the spot where the river begins. This alone would diminish the volume of the water by five or six feet, and afterwards when the land drained had time to consolidate, and if it were found to be good for cultivation, and the vapour did not prove un-healthy,[1] the waterfall at Lough Beg could be attacked, and communicating canals could be made at other parts of the river where there are rocky obstructions. The sea is about thirty miles off, and there are not more than seventy feet of fall in all that great length, and the river, except at the rocky portions, hardly seems to flow. Through some of these obstructions, it seems to me quite feasible to cut passages for boats— a lock at each place would do all that is wanted—and then there would be communication by water between the principal towns of the North of Ireland, for Belfast has a canal to Lough Neagh, and there is another which goes to Newry.

The Bishop of Derry has built a magnificent palace on the other side of Lough Beg. The architecture is

---

[1] The doctor to whom I spoke about the possibilities of draining the lake, after making many objections, all of which I met, said: ' To tell the truth, it is not in my own interest that I am speaking, for the draining would produce a delightful fever, which would make my fortune.'—*Note by Author.*

rather singular for a country house. It seems to be modelled on that of the Pantheon at Rome. Bally-scullen is absolutely circular, and light comes only from the roof. The edifice indeed has the air of a public building rather than that of a country house. The apartments of the interior are very richly furnished, and decorated by a great number of valuable paintings and pieces of sculpture. I am told that this house has cost Lord Bristol nearly eighty thousand pounds sterling. His Lordship has a mania for building superb palaces in Ireland and England, while he lives in ugly rat-holes on the Continent.

The spirit of the people was here in such a state of fermentation that it could easily have become dangerous in the absence of precautions. However, I am satisfied that there was not so much danger as some people pretended, although, certainly, there were some assassinations and other crimes, the authors of which cannot be traced. It would, however, be an injustice to accuse the entire mass of people for these crimes of a few individuals, and the greater part of them appear to have been committed through fear of being denounced by the persons who suffered. I have seen suspected persons arrested without the least difficulty and taken to prison, crossing, on the way, a market filled with country people, not one of whom showed any disposition to interfere. I saw here examples of excesses, but they are to be characterised as ridiculous rather than criminal. The curate of the parish had been a Catholic, and had been employed as chaplain in France and in Ireland. Seeing himself abandoned by his patrons, he renounced what are called the *abominations of the Babylonish Woman,* and immediately obtained a pension of £40 sterling per annum and the first vacant curacy.

The peasants, who always judge actions and their motives in a matter-of-fact, common-sense way, left him in peace, and contented themselves by staying away from his church. But he, wishing to show himself at this time ardently in favour of the Government and taking its side openly, they took a dislike to him, and hardly allowed a day to pass without showing him some insult or impertinence. They cut the tail, the horns, and the ears off his cow, and nailed them to his door. The poor beast, being no longer able to show itself respectably in public, he bought another, and four days after, it suffered from the same operation, and so a third. In the end, however, he thought it better to keep this last as it was, and when it was allowed out in a field, the people sent dogs after it. The curate complaining and protesting, they broke his windows and stopped his chimney.

The town of Antrim, capital of this county, is a poor little market-town without any appearance of trade or industry. Some distance off there is a round tower, which, according to the country folk, was at one time in the centre of the town. At present it is at least a mile from that centre, in the park of a country house. To go from here to Belfast, it is necessary to cross the mountains, which follow the coast round nearly the whole of Ireland.

I had heard so much about the troubles, the assassinations, and the conspiracies of which Belfast was the centre, that I felt considerable reluctance to proceed there. I was, however, agreeably surprised to find the town in perfect peace and quietness.

Thus wags the world : if a storyteller, in going along the street, knows that there is in a building some six or seven hundred persons, and passing beneath the windows hears some noisy talk, he will say, and naturally, that there were seven hundred persons there making a frightful noise, while really the noise perhaps proceeded only from four or five excited persons, although it is put to the debit of the 695 quiet people. So it was at Belfast, the inhabitants seemed perfectly calm, and even less occupied by thought of politics than was the case in many other parts of the country.

Belfast has almost entirely the look of a Scotch town, and the character of the inhabitants has considerable resemblance to that of the people of Glasgow. If you start a conversation with them about the Emperor or General Clairfaix, they will possibly talk about the prices of sugar or linen, according as they are trading in one or other, or may remark that if peace is not made promptly they do not know how they are going to get rid of their muslin or how they are to buy wine. I do not say that they are wrong. I wish for peace, but, at the same time, care must be taken not to excite civil war in the country in order to have peace abroad. In any case, like marrying, the making of peace is not a thing to be done by one party ; the other party must consent.

One day I went to Carrickfergus to see the castle that Thurot surprised during the late war. It is situated on a rock near the mouth of the bay of the same name. The French, to the number of 3000, arrived in two vessels, and within an hour or two took the castle by assault. If the commandant had known to profit by the terror which his expedition caused in the country, he certainly would have put Belfast under contribution. But he had with him an officer of genius, his superior, who was not willing to hazard the attempt until he had further support. His delay gave time for troops to arrive, and he was obliged to re-embark. At some distance by sea, he met the English vessels and fought them ; the two French frigates were taken, and he himself was killed in the fight. The prison of the county is situated at Carrick-fergus. It was at the time of my visit full of State prisoners, arrested on charges of murders which had been committed in the neighbourhood of Belfast. I remarked with pleasure that the town seemed per-fectly peaceful, and that justice was allowed to have her way ; further, that there was only a single sentinel at the prison gate.

It is said that it was near this town that the first King of Scotland was drowned in returning to Ireland.

Belfast is a rather pretty town, and trade in it seems to be very flourishing. Its principal industry is the manufacture of textiles ; the Linen Hall is a building of considerable size. I have already men-tioned that it is to the French refugees under Louis XIV that Ireland owes these establishments. More than once the ills of France have been the benefits of her neighbours.

In a terrible frost, which made me think that it was time to finish my travels, I returned to the house of Mr. Birch near Comber. The proprietors in this neighbourhood were this day assembled in order to take measures for the surety of the country, in case of riot. The peasantry had stolen the arms of a party of cavalry a few days earlier. I cannot, for the life of me, understand how troops can allow their arms to be stolen. Perhaps it was here due to great confidence in the people round them. The thing might happen once—but twice—but thrice— ! ! !

All this country is made up of little hills of nearly equal height, and these continue on to Lough Strangford, which is nothing more than an arm of the sea, very wide, but with very little depth. The little town of Newtownards at the end of the lough is fairly well built, but it must suffer from the damp rising from this arm of the sea at low tide, when much of it is almost entirely dry. I may be reproached with having introduced this subject of drainage and drying lands too often, but certainly there is no country has such need for it. I shall repeat here what I have already said twenty times, and that is, that it is a shame to allow all these lakes and arms of the sea to exist, when the ground below them could be turned so advantageously to account. Nothing will better indicate the quantity of good land, which might be taken here from the sea, than the statement which I can make, that at four or five miles distant from the town it is customary, at low tide, to cross the bay on horseback, and even on foot. Although on this great space there may be certain stony places, by far the greater part of it is made up of a mixture of loam, sand, and shells.

I was received at Mount Stewart with much kindness by Lord and Lady Londonderry. My Lady is sister to the Viceroy of Ireland. She lives here a very retired life in the bosom of her amiable family, to the education of which she devotes the whole of her time. Lord Londonderry and his son were at this time raising a corps of volunteers and administering the oath of allegiance to peasants who presented themselves. Man is a sheep everywhere ; they had much trouble in getting the first ten or twelve to join, and in the days following, seven or eight hundred came forward. The peasantry in this district seemed to be comfortably situated and are well clad. Not far away are the ruins of Greyabbey ; the minister's house, which looks like a fine castle, is in the enclosure. I saw a spring which had some resemblance to the holy wells of the west, and I asked if it wete customary for the peasantry to come here for devotions ; but here the inhabitants are for the most part Presbyterians. They told me that the common belief is that any person drinking the water of this spring will never leave Ireland. As it was my intention to leave in a couple of days, I took care not to take it. Going back to Donaghadee, I was received by the postmaster, Mr. Smith, whose assistance in arranging my passage was very valuable. The number of cattle taken from here to Scotland is something inconceivable, and the farmers are obliged to submit to the impudent impositions of the owners of the boats which take the cattle. They ask as much as twenty guineas for a crossing, and as they hold the farmer in the hollow of their hands, he is obliged to pay what they ask, and this means that the cost of transport for horned cattle is as much as one guinea per beast. It seems to me that the country authorities ought to establish a regular tariff as is done at many places. Here the distance is scarcely twenty miles.[1]

[1] On the day I crossed there were four hundred horned cattle taken over to Scotland, and in the six weeks previous there had been transported nearly thirty thousand.—*Note by Author.*

In two hours and a half I was carried to the opposite side of the water, saluted anew the coast of Scotland, and counted myself happy that I had at last arrived at a place where I could rest in peace.

I had left Dublin on May 25, and I landed at Portpatrick on December 21, so I had spent more than six months on this walk, travelling without provisions, without cares, and without any baggage beyond what my pockets were able to contain.

My time, I must say, had been well employed; I had never spent time, indeed, with greater pleasure; my ideas had been enlarged; I had made the acquaintance of an interesting people too little known of their neighbours, and, unfortunately, too often the prey of avidity and caprice, leagued together during centuries for their vilification.

The surprising advance which this country has made during the last fifteen years leaves no doubt of the certainty of the prosperity which awaits it if the system of moderation lately adopted should be continued. Far be it from me to encourage any idea of revolt. The moderation of which I speak is that which every wise Government should exhibit in dealing with its faithful subjects, no matter what their religion may be. Too long these fatal quarrels have torn the bosom of Ireland. The cares of Government now are doubtless employed to extinguish them entirely. A happy experience will prove to England that the prosperity of this beautiful kingdom, far from being hurtful to her, will increase her own, and that in destroying the ridiculous prejudices which have been for ages existing against the most beautiful and richest part of her possessions, and in really making Ireland share the advantages of the beneficent laws by which she is, herself, governed, she will acquire the love of 4,000,000 of subjects, which her armies have conquered, but which justice alone will bring to submission.

CHAPTER XIII

SHORT VISIT TO SCOTLAND—EDINBURGH

THE Scotch accent appeared very strange to me, although I had been accustomed to it during my previous sojourn, but while their tongue may be uncouth, it must not be denied that the cleanliness and air of industry apparent everywhere are extremely creditable to the inhabitants who use it. I travelled through Stranraer, and following my way along the coast I had soon from the heights a magnificent view of the sea which separates Ireland from Scotland, and of the passage which opens to the ocean between Fair Head and the Mull of Cantyre. It seemed to me, almost, that I could distinguish the surprising columns of Fair Head, and spite of the hard frost, and that I was obliged to conduct my horse by the bridle on account of slippery roads, I took a singular pleasure in the outlook. Doubtless there are many folk who, in a similar case, would think only of the pleasure of being opposite a good fire.

I crossed the pretty town of Ayr, paying toll at every step, and when I asked a passer-by for direction to the house of Mr. Reid at Adamton, I was told 'Tak the corner o' the hoose when ye'll be to the end o' the toon, and ye'll gang stracht for it.' An Englishman hearing such a jargon would imagine that he heard Greek, but having spent two years in Scotland I understood perfectly well what it meant.

An Englishman who had lived long in Scotland pretended to know the language perfectly. A young and pretty girl for whom he had an attachment, having bet that she could say to him something that he could not understand, said, ' Ye're a canty callant, will ye pree mee mou.' He could not make any meaning out of it, and when it was explained to him, he had the double sorrow of losing his bet and the happy occasion. But when I come to think of it, neither English nor Irish will understand the phrase, and I am not going to take the trouble to explain it. But if they wish to know its sense, let them say to the first Scotch girl they meet, ' Bonny lassie, pree mee mou.' If she is pretty they will have something to laugh at, and if she is not, they will remember it at another time.

On the way to Glasgow the frost was so violent that, they say, it split rocks. I ought not, therefore, to be astonished that it split my riding-breeches so badly that, notwithstanding the handkerchiefs and hay I used, I was nearly frozen. Passing the night at Cathcart with the Rev. Mr. Dour, I came to Glasgow, where I had already been in my Scotch journey. I admired its beauty as much or even more than at the time of my first visit, and saw again with pleasure the people who had welcomed me then, among others, the family of Mr. Oswald, to whom I paid a visit at Scotstown. It is but just to acknowledge that, failing the kindness which he and his family showed to me, the cold passivity of other people in Edinburgh to whom I was introduced would have left me without means to carry out my project. I had anew on this occasion a proof of this friendship, for, the frost continuing, I had the shoes of my poor companion in the journey sharped, and the smith in the operation lamed the poor beast badly. Not knowing what to do, and the expense of keeping it at the inn being very considerable, I thought of ridding myself of him by simply leaving him behind. I spoke about the matter to Mr. Alexander Oswald, who came to see the horse, and having examined it, he asked me what it was worth. I said to him that, wounded as it was, it was worth nothing. ' In the situation in which it is,' said he, ' would twelve guineas suit you ? ' ' They would suit me perfectly well,' I answered, and the bargain was made. This frank and generous way of acting, made me wish that my poor beast should become in his hands a courser of Araby.

I think I really feel more pleasure in acknowledging a benefit than in reproving an impertinence. I may be found sometimes biting, but I shall never be found ungrateful.

Being at Scotstown, I crossed the river on the ice, although it was entirely concealed under water, and went to see the manufactories at Paisley. They are truly surprising in their immensity. The machines, alone, in the manufactory which I visited, had cost more than twenty thousand pounds sterling. It must take a devilish lot of muslin and ties and petticoats to make this pay, and yet this is nothing compared with what I saw at Lanark, of which I shall speak later.

I quitted Glasgow, alone, and contrary to usual custom I took a place in the coach which travels to Falkirk ; the rest of the way I accomplished on foot, crossing the Forth in spite of the ice at Alloa. Here I had the pleasure of finding myself again in a country where I had received hospitality, and happily it was again forthcoming from Mr. Bruce of Kennet and Major Mayne, with whom I had lived a long time. Leaving there, and following the line of the Forth near the iron mines, or rather iron earth, for at certain places the whole soil seems to be iron ore, I crossed the river at Queensferry, and arrived, at last, at Edinburgh.

It was the same town, the same buildings, the same places, but manners had changed very much since my departure. Everybody was armed ; the doctors, the barristers, the attorneys, even the ministers of the Gospel, and professors of colleges were exercising and sweating in the uniforms of grenadiers.[1] I do not say that this was anything but very honourable on their part. All I have to say is, that it made a great difference in society.

All the street porters, the chairmen, the lackeys, and artisans of every description had been forced to carry arms, and the sum of two shillings per week was paid to them by way of compensation for time lost in going through exercises.

This singular energy certainly did honour to Great Britain, but remembering what has been said to me so often when I first set foot on English shores, I cannot see the necessity for it. I had been told then that one Englishman was always as good as three Frenchmen, and in the north it was held that one Scotchman was as good as three Englishmen.

---

[1] A corporal who wore himself out without success in endeavouring to teach manœuvres to a professor, became very angry, and, swearing at him, said, ' I would rather teach fifty ragamuffins than one philosopher.'—*Note by Author.*

It is very strange, when one comes to think of it, to find the menace of invasion renewed in every war with France, and always with the same success. These menaces do not lay any burden on the Government, beyond the maintenance in the Channel of twenty vessels of war which perhaps could be employed elsewhere ; but, after all, they make access to the purses much more easy through the terror which they inspire. ' The secret of Government,' said Cardinal de Rets, ' is to govern by terrors of which the governed make themselves the instruments.' This secret is known in Great Britain.

The spirit which reigned among the inhabitants of Edinburgh at the time of the formation of the volunteer forces was very like that which influenced our people at the time of the formation of the National Militia, although in a different way. Some people suggested to me that I should be enrolled among the volunteers. It was vain for me to say that when I came to England or Scotland it was in order to submit myself to a policing force, and not to become a member of it ;—to be protected myself, and not to protect. These reasons seem to me very good, but they were not accepted. I was pressed to take sides, and was seriously reproached for abominable conduct in eating, without remorse or prick of conscience, a good dinner with the partisans of the Opposition, with as much appetite as if the hosts belonged to the Ministerial side.

Unless one has been in Great Britain at a stormy time, it is impossible to conceive of the animosity between parties, and the bitterness with which they defend their two patrons ;—the one side has done all the wrong, the other alone can repair it. If the king himself should make choice of one or other of these two precious mortals, I should not be very much astonished to see the two parties unite against him, and perhaps there might follow a revolution if the new Premier should not be able to get a majority.

It is not for the principles of a Minister that the people plague themselves. It is simply a matter of persons, the reason being that one has received a favour or hopes to receive one. There are, of course, people who without any thought of self-interest take sides violently, but these are rare. ' He is the greatest man that ever was at the head of the nation,' say one set, while the people on the other side cry ' Oh, the monster, the rascal, he has dragged the nation to the brink of ruin—we are lost. There is only one thing that can save us, and that is to hang Mr. Dupuits, and put Mr. Renard in his place.'

During the course of the winter the Anti-ministerialists at Edinburgh and over Great Britain made a humble petition to the king to dismiss his ' weak and wicked ministers.' Signatures were received to these documents at every public-house, and in order to encourage the people to add their names, I am told that a glass of wine was given to every one who signed. It is said that some people signed so many times on the same day that they were drunk in the evening. The partisans of the Opposition on this occasion only did what others had taught them, for when the corps of volunteers was being formed from the lower classes, a great hogshead of porter was drawn through the town, and some of its contents was given to everyone who presented himself as a defender of his country.

There was here a great cry of misery, nevertheless there were seven or eight balls daily ; comedy, concert, circus, panorama, wild beast show, all were filled. A certain Italian who knew how to attract the help of people in high station drew crowds to what he called his ' Literary Exhibitions,' at which he read, with a Milanese accent, the tragedies of Corneille and the comedies of Molière. This country is really the Promised Land for charlatans. This one made use of a little Italian compliment, changing the name of the country to the one in which he happened to find himself. Here it is : ' Foolish lovers, why do you go to Paphos ; Venus is no longer there, she has fixed her dwelling among the charming women of Scotland.' My word ! Reading this, I was charmed and thought how happy I should be at Edinburgh to have the chance of meeting the beautiful goddess. In the middle of these diversions there was a movement to send missionaries to the Indies, to preach the Gospel to the Gentous, Arabs, and Chinese. There was a subscription even got up for this purpose.

The circus where Astley exhibited his wonders of horses was changed to a church on Sunday, and I have seen in it nearly two thousand persons, the stalls (although they smelt of the stables) being filled by the fashionable folk, and the minister preached from the prompter's perch. How everything passes, everything changes ! Twenty years ago, the people of Edinburgh demolished and burnt the theatre, as the work of the devil, and now they go there for the Lord's Supper. Another twenty years and perhaps they will be playing comedy in the churches.

Several sects have been formed, even since my first

visit, among others one (the name of which I have forgotten), disdaining the sombre carriage of Presbyterianism, pretends that God is only to be honoured by gaiety. This sect sings the Psalms in the gayest manner, and, for Anthem, laughs most seriously.

People who had not taken orders were often to be found preaching in public. Sailors in the pulpit dealt warningly with the fire of Hell, and I myself have seen —oh, strange thing!—an attorney discourse to his clients on the precepts of the Gospel.

I am much astonished that ministers do not discourage such work, seeing that it will take the bread from their mouths, if the people should come to understand that without their aid they can enjoy a sermon of six or seven hours, and for nothing. With this understanding will come an end to benefices—in Scotland at any rate, where it is the people who pay.

Sunday was still observed with the same regularity ; that is to say, the ladies spent it at church, and the men over their bottle. I knew one minister who shaved on Saturday, because shaving is labour, and labour should not be undertaken on the Sabbath. Happily he did not class the putting-on of one's trousers as labour. It is not so long since there was a law which prevented barbers from exercising their profession on this day. However, nobody says anything about stopping the work of the chair-porters, the cab-drivers, nor the cooks.

I have heard that some twenty years ago, an enthusiastic minister made a journey to Rome with the laudable intention of converting the Pope to Protestantism. When, at a certain moment, the Pope lifted his blessed fingers, and the audience bowed to receive the benediction, he, instead of abasing himself, cried out with anger, 'Abomination of abominations ! Behold the Babylonish woman about to accomplish her work of iniquity ! ' Everybody was confounded, and the man was arrested. The Pope, knowing that he was a subject of Great Britain (for which country, although it condemns him and his work, he has always a paternal tenderness), had him brought before him, and questioned him. The minister avowed his intention naïvely and commenced to preach. After the Pope had listened to him very patiently, he said : ' My dear son, what would you think of me, and how do you think I would be received, if I went to Scotland, and shouted suddenly in the middle of your preaching, that you and your people were heretics doomed to everlasting burning ? Moderate your zeal, go back to your own country, do the best you can for the flock over which you are set, and which you have left for the moment without a shepherd. I have given orders that you shall not want for anything on the way.' Leaving the audience, the good minister found a person waiting for him, who conducted him to Ostia, handed him some money and saw him embark on a vessel for Edinburgh.

I have seen the King's birthday celebrated in this city with remarkable solemnity. The Lord Provost (Mayor of the City) and the other magistrates invited the Judges of the Court of Session, the Officers of the different Corps, and many other persons to solemnise the day of the King's birth in the Grand Hall of the Parliament House. There were four or five tables, one of them among others large enough to allow nearly two hundred persons to stand round it. All were covered with dried fruits, bon-bons, and, especially, with bottles. The Lord Provost, at the head of the table, in the costume of office (which, parenthetically, I may remark is very like that of Nantes), cried with a loud voice, 'Gentlemen, fill your glasses.' The request had not to be repeated, and he then said, 'The King,' which words everyone repeated, and then drank. The Lord Provost did not allow much time to pass before he said again, 'Gentlemen, fill your glasses,' giving an other toast, and this went on for three full hours. I should add that, although everyone present had at the end nearly three bottles, I do not remember to have seen a single person drunk, nor even tipsy, which goes to prove that the Scotch heads require a great deal to upset them.

I had not noticed on my previous visit a courtesy intended as a compliment to the Royal Family, and to celebrate the Union of the two Kingdoms. It consists in the nomenclature of the five parallel streets in the new town. The southern one has been called 'Princes Street' in honour of the Prince of Wales ; that to the north, 'Queen Street' in honour of the Queen ; one of the two smaller near that of Queen Street is named 'Thistle Street,' because the thistle is an ancient device of Scotland. The other near Princes Street is 'Rose Street,' because white and red roses are heraldic devices of England (I may say that there are few streets smell less of roses). To that of the middle, between England and Scotland, they have given the King's name—George Street, which street, at the end, touches on the place called after the Queen—Charlotte Square, and at the other end touches on one called after the Patron Saint of Scotland—Saint Andrew Square.

Behind this fine quarter, and as if out of the way, they have hid poor James—James Square—which is not to be reached until after one has made the grand tour over a hill, and a rapid descent down the side, next the sea. It will be seen that the folk who planned this out were very ingenious.

I went to see an establishment which cannot be too highly praised. It is an institution for the maintenance of the blind, who by their labour are able to pay nearly the whole of the expenses. There are also charitable establishments which supply work at one shilling per day to poor people and old men. There are always one hundred or more employed here in breaking stones and preparing them for the roads. A great store of these has been accumulated, but they find means to employ all who present themselves, and the poor folk are able to live. The greatest security reigns in this city at all hours, although there are very few watchmen ;—it is due to the good disposition of the inhabitants that more are not needed.

I do not remember to have heard of any theft during the whole of the time I was in Scotland, and although I have permitted myself sometimes to make certain little jokes—for which I hope no one will censure me too much—Edinburgh is certainly the best-informed and most agreeable place of habitation in the whole of Great Britain. It can show at present something rather remarkable. The Professors of the College are not only very learned, they are, also, nearly all celebrated for their works.[1] The greater number of famous

[1] Mention may be made of the works of several of the professors : Ferguson's *Discourse on Roman History* ; Stuart's *Moral Philosophy* ; Munro's work on Medicine ; Black's *Chemistry* ; Blair's *Sermons*, &c., &c.—*Note by Author*.

authors who have appeared in Great Britain during the last century were Scotch. It suffices to mention the names of Hume, Robertson, Fielding, and Smollett. I have often thought that the most generally well-informed and at the same time most sociable class is that of the lawyers of Edinburgh. A stranger who would desire to know the best of the inhabitants of the three kingdoms should try to become acquainted with the rich merchants of London, the lawyers of Edinburgh, and, in their country houses, the landlords of Ireland.

I should be ungrateful if I allowed this occasion to pass without offering my thanks to the amiable family of Mr. Clerk of Eldin, to Baron Gordon, Lord Ankerville, Sir Henry Moncrieff, the Lord Provost, Mr. Elder, and other esteemed persons who treated me with so much kindness, helping me in all the little troubles and bothers which attended the printing and publication of my first volume.[1]

Having then rested as long as my business required, I started one fine morning with the intention of returning to Ireland, there to finish my travels and fulfil the engagements I had entered into with the persons who had received me, by publishing the reflections which my journey had occasioned, and the details of matters I had observed.

According to my usual custom on leaving or returning to Scotland, I went to pay my respects to the persons who received me on my first arrival. I took, therefore, a place in the Stirling coach, and seeing a young and fairly well-clothed man disappointed of a place on the imperial, without saying a word I took

---

[1] Referring to his book entitled *Promenade d'un Français dans la Grande Bretagne.*—Tr.

him by the hand and made him sit down in my place on the coach, while I took his place, to the great astonishment of my travelling companions, who were astonished that anyone could be so polite. However my action in the end touched them, and one of them at the first change of horses offered to take my place, for there is really good material in these folks, and you only need to get at it to make them do what is right.

The coach stopped at Linlithgow, a little town prettily situated on a lake. After the battle of Falkirk, the Royalists were so terrified that, without stopping, some of them ran to Edinburgh, others passed the night in this town, and by misadventure set fire to the Royal Palace, the walls of which are still standing. In the middle of the street there is a fountain with this inscription below the figure of an angel—' St. Michael kind to strangers.' It is really very kind, although the beverage which it offers to a traveller is not much used in this country. The offer is at any rate generous, and it is offered to all comers for nothing, which is an act rare enough in all countries, and not very common in Scotland.

Falkirk was what it was when I had passed before, a rather ugly hole, and the Carron works always smoking. I saw again with pleasure the persons who had been kind to me in Stirling. There was competition as to who should take me to church, but I gave the preference to the Established religion, and I had the pleasure (?) of hearing in the society of the faithful a sermon three hours long.

It was a great pleasure to me to see again the places I had frequented two years before. I found an inscription upon the door of the hospital at Stirling which had escaped me on my earlier visit, and I think it merits quotation here. Three or four hundred years ago a certain tailor having, by his industry, amassed a considerable fortune, left part of it to the hospital, and this legacy is the reason for the existence of the inscription I have mentioned. Round a pair of scissors, cut on white marble, there are these remarkable words—

> Remember, you reader,
> That the scissors of this honest man
> Do more honour to human nature
> Than the sword of the conqueror.

The view from the castle here to me is beautiful as ever. I made a little excursion to the summit of Craigforth, and remarked with much pleasure that the great works on the Blair Drummond moss were proceeding, and promised the entire uncovering of this immense area. Passing the Abbey boat I heard, with pleasure, a discussion among the boatmen on the mutiny in the navy, which was then at its worst, and it was said that the sailors had hung their Admiral. ' Weel, mon,' said one, ' I'se warrand ye mony a ane'll swing for this.'

' But, dear mon,' said another, ' it's no' that they want, they're only seekin' bread and drink.' ' Weel a weel, Jock will gie them that,' replied the first speaker.

As a matter of fact this ' Jock '[1] had really the last word in the matter, as he must have in any Government that is absolutely determined to maintain established order. Revolutions never come unless the Government believes itself to be stronger than it

[1] The hangman.

241   R

really is, and is glad to profit by the effervescence of the populace to overturn its opponents. At this moment the example of France was too recent for the Government to draw any conclusions from it, and the chiefs of the insurrection were hung. If the Government had been weak enough to *Machiavéliser* with them, as did the French Government, they would have been treated exactly as the latter has been treated.

I went to see my old host, Major Mayne, with whom I had passed a time of peace, and during the few days of my sojourn I travelled the country round about. It is always a great pleasure to one to revisit the places where he has already spent some time, it is a sort of gratitude or homage which should be rendered to Nature.

The adjacent mountains are full of veins of copper. There is, however, only one mine open, and that has been working but a short time. A short distance from the Devil's Bridge, there was found here in the time of Charles II a mass of silver, which produced, I am told, more than fifty thousand pounds sterling, but it was what the mineralogists call a *nest* of silver—there was no vein.

This part of the country is cultivated to great perfection. In order to encourage emulation among the labourers, the proprietors organise, annually, a ploughing match ; that is to say, they choose a field and turn into it all the ploughmen of the neighbourhood with their ploughs, these and the horses being decorated. The men and ploughs are ranged in line and are started together—he whose furrow is the best and straightest, in the judgment of the other ploughmen and the owners, receives a prize of some value, a profusion of

compliments, and is sure never to want a place. One
can easily understand the emulation which this ceremony or practice encourages among the ploughmen of
the country, and of the good effects it must produce.
Certainly, I have never seen better cultivated or more
fertile fields.

During the troubles of the invasion of Prince Charles
in 1745, a lady of the country, according to the story
told me, used a singular method to prevent her husband
from taking any part in the operations. The husband
was a partisan of the house of Stuart, and had announced
his intention to join, next day, the last Prince of that
House appearing in Great Britain. After having
exhausted her rhetoric in the effort to dissuade him,
his wife begged him, as a special favour, that he would
breakfast with her before setting out, a favour which
the husband could not well refuse. Next morning he
was booted, spurred, and ready to start, his horse
already at the gate. The good lady, under the pretext
of making the tea, took the boiling kettle from the
fire, and by a sudden movement overturned it in one
of his riding boots. These, at that time, were made
with a wide leather expansion above the knee. The
anger of the man and the pain caused by the burning
can easily be imagined. ' Kill me if you will,' said the
woman, ' this was the only way to save you from the
rage of one or other of the parties. Neither of them
can complain that you have not appeared, since for
a long time you will not be able to budge.' There are
a good many people who would not have been sorry
to have been scalded in this fashion.

Shocks of earthquake accompanied by subterranean
noises occurred regularly near the Roman camp of

Ardoch ; I have described them on page 232 of my 'Promenade dans la Grande Bretagne.' This phenomenon should attract the attention of the learned of the country, and they should endeavour to discover the cause of it. I myself have felt the shocks in the mountains in the neighbourhood ; the water of the lakes is sometimes visibly agitated, and it has often happened that it has fallen or risen several feet at such times. I have often wished for the country that a brave volcano would break out in the middle of these desert mountains ; it would attract the curious from all parts of the earth.

The inhabitants of the mountains are reputed to be subject to a malady, which is politely called 'Scotch Fiddle.' One of their kings, who seemed to have known something of the malady, asserted that the rubbing of one's back against a stone was an enjoyment too great for a simple subject. I should say that I have not seen more of this instrument of music in Scotland than elsewhere ; and, in spite of the long time I have spent in that country, I left without learning to play.

It is hardly forty years since tea was first introduced into Scotland. Some one in London, having returned from China, sent four or five pounds as a rare gift to a lady of his acquaintance. She, as the story goes, boiled the leaves a full hour, then threw the water away and dished the leaves with melted butter.

Everywhere throughout Great Britain little use is made of vegetables, especially in winter. I have been told, however, that a certain man called Montrose, not being able to do without them, kept asking his wife continually, ' Give me something green,' even when she had told him that vegetables were wanting. In the end the good lady, to try and satisfy her spouse, boiled an old pair of green velvet breeches, and placed them on the table round the beef !

It is perhaps fit that I should not indulge here in jokes about Scotland, for the bile of these honest folk is easy to raise, and I am here reminded of a story. One of the chiefs of the American League having said in a joking way to a Scotchman who was dining with him, ' I hope, Sir, that you will not be offended if I speak ill of the Scotch when I am a little tipsy, it is my custom, and I cannot help it,' the other replied, ' I hope, Sir, ' that you will be good enough to excuse me a rather bad custom which I really cannot help, and that is to slay anyone whom I hear saying a word against a Scotchman.' The ill custom of the Scotchman freed the American from liability to indulge in the practice of his bad habit. I left here, after having passed a little time in this beautiful and good country in the enjoyment of rest which was so necessary to me after my winter's work. Well received, well treated by persons whose goodwill and esteem I had the good fortune to gain, my sojourn would have been extremely agreeable, but for this cruel division of the people into partisans of Mr. Pitt or Mr. Fox. Always it was Mr. Pitt and Mr. Fox, and I, as a foreigner, found it impossible to take any more interest in them than I did in Mahomet or Ali. Like these rival prophets, Pitt and Fox are no doubt very clever men, but I must admit that the weariness which their follies caused to me made me (I beg their pardon) wish them many a time with the devil for company.

It is strange that in all these disputes I never once heard the name of the King mentioned. What is heard

of him is—the King took a walk on the terrace at
Windsor—the King eats—the King drinks—the King
gets up—the King goes to bed—everything else is Mr.
Pitt and Mr. Fox.

I had the chance at Glasgow of being presented to
Mr. Dale, one of the most extraordinary characters
I have seen. He began as a simple weaver, and by
long continued industry he has acquired a brilliant
fortune. He was good enough to take me, with a
Glasgow merchant, to his cotton mills at Lanark, near
the Falls of Clyde. Passing through Hamilton, he
showed me a house, saying, ' There is a house where
for many a year I worked at a loom.' His mills consist
of four great buildings each of four storeys, and each
storey with seventeen or eighteen windows in line.
I saw here more machines, more wheels, and more
cotton than in any other place I had visited.[1] All
the machinery is put in movement by water power
drawn from the Clyde, the water carried at great cost
through a rock of more than two hundred feet thickness.
Before there were any manufactures here, the place
was wild and desert. Now it has two thousand
inhabitants.

Mr. Dale maintains at his own charges nearly five
hundred children who work for him, and whom he has
taught to read, write, and to know arithmetic. They
are all kept in excellent trim, well dressed, and well
fed. When they have attained the age of fifteen or
sixteen years, and after they have acquired the
taste for work and industry, they leave and easily

[1] The Manchester people make a great many faces if they
are asked to show their mills, some of them absolutely refuse. But
what are their mills in comparison with those of Lanark ! !—*Note by
Author.*

246

find places. It is on account of this that I find the
mills of Lanark so very interesting. This is the real
glory of the merchant. Mr. Dale has the praise of
maintaining more than two thousand persons, and of
turning into useful members of society a prodigious
number of little friendless orphan children, who are
for the most part simply a charge on him.

Several persons in Ireland having appeared to me
to wish to form such establishments in which to give
occupation to the children of their neighbourhood,
I took the liberty to question Mr. Dale as to the best
way to make use of his plans in a small way. He has
assured me that it is impracticable, and that the best
way to employ the children of the poor in spinning
cotton is for a simple individual to follow the old
method unless he can bring together a great number,
and make the enterprise his sole business. The smallest
establishment of the kind I saw would cost at least
seven or eight hundred pounds sterling—the Lanark
Mills have cost over one hundred thousand pounds.

The Falls of Clyde are two miles from these mills.
They are reached by a charming promenade cut
through the woods of the park of Lady Ross. I have
seen waterfalls much more considerable, but never any
so romantic. On my way I found a little key. ' Oh,
you are a happy man,' said my conductor, ' that's a
sign of good luck.' ' Good or bad,' I answered, ' it is
certainly a sign of a lock.' Returning to Glasgow,
my travelling companions, as is the custom in this
good city, overwhelmed me without mercy with their
talk of money, banks, cotton, goods, bills, &c., until
I wished to have my ears stopped. Money, money
was always there. If, instead of taking the way to

my ears, it had found its way to my pocket, I might have become accustomed to it in the end.

Again I had the pleasure to pass two or three charming days with Mr. Oswald at Scotstown. I think I may say without vanity that I have profited by my exile. There is not a corner of Scotland or of Ireland where I have not been received with politeness, and often with most remarkable kindness. Besides the amiable family at Scotstown, Dr. Wright and Mr. Brown treated me in a very friendly way. If ever the glorious days of France come back, and if I am able to return to my *penates*, I shall have very agreeable remembrances of my days here.

Trade in Glasgow was pretty good in spite of the war. The shows were all going as in ordinary times, and I had the pleasure to see an audience bursting with laughter at the agonies of Beverley, and nearly weeping at a farce. It must be horrible for an actor to find his efforts accepted in this manner. Next day I travelled in the coach to Ayr with the comedians I had seen playing, and they were still stunned. They found at Ayr a vessel which took them straight to Dublin, the voyage lasting one or two days, and the charge for the passage very moderate. But I, wishing to finish my travels, let them go that way while I proceeded to Portpatrick, and embarked there. After being tossed for thirteen or fourteen hours I found myself again in the land of St. Patrick.

CHAPTER XIV

THE importance which was given in Scotland to the Irish troubles made me almost fear to set foot again in the country, but at Donaghadee I was happily reassured, and welcomed by Mr. Smith with the same hospitality which I had experienced at the time of my first crossing. Although the country was ' out of the King's peace,' it seemed to me that everybody was perfectly calm. During the two or three days which I stayed in the little town, I had opportunity to take note of a custom which had hitherto escaped me. Spite of the facilities for marriage-making in Scotland, since a single word there is sufficient to make a contract valid, there are not a few illegitimate children. The minister of Portpatrick, a holy man of God, not being able to punish the guilty parties as they deserve, makes the chastisement pass to the unfortunate child, and absolutely refuses to him the rite of baptism. The parents, however, sinners though they may be, do not like to have their children deprived of this benefit, which perhaps they have more need of than others, and so they send their children over to Ireland, where it is not difficult to find an Anglican minister who is more reasonable.

On the other hand, the Anglican minister is ex-

tremely reluctant to marry persons who are not known
to him, and requires all the formalities of banns, &c.
And so, for the purpose of avoiding delay and ceremony,
the marriageable people go over to Scotland, and if the
couple, with the fathers and mothers, present themselves
to the minister at Portpatrick, he questions none and
says, ' You men and women I declare you married.'
As a matter of fact, his refusal, if he made it, would not
amount to anything, for in Scotland, as I have already
stated elsewhere, a word before witnesses, even in
joking, or a letter by way of joking, suffices to render
a marriage valid.[1]

I learned here something of a trade of which I had
previously no knowledge, the trade in rags. I had
indeed seen, at Edinburgh, different houses with the
inscription—

RAG WAREHOUSE

or

MONEY FOR RAGS,

but I always thought that the rags were intended for
paper making. I have since ascertained that there

---

[1] In the month of June 1795 the Court of Session at Edinburgh
decided a case of this kind in favour of the plaintiff. A young
man, falling in with the wishes of his family, was accustomed to
write to a young girl living more than two hundred miles away,
and in his letters commonly called her ' my little wife.' She in
return called him in her letters ' my little husband.' Correspond-
ence went on for two years, at the end of which time the young
man tired of the distant intended whom he had never seen, and
fell in love with a girl he saw very frequently at home. The distant
young lady soon heard of this and in the end a lawsuit was entered.
The Court of Session decided in favour of the young woman, who
was then duly recognised as married although by letter only.

Will it be believed that with all the facilities for marrying,
Scotland is the country of the world which has the greatest number
of old maids ? The number of them is truly frightful.—*Note by
Author*.

are people who go about buying from the lower classes the clothes which they think not good enough to wear (the Scotch peasant is always well clad), and these they send to Ireland, where they are sold with a large profit.

Feeling partly reassured as to the danger to which a traveller on foot might be exposed in proceeding through a country where the Government were obliged to act rigorously, I slung my small baggage over my shoulder and started for Newtownards. About half-way on the road I found a man who had a *car* laden with turf, and who seemed to be in some embarrassment. He called out ' Pray, Sir, will you push my cash.' My head still full of the terrible stories which the Scotch had told me about poor wretches in Ireland, I took this to be an Irish way of asking me to push *my* cash ; that is to say, I interpreted his saying as a demand for my purse. Taking care, then, to stand at a respectful distance, I asked him what he meant. ' I want you to help me up with my turf cash,' he said, and then I learned that the basket or pannier which carried the turf is called a ' cash.' ' With all my heart,' I answered, and with a lift and shoulder-push, the pannier was placed in proper position.

Entering the inn I saw a notice fastened to the door which read, ' If there is another shot fired over the sentinels, orders will be given to burn the town.' ' The devil ! ' I said.

I was received with much kindness by Mr. Birch, whom I had seen on my first arrival, and I proceeded again to Belfast, where I arrived in time for the celebration of the King's birthday, and heard the volleys fired by the garrison in honour of His Majesty. The people of this town, who were represented some time ago as about to rise, appeared now in a sort of stupor hardly distinguishable from fear. In the evening the town was illuminated, and the soldiers ran through the streets armed with sticks, breaking the windows of those who had not lit up their houses, and of a great number also who had done so. They went into all sorts of holes and corners breaking back-windows and the fanlights of doors. They seized their officers and bore them, in turn, on their shoulders through the streets. The yells, coming from the soldiers, and the huzzas were simply terrible. Three weeks earlier it was the people who assembled tumultuously and made a racket. If I may say it, I think a crowd of soldiers and a crowd of people differ very little in point of the danger to be expected; in the former case, however, if the officers have their soldiers well in hand there is less danger, as by the terror they inspire they are able to prevent the excess to which the populace might give way.

I imagine that the people of Belfast will not for long forget the terror in which I found them. General Lake, however, walked the streets the whole night and arrested some soldiers who were becoming unruly; he dispersed the crowd, too, as soon as the time fixed for the illumination was past. The row was so agreeable and entertaining to the soldiers that they would have been very glad to begin it again; a report was, indeed, circulated that there would be a second illumination next day. In every country soldiers are delighted with the chance of making a rumpus, than slashing and cutting they like nothing better, and it required all the activity of General Lake to keep them within bounds.

The next day, desiring to see the Sovereign, as the first Magistrate or Mayor is here called, his house was pointed out to me by a poor woman who was near the door. ' There it is,' said she, ' but he is not in, and I am waiting,' she added, ' to make him pay for my broken panes.'

On the same day a man with whom I dined, and who was in a state of alarm, said to me : ' France is in great trouble, Italy is ravaged, a revolution is coming in Spain, Germany is ruined, Switzerland is about to declare war, Holland no longer exists ; here we are breaking our windows, and we shall finish, perhaps, with slaughter ;—where is peace to be found ? ' ' Faith,' said I, ' I know one sovereign who has not been troubled, and to whom anyone can go very quickly.' ' And who is he ? tell me, Sir.' ' The big Devil in hell,' I answered.

The troubles, however, having made Belfast a somewhat disagreeable resting-place, I provided myself with passports and started out. I was much surprised to see that the soldiers had taken the trouble to break windows as far as two or three miles from the town. I travelled by coach, thinking it not desirable to risk myself on foot, on the road, after what I had seen. I passed successively through Lisburn, Hillsborough, and Dromore ; the two first-named are situated in beautiful and perfectly-cultivated country. Hillsborough, where is the castle of the Marquis of Downshire, is on a height dominating a most fertile and rich country. It was at Lisburn that the French refugees first established the linen manufacture which has become the principal industry in Ireland, especially in the north. The three towns were full of soldiers and volunteers. Although I regretted that I could not stop in them a little while, the thought that my stay here might be very far from agreeable, made me push on to a place which I thought might be more settled, or, at any rate, to the place of residence of someone to whom I had a letter of recommendation. Influenced in this way, I came to Banbridge, and was there received at the house of Mr. Ross Thomson.

This country is entirely occupied in the manufacture of linen, but the late troubles have made trade to languish. The mills, however, are still going, and it is hoped that a year of peace will restore order and prosperity. Military law was rigorously enforced here on the inhabitants ; they were not permitted to have lights in their houses after nine o'clock, and any person found in the streets after that hour was in danger of being arrested. A fair was held during the time I stayed in this little town, and it passed over quite peacefully ; the soldiers promenaded through the market-place and obliged women who wore anything green, ribbon or otherwise, to take it off.[1] Had one-fourth of the precaution taken here been observed in France, there would certainly have been no Revolution. I was much struck here by the thought of the different results which different characters in government may produce. It is remarkable how in France a weak government and foolish ministers have led a people entirely Royalist to slay a King they loved, and whose good qualities they respected, and to destroy a flourishing monarchy for whose prosperity they had been enthusiastic ; while here, surrounded by enemies,

---

[1] The green ribbon was the distinction adopted by the United Irishmen.—*Note by Author*.

a vigorous government in Ireland has been able to repress, and hold in the path of duty, a people discontented and seduced by the success of the French innovations.

The boldness of the United Irishmen increased each day as long as the Government did not interfere ; many who had joined them had done so out of fear, and there were with them a number of weak, undecided people ready to range themselves on the winning side, and so immediately on the Government's determination to act vigorously, it was only necessary to let the soldiers appear upon the scene, and the difficulties disappeared.

The poor peasant on this occasion, as in so many others, was the dupe of rogues, who put him in the front, and were very careful themselves to stay behind the curtain. The troops went through the country, burning the houses of those who were suspected of having taken the ' Union ' oath, or of having arms, and on many occasions they acted with great severity.

On the way to Armagh I passed through a superb country ; there is a charming valley, and well-wooded, near Tandragee. Between this town and Armagh I met a company of Orangemen, as they are called, wearing orange cockades, and some of them having ties of the same colour. The peasantry seemed very much afraid of them. I went into one or two cabins to rest myself, and was offered, certainly, hospitality in the ordinary way, but it did not seem to be with the same air as before, and at last, near the town, a good woman said to me, ' You seem to have come from far, my dear Sir, I hope that your umbrella or the string of it will not bring you into trouble.' I laughed at the good woman's fears, but, on reflection, I felt that since she had remarked that my umbrella was greenish, and the cord of a bright green, soldiers might make the same observation, and that in any case it would be very disagreeable to have any trouble over such a silly thing, and I cut the green cord off my umbrella.

Arriving in the town of St. Patrick, I went immediately to pay my duty to his metropolitan church. The foundations of this, they say, were laid by the Saint himself on the ruins of a Druidic establishment. History relates that there was here a lively passage at arms between the Saint and the Druids in presence of the great monarch who was then King of Ulster, and the Saint, having convinced his Majesty, baptised him and all his court, and afterwards sent missionaries into the other kingdoms of Ireland. The old cathedral has been destroyed and burned several times, and has been rebuilt always on the same spot.

The city had been reduced to the miserable state of a little country town, but the last Archbishop, the Rev. —— Robertson, being a man of learning and friend of the public welfare, liberal, and without family, set himself to improve and increase it, so that at present it is really a very handsome little city. The cathedral is situated on a rocky height (as the name Ard indicates), and here, a few years ago, among some ruins was found an ancient cross of stone in one piece, with strange looking figures thereon carved, and appearing to be a representation of a man baptising converts. It has been erected in the market-place.

Primate Robertson has built at his own charges an observatory, and has furnished funds to give it an annual income of £300 sterling, which is paid to the person in charge. He has also established, at great cost, a well-furnished library, which is open to the public four hours every day. He has erected a hospital and several other edifices, and certainly merits as much gratitude from the inhabitants of the diocese as may be considered due to St. Patrick himself.

The revenues of the Archbishop amount to eight or nine thousand pounds sterling per annum, but it is known that the estates belonging to the seat bring in to those who have farmed them £150,000 (3,750,000 francs). If the Archbishop had such an income, it might well excite the jealousy of the Government, as well as the discontent of the rent-farmers, who regard these estates as heritages belonging to their families, thus, prudently, the leases are renewed every year at the same price, plus a considerable *pot-de-vin*. The demesne of the Archbishop is superb ; the Palace, although very large and well built, does not seem too magnificent for the embellishments of the park surrounding. There is in it a chapel, brilliant in architecture, in which there is some very fine stained glass.

There are four Archbishops in Ireland, who all take the title of Primate. He of Armagh is called Primate of All Ireland, the Dublin Archbishop is called Primate of Ireland, that of Cashel, Primate of Munster, and that of Tuam, Primate of Connaught. This is pretty well for Primates. In England there are only two : the Archbishop of Canterbury, Primate of All England, and that of York, Primate of England. I am sorry I cannot remember how many there were

s

in France ; but perhaps the reader is pleased to be
without the information.

The country in the neighbourhood of Armagh is
charming, full of little hills and plains and pretty little
lakes. Among the places I saw I remarked, especially,
Castle Dillon and Drumilly, where I was received by
Colonel Spencer, whose acquaintance I had made at
Westport in the summer. Certainly there could not
be a more agreeable quarter ; the country is a little
paradise, it is impossible to conceive anything better
cultivated or more romantic. What a pity then, that
the spirit of discord and fury has laid hold of the inhabitants to a point that might well make one fear to live
among them. Every morning there is news of crimes
committed during the night. Not a day passes without murders or the burning of houses. For the sake
of a walk I accompanied one of the officers who was
going to verify information by visiting a man who had
been beaten. We found the man with one eye punched
in, it is true, but I thought the injury might just as well
have been the result of a private dispute with which
politics had nothing to do. The house of one good
woman had certainly been ' wrecked,' as they say,
by some armed men, but that was all we were able
to learn.

I think it my duty to give here a little information
on the subject of the troubles, which for so long have
desolated this beautiful country. The quarrel between
Catholics and Protestants of this county began with a
private dispute between two peasants at a fair. The
one was Catholic and the other Protestant. During
the fight ill-advised words passed from one side to the
other, and these had the effect, as is unfortunately the

custom at most fairs, of ranging the friends of the
two combatants into parties who fought each other
with sticks. That day the Protestants were beaten,
but at another fair they took their revenge, falling,
armed, on the Catholics, and a number were killed.
The animosity between the parties manifested itself
for a long time before the Government appeared to take
any notice ; in the end, however, the magistrates,
although not very energetically, took certain proceedings, and put into execution a part of the law which
at that time forbade Catholics to have possession of
arms. It followed that, as there was no power to disarm
the other side, the former were entirely at the mercy
of the latter.

I have been assured that there were certain persons
who thought it their duty to take the Protestant side in
order not to lose their votes in the parliamentary elections. This unfortunate partisanship increased the
audacity of the triumphant side, who formed a military
corps, to which they gave the name of ' Orange Boys,' in
memory of the Prince of Orange (King William) and
of the Revolution. The other side took, correctly
enough, the name of ' Defenders,' for it is true that,
at first, they only thought of defence. The Orange
Boys had the advantage over their adversaries, seeing
that they were armed, and the others were not.
Matters came to such a point that Defenders, who
were obnoxious, received letters in these terms :

' Peter —— or James, —— you have —— time
to sell your things and go to Connaught, or you will
go to Hell.'

Some disdained to submit to these barbarous orders,
and during the night their cabins would be overturned

or demolished over their heads, or a dozen of shots would be sent into a bedroom. These horrors started the Defenders to commit excesses no less cruel. The atrocities were not repressed with the necessary vigour to put an end to them, in fact it seemed as if very little attention was given to them. Peaceful families of both religions, frightened at these disorders, hastened to sell their effects at loss, and retired to the province of Connaught, where I have seen a number of them welcomed by Colonel Martin and Lord Altamont.

While, here, matters were in this distressing state, it is very singular that troubles of a totally different character appeared in the neighbouring counties. Those of Armagh really belonged to a religious war, those of the Counties of Down, Antrim, and Londonderry had, for pretext, the reform of Parliament, and the discontented affected to speak with indifference of all religions. I have known cases of men who, having practised the most barbarous cruelties on their compatriots on religious pretexts, affected, in the name of United Irishmen, to say that all religions were equal, while they appeared not to believe in any.

They assembled, appointed chiefs, announced republican opinions, and declared that they only waited the arrival of the French to join them.

It is certain that this new spirit of dissension by throwing ridicule at, and treating with contempt, the troubles of Armagh succeeded in settling these to a great extent. But the new ideas, by their immediate connection with the revolution in France, were likely to become much more dangerous than the first. It is well known to what indefensible excesses the United Irishmen proceeded. I have mentioned some of them which happened before I reached Scotland. I was convinced then, by the knowledge I had of the people of this country, that this frenzy would calm down, and that unless there were really an invasion on a large scale, there was absolutely no fear about the surety of the Government. Such was the situation of the country at the time I started for Scotland. Perhaps on my return I would have found things in the same state, if the arrival of the French Fleet in the bay of Bantry had not opened the eyes of the Government as to the dangers they ran, and convinced them of the necessity for rigorous methods in dealing with the dissatisfaction.

Before the French appeared off the coast of Ireland, although the project of the invasion had been much talked about, little or no precaution against it had been taken. After the disorder occasioned by the first moment of alarm had commenced to disappear, the Government set themselves, seriously, to take efficacious measures for putting Ireland into a respectable state of defence. Volunteer corps were formed in all the different towns. Many troops were sent over from England, and these were quartered particularly in places in the north where there had been any manifestation of seditious inclination. These troops were commanded by active and experienced men, and it was only at last, after the Government had wisely and prudently taken all the steps necessary to ensure success, and not before, they set themselves to act with severity against the discontented.

Orders were issued by all the generals to the peasants in the districts under their command to deliver up their arms and take the oath of allegiance. The

United Irishmen, who for long had been accustomed to obey no orders but those of their leaders, and to despise the soldiers and the Government, paid no attention at first to these commands; but finding soon that the Government had serious intentions, and seeing that their houses were burned and that imprisonments followed illegal assembling, they broke up immediately, passing, it may be said, in the winking of an eye, from audacity to fear, most of them hurrying to make submission and to do what was required of them.

It is an extraordinary thing that just at this moment the troubles at Armagh recommenced, and the religious quarrels helped powerfully to neutralise the political troubles caused by the United Irishmen, as these latter some months earlier had almost made the religious difficulties of Armagh to disappear.

The renewal of religious strife at Armagh was followed by frightful excesses on both sides. The Orangemen accompanied the magistrates when these went on an expedition, and some of these having been previously of the Society of United Irishmen, they knew where to discover arms, and often committed such excesses as may always be expected in the action of the lower classes of people when they are allowed to have arms and to feel themselves under protection. The Catholics could not be received amongst the Orangemen, even if they were willing to take the oath of fidelity. The greater number of the inhabitants of this faith swore that they had never been United Irishmen, and that they would not become such; perhaps they spoke truly, for their quarrel was entirely of a different nature, and it could be understood that they had not abandoned one trouble in order to take up another. I knew one brave commandant who tried to steer clear of favouritism in any shape or form, and who was always ready to succour the oppressed or weakest, without regard to party. This was very good in him, but it was necessary for him to have a strong force in command to deal with the mutinous, for otherwise there was a risk of the two parties joining against him. Although such divisions are a great misfortune, they are, in certain circumstances, of value to a clever government which knows how to manage them, and to make use of these animosities to keep different parties in check through their own action, and to prevent them from combining against the Government.

Although I did not hear, this time, that the Orangemen used the old menace of Connaught or Hell, it was easy to see that their dominating idea was still the expulsion of the Catholics, but their manner of action was no longer so terrible. Trade was at the time, in the north, in a very bad state, and many of the workers, being idle and exposed to the fury of their opponents, they circulated adroitly among the peasants an old prophecy of St. Columba which warned the faithful that ' A time will come when war and famine will destroy in this part of the country all those who have not embraced the new errors,' but, adds the prophecy, ' the massacre will not extend beyond the Shannon, where the faithful shall prosper.'

It was also stated that everything was very cheap in the neighbourhood of Limerick, Galway, and Westport, and that the workers would there find all the industries they could desire, and at good wages. The poor folk, who are after all the most timid and credulous

of the universe, with their families and small remains
of furniture, started in crowds to put themselves in
safety on the other side of the Shannon. I myself
have met often these wandering families moving to the
line of safety ; the father and mother carrying, with
their few effects, the children unable to walk, and
followed by others carrying part of the baggage, and
accompanied by the faithful pig and often a few
fowls. It was in talking to some of these on the
road that I learned of the prophecy of St. Columba,
and the tempting reports which had been circulated
about the country to which their faces were turned.

The inhabitants of the city of Armagh were so
accustomed to hear, in the morning, of excesses committed during the night, that they spoke about them in
a very indifferent manner. The neighbouring country
had very little information about them, and I imagine
that not a hundredth part of the knowledge filtered
to Dublin. Revenge was always the motive where
the crimes were committed by one party or the other,
and the complaints that the peasants came into the
city to make were always presented in the way least
effective to excite interest. I saw a man, absolutely
drunk, coming to complain that his brother-in-law
had been murdered by a party of four or five hundred
men who were marching into the city. His brother-
in-law had indeed been killed, but it was in a private
quarrel, and the troops found no one to oppose them.
It happened also, at times, that through sheer wicked-
ness, the peasants sacked and burned their own houses,
to throw the blame on their enemies. The following
story may appear incredible. I am told that a peasant,
who had been obliged by the magistrate to come to

terms with another, returned the next day, accusing
his adversary of having torn his ear off with his teeth,
and in proof of his story he produced, from his pocket,
the ear, which he showed to the Judge, who, as may
be imagined, was much shocked, and who, without
asking proof, sent at once and seized the offender and
put him in prison.   The poor man denied all that
had been alleged against him, and a surgeon being
called, it was proved that the ear had been cut off
with a razor, and not torn by teeth.   In the end it was
proved that the man to whom the ear belonged had
cut it off himself, in order to get his opponent punished.

This country, which is, certainly, the most beautiful
in Ireland, is also that in which the inhabitants
are the least tractable, and approach nearest to the
character which the English call ' Wild Irish.'   The
animosity between the different sects certainly contributes to this savagery, but if this pretext for it were
not available, another would soon be found.   The real
reason is that the fertility of the country attracted a
great many strangers, who, having multiplied exceedingly, have become too numerous to allow of equitable
division of the land with the descendants of the ancient
stock, and therefore wish to expatriate these, and to
remain alone the occupiers.   The others, naturally,
wish to see the expulsion of the colonists or settlers,
and the land remaining in their sole possession.   Hence
the continual quarrels between neighbours, such as
are not found elsewhere.   Sides are taken, disputes
multiply, the sticks rattle, and the side which the
Government for the moment favours profits by the
sense of protection, and does its best to inflict the
greatest possible injury on the other.

Charlemagne conceived the idea of transplanting a part of his subjects from a too-populous area, in which he feared the spirit of insurrection, to another insufficiently peopled, and where he had nothing to fear, and without ceremony he ordered the inhabitants of the one part to leave their country and proceed to another indicated. This method of dealing with subjects would seem very cruel and arbitrary in a country governed by the British Constitution ; it would, however, spare a great many rows, and would prevent the interminable quarrels which will end in ruining this beautiful country.

I have hesitated for some time in deciding whether I should publish these details, but as the Armagh troubles have excited the most lively public curiosity, I have thought it my duty to explain the situation frankly and freely. An honest man may keep silent, but if he speaks, he should tell the truth.

It is somewhat strange that these animosities, being such as I have described, have not however destroyed the safety of the roads for the traveller, nor indeed for anyone during the daytime. Being assured of this, I resolved to continue my travels, on foot, in my accustomed manner, and made my way to Newry. I spoke to several peasants on the way, and went into one house on the road where they gave me milk and potatoes in the same frank way as they are offered in other parts of the island. If I had not known of the night troubles I would have taken the country to be in a perfectly peaceful state. I fell in with a car returning empty to Newry, and the driver offered me a seat. He told me that his business was the carrying of goods from one end of the kingdom to the other, and that he was returning from Westport at the moment. When this good creature caught sight of the Newry clock-tower, he took off his hat and cried 'Huzza! I have been fifteen days away from my folk and it revives me to see the steeple of my place.' It was impossible not to see that the man was really happy.

When we had nearly reached the town, following usual custom, he asked my name and what was the country to which I belonged. I following my usual custom told him I was Scotch, and that my name was MacTocnaye.

Newry is situated among high mountains, and nevertheless enjoys all the advantages of the plain. The sea is only at three or four miles distance, and vessels reach the town easily by the river mouth and the canal, which is continued from here to Lough Neagh. There is here a very considerable trade in linen,[1] but the late troubles have reduced it.

The divisions here have very little connection with those of Armagh; they were more like those of Belfast, being entirely political. Some time before my arrival, the military had used severe measures, and once, unfortunately, on false information and inconsiderately. On this occasion eighteen men were killed. Some story-tellers came to the town saying that a troop of the United Irishmen were encamped in a little wood, that they had committed various depredations, and had attacked the militia. On this information the troops took horse, and going to the place indicated, sacked several houses and shot a few unfortunates,

---

[1] The year before the troubles, in 1794, a Newry merchant sold, to my knowledge, to the value of £80,000 sterling in linen, and made on it a profit of £30,000.—*Note by Author.*

who fled before them. The gathering in the wood turned out to be merely a number of people who from fear had there sought shelter. They were neither armed nor provisioned, but before this was discovered eighteen were shot.

The cavalry regiment then at Newry was Welsh, a newly raised troop. When they came to Ireland they came with all the English prejudices, expecting to find the Irish to be half-savages, in complete insurrection. In consequence, they disembarked with the idea that they were in an enemy's country, and at the commencement of their stay made themselves much to be feared by the inhabitants. With all that, it is to be admitted that the terror which they inspired was perhaps in many cases salutary, and I have no doubt that the inhabitants of Newry for a long time will remember the ancient *Bretons*.

I left these parts, and although I had been politely received, it was with pleasure, for I hate quarrels. Mr. Pitt and Mr. Fox had tormented me enough during the winter. In politics it must be said that the people are fairly reasonable in Ireland, and little division from this cause is found in the middle classes of society, among whom everyone is supposed to be of the same opinion. There is not much talk about the troubles, certainly there is less than in Great Britain. My letter of recommendation to Newry was addressed to a man who had been arrested some time before, and was now out on bail. Far from wishing me ill because I had accepted the hospitality of his house, persons of entirely different opinions said to me, ' It's all right ; when you get the chance to take anything from the devil, take it.'

I crossed the narrow chain of mountains near Newry, and perceived with sorrow that the inhabitants had there suffered much more than their neighbours. I saw many houses which had been burned in order to force the owner to give up his arms. The peasant conducted himself in a peculiar way on these occasions. First of all he would deny that he had any ; then he would be threatened with the burning of his house and unshrinkingly he would stand by to see the act performed ; but when it was really burned his courage would abandon him, and it has happened more than once that he has gone quietly to unearth from the ruin a gun, which he would hand over to the magistrates. One would think it would have paid him much better to have found it before the fire.

It cannot but be true, however, that many innocent people have suffered through false information supplied by rascally enemies ; these destructions of the property of the innocent are very regrettable, but it is absolutely impossible that there should not be some such cases in such time. It seemed to me that the peasant made the difficulty about giving up arms simply because he feared to lose their intrinsic value. If they had offered to pay him even half the cost, there would have been no trouble.

CHAPTER XV

To be in the middle of such disorder was very disagreeable to me, and I saw myself, with great pleasure,
on the other side of the mountains. If I presented
myself to a man in favour of the policy of the Government, the name of Frenchman was to him suspect ;
if I went to one of contrary opinions, he did not know,
at first, on what footing to receive me, and when he
had seen my passports he did me the honour to believe
me an agent of the Government sent to inquire into
the conduct of the discontented, and to terrify them
afterwards. A certain man with whom I talked on the
way gave me in a very confidential manner his opinions
on *Union*, whereupon I advised him for his good to
be very careful as to whom he talked before opening
his mind in this way. I saw his eyes sparkle, and had
I not quickly, by way of changing subject, called his
attention to my umbrella invention, there might have
been an unpleasant union of his cudgel and my ears.
As it was, disunion was effected promptly, for he
cleared off.

Dundalk is a rather good-looking little town situated
in a charming plain on the margin of the sea, and near
the foot of the Newry mountains. It was fair day,

and patrols were in the market-place, but there did not seem to be much uneasiness. The idea that the farther I should get away from the country I had just travelled the less should I find of that air, terrified on one side, defiant on the other, made me set out immediately. I passed by Castle Bellingham and did not stop until I came to Dunleer—twenty-five Irish miles —not a bad day's walk. Nothing special happened on the way ; I went too quick for investigations, and really did not wish to investigate closely.

I remarked at Dunleer that it was not linen which was being bleached, but yarn. The cloth is not so white as what has passed through the mills in the north, but it ought to be more durable, for the beetling in the mills is very severe.

The inn where I put up was really good, nevertheless a big Englishman there was disgusted, and could find nothing to his taste. He stormed and swore and longed for the roast beef and plum pudding of Old England. His conduct made me think of a certain story well known in the island of St. Patrick, and which does honour to the subtle wit of one of its children.[1]

Spite of the rain I went on to Drogheda, and amongst the arid mountains which separate this town from Dunleer saw, at some distance, a round tower, which seemed to be very high and very well preserved. By the wayside a good, benevolent soul had placed the inscription ' THIS IS A SPRING OF WATER ' over a well. The words are in large characters, and on a pole carrying a board just like the finger-posts at the partings of roads. If it had been a spring of whisky,

---

[1] The story, which is given in the original at a length of three pages, is not worth the space occupied.—Tr.

it would have been more uncommon I thought, and certainly more frequented.

Drogheda was formerly a place of great strength. At present it seems to have a fairly good trade. Its situation is most agreeable. I should certainly have stayed here for some time had the persons for whom I had letters of introduction been at home. As, unfortunately, they were absent, and I am not gifted, like my brethren the professional travellers, with the art of talking to stone walls, I thought it well to decamp.

I went up the Boyne which passes through the town.

As is well known, it was on the banks of this river that were finally determined the fortunes of King James. His partisans accuse him of losing this battle through the same weakness which cost him his throne —he ran away long before the issue was decided. Some days after his flight his generals gave battle for the second time, and succeeded in effecting a retreat to Limerick. It was with a sad kind of pleasure that I trod this soil, witness of such high deeds a century ago. A peasant pointed out to me the position occupied by the two armies, the place on a height from which King James watched the progress of events, and the place where King William crossed the river at the head of his troops and routed the opposing forces. An inspection of the ground makes it difficult to conceive how King James' army could have been forced to fight, and still less how its retreat could have been cut off. It is an indubitable fact that on its side were all the advantages of numbers and position. A high obelisk has been erected at a short distance from the spot where King William crossed the river and where his general Marshal Schomberg was shot. It is situated on a rock which juts out into the river— the pedestal covered with inscriptions in English and Latin.

Whatever the issue, an obelisk on this spot was inevitable. Had King James won, what high-flown words in his honour would have been here for the traveller to read !

Success decides all ; justifies all. A hundred years hence, if the republic maintains itself, monarchy will be abhorred by everybody. If, on the contrary, royalty is restored, the abhorrence will be of republicanism.

The peasant who showed me the different places in a routine way had not the least idea of the story of the battle. ' Why was this obelisk erected ? ' I asked. ' Oh,' he replied, ' that's the place where the man was killed.' ' What man ? ' I queried, and his reply was ' Why, to be sure, King William.'

Voltaire records an original epigram current in Paris on the subject of the piety of King James when he was at St. Germain. Here it is as I remember it, but it is eight years since I read it :

> Quand je veux rimer à Guillaume,
> Je trouve qu'il a conquis un royaume
> Qu'il a su soumettre à ses lois.
> Mais quand je veux rimer à Jacques,
> J'ai beau rêver et me tordre les doigts,
> Je trouve qu'il a fait ses Pâques.

Leaving, at last, these places so famous in the history of Great Britain, and continuing my walk through the fertile valley of the Boyne, I arrived at

Slane. To leave the sea coasts is to find oneself, immediately, among a people differing from those who inhabit them. It was not without pleasure that I found again the extraordinary customs and the singular monuments which had excited my interest and curiosity in the south and west of Ireland.

I met a funeral. It was preceded by a child carrying a white rod decorated with paper cuttings, and followed by a number of wailing women. The procedure, however, was not exactly like that of the south. More order was observed ; the women paused in their cries, at intervals, and did not beat their breasts or tear their hair. The cries too were not the same, and instead of the *pi lu lu* or *hu lu lu* of the south, the sounds were more like Presbyterian psalm-singing.

I could distinguish *Oh*, *Ah*, *Oh*, *Ah*, *Oh*, *Ah*, and then followed an interval of silence as long as the time required to sing the melancholy notes, which at a little distance were not unmelodious. The cut papers carried by the child are placed at the head of the grave, with a handful of osiers, and if one of these take root I imagine that it is looked upon as a happy omen, for the tree is allowed to grow.

The town of Slane was built by Mr. Burton Conyngham. He had a park, and a superb house on the smiling banks of the Boyne. Here I was received by Lord and Lady Conyngham with the most kindly hospitality. My first act after arrival was to go and pay a solitary visit to the tomb of the honoured and honourable man who had befriended me, and whose loss to Ireland cannot easily be repaired.

On the summit of a hill near the little town there are extensive ruins of what was, anciently, a college.

From the top of the bell-tower, still in a tolerable state of preservation, is to be had an extensive view over the field of the battle of the Boyne, and in sight are two of those round towers of which I have had so often occasion to speak. Near the seminary there is a rath or Danish fort with very high breastworks. I imagine that, on the south side, there has been a little Druids' altar, for two of the side supports are still standing, and the principal stone now covers a vault inside the ruins of the church. It is in this neighbourhood, at New Grange, that is to be found the most extraordinary remains of the constructions of these ancient priests.[1]

. . . .

But I wander too often, carried away by interest in a subject about which, in commencing my journey, I had not a single idea . It is time to get back to my journey and wind up its story.

The Boyne is a charming river. It is well supplied with fish—the salmon are caught in basket boats such as are used at Carmarthen in Wales. Coming back from the monument I have been describing, I saw a fisherman who, seeing a storm approaching, landed and turned his boat over his head as an umbrella. In partnership with three others, Mr. Burton Conyngham had built on the river bank an immense flour-mill, which supplies the needs of Drogheda.

Inside the park of Slane is a fountain round which the inhabitants perform their devotions. Although the well has been filled up, and water is not to be seen within a considerable distance from it, the poor folk

---

[1] At this point are omitted several pages of the original, descriptive of New Grange, with further speculations of the author's friend, General Vallencey, based on the similarity of Irish and Sanscrit.—Tr.

still come and go through their performances on their bare knees, circling the space where once was the well and hanging rags on a neighbouring tree afterwards. On the height, near the remains of the ancient college or seminary, is another well, its virtuous quality being the removal of the curse of sterility. The women here, it seems to me, have no need to use its waters. It is dedicated to St. Patrick, and this great saint, to whom the Irish owe so much, still assures to those who render homage here a numerous posterity. It is stated, however, that the well has lost credit to some extent in modern times. It would really appear that it was more efficacious before the destruction of the college.

I remarked that some of the children of the neighbourhood wore round their necks little linen bags hanging by woollen thread. A good countrywoman explained to me that these are Gospels, given by the priest of the parish for the prevention of many evils. There are countries where the priests excite the people to superstitious practices—there is one, evidently, where the people oblige the priest to lend himself to such doings.

I continued to follow the smiling banks of the Boyne, and saw, near Slane, a pillar of stone carved with strange figures and some Irish characters which I could not read or have explained to me, for here it is difficult to find an English-speaking person when the workers are at their employ. A mile from Navan I saw, at Donaghmore, the round tower I had seen from the heights near Slane ; this one has something about it which makes it appear that it has been built since the introduction of Christianity. On the keystone of the doorway, here, as in others, fifteen or twenty feet above the level of the soil, is carved a crucifix, but I have been told since that the date of placing this stone on the curve is very well known. It is generally believed that these round towers existed long before the Christian era ; their use is differently interpreted by antiquaries, some holding that they were the receptacles of the sacred fire, others that they were the abodes of hermits living in far retirement from worldly things, and the story of St. Simeon Stylites owes its origin to the fact that he lived in one of these towers. I have no carefully thought-out theory on the subject; I would observe, only, that among the peoples of the Levant there have been, from time immemorial, round towers, called minarets, near temples, mosques, and churches, and other large buildings, and that at the hour of prayer a Dervish mounts to the top of one such, and by instrument of some kind, or by voice, calls the people to their duty. I shall not be far wrong, I think, if I hazard the guess that the use of these was similar, let the time of their building be what it may.

The only difficulty persons may have in accepting my theory is, that the windows near the top are very small—the tower of Swords, near Dublin, is the only one I have seen with large windows at top, opening to the four points of the compass. It would seem that its construction is different from that of others, for its door is at the earth-level, and looking into the interior one can see holes cut in the wall, evidently with the intention that beams should be placed in them.

In the cemetery, in front of the stone on which is carved the crucifix, is a large boulder on which the people of the country have knelt so often that it is worn hollow. On a neighbouring tomb I saw the inscription :

' Here lies O'Connor who was gathered here at the age of 104 years.' ' Gathered ' I thought rather good.

Navan is an entirely Irish town, and although that does not mean that it is either beautiful or clean, I must say that I like it better than many others. I wish the tastes and customs of the country could prevail in its buildings and other matters. Let them be bettered, certainly, but don't destroy to replace them. I believe sincerely that the course I indicate would be the best and shortest way to improvement, but here England is thought of in everything, and for everything, and I do not think this to be for good.

By means of a canal it is intended to carry the navigation of the Boyne to Trim, and afterwards to the Grand Canal of Ireland, which will cross the country from Dublin to Limerick.

Returning to the Boyne, I trod its picturesque banks for three or four miles to reach a bridge, by which I crossed to take the Dublin road. Indolence is figured for us in many ways—lying on a flower-covered bed for one example. I saw here, below the bridge, a sight which might have served as an entirely novel and hitherto unthought-of model. It was a worthy Irishman who had brought his horse, harnessed to a car, to the water, and who, while the animal drank, had fallen asleep. The poor beast having finished, and hearing no word from his master, rested tranquil and motionless in the middle of the river.

At a little distance I saw an immense rath called *Rathlema*—the only one I have seen of such size ; it covered a considerable stretch of land, certainly the circumference of the circle must have measured a full mile. Certain worthy folk told me that, here, in ancient times, was the dwelling-place of the King. It is not far from the castle of Fingal, near which the inhabitants, it is stated, belong to the ancient Irish race.

Not feeling very much fatigued at nine miles distance from Dublin, I thought of going farther, and inquired if there were any inn on the road. I was told 'Yes—at Cluny.' 'Cluny,' I said to myself, and certain remembrances made me accept the name as one of good augury, and I proceeded. But, alas! Cluny no longer existed, I found only a most miserable village. I went farther and found nothing—it seemed as if I should have to finish my journey just as I had commenced it, and pass the night in a cabin. I was not more than four miles from Dublin, but it was already eleven o'clock at night, and the remembrances of the martial strictness I had observed in the north made me fear an encounter with road patrols, which might prove rather disagreeable. The knowledge, too, which I had of the frightful number of mendicants in the capital was not reassuring, and I knew that I should hardly reach my destination before one o'clock, and then only to find all the inns closed, with the prospect of spending a night in the open. While I pondered, a chaise came along, travelling northward. I stopped it, bargained, and retraced my path.

Starting early next morning I made my way to the capital, crossing immense plains sparsely inhabited by a people who have absolutely no ordinary fuel, and are obliged for heat to burn the weeds they gather in the fields. I have seen a pot of potatoes boiling on a fire of hay.

Near ten o'clock I found myself in the pretty village of Finglass, and had just stepped into the shelter of a

great door to avoid a rain-storm when a man came out
of the house, pressed me to enter and to take breakfast.
I do not believe that there is another town in Europe,
especially among those of 300,000 inhabitants, where
a traveller on foot could hope to experience a similar
politeness.

I pushed on, and eastward, to Clontarf, to the
field of the battle in which Brian Boru defeated the
Danes on April 23, 1014. From here is a fine view of
Dublin Bay and the Hill of Howth, which juts out into
the sea, and has a certain resemblance to Gibraltar as
we see it in picture. From here, too, the eye can follow
the line of the immense embankment constructed to
prevent accumulation of sand at the mouth of the
river Liffey. Not far off is the charming park of
Marino, and in it the temple built by Lord Charlemont,
a gem of architecture in which I think the most critical
eye will fail to discover any defects and negligences
such as disfigure several of the public buildings of
Dublin.[1]

And so I re-entered, from the north, this city from
which a little more than a year earlier I had departed,
travelling southwards. And there was this agreement
of circumstance in my outgoing and incoming, that
on the day of my arrival I was invited to dinner at
the house I quitted on starting my journey, I took tea
with the person I had seen on the eve of my departure,
and was housed at night in exactly the same quarters
which were mine at the beginning of my journey.

I shall think little of the fatigues of my journey if

[1] The Parliament House, Dublin, is a magnificent building, but
through a strange remissness in its design a Doric entablature is set
on columns and capitals of Corinthian order.—*Note by Author.*

any expressed ideas of mine can be of service to the country of my exile ; at same time one must think, at least a little, of personal matters, and unless the friend persuading and encouraging me to further travels of this kind will give me his word of honour not to die before the journey be completed, I shall not be found tramping the highways in like manner again.

The changes brought about by the critical state of circumstances seemed to me to be less marked in Ireland than in Great Britain. The inhabitants of standing had enrolled themselves as volunteers, and formed companies made up of members of various professions and trades. Thus, there were the Companies of Barristers and of Solicitors,[1] foot and horse, of Custom-House Officers,[2] of Merchants, of Students, &c., all of them commanded by principal men of their own calling. The students had for colonel one of their professors.

Among these companies were several which, on several accounts, must be considered as excellent. The cavalry especially, mounted on horses accustomed to the dangerous hunting of the country, deserve notice. More than once has the spectacle been presented of an entire squadron jumping hedges, ditches, and walls on the way to disperse gatherings. The formation of a Volunteer Corps here bore much resemblance to that

[1] I have been assured that there were five hundred persons in the Foot Company of Solicitors, and there were many who did not enrol themselves. The Horse Company of Barristers or Pleaders and Solicitors appeared much in exercises, and a current pleasantry explained the excellence of their horsemanship by asserting that before their enrolment *they knew pretty well how to charge.*—*Note by Author.*

[2] The joker also said that it was wise to form a corps of Custom-House Officers as they were adepts in hindering or preventing a landing. Joking aside, the Companies were really very fine, and would have done credit to any army.—*Note by Author.*

of the *émigrés* at Coblence. No one entered a company otherwise than by right of profession, that is to say, it was never attempted to increase the size of a company by drafting to it men not of the profession giving it a title. Society was therefore much less mixed than at Edinburgh, where the volunteers formed only a single corps. The city seemed to be perfectly peaceful, spite of the severe measures which troubles in adjacent counties had obliged the authorities to take. Although Mr. Grattan and the other members of the Opposition exhibited much passion, and even left the House of Commons, their partisans were not nearly so hotheaded as those of Pitt and Fox. The opinions of persons in society seemed to approximate ; one might have said, indeed, that the Ministerialists leaned to the Opposition side, and that the partisans of the Opposition favoured the Ministry. This *rapprochement* of opinion calmed passion—there was no such pronounced division as in Great Britain—and, consequently, the opposing parties treated each other with respect.

Charity sermons were still in fashion and produced large sums. There is perhaps no city which does more in the way of public charity than this, and as a consequence there is no city better supplied with beggars. The late troubles, and the continuation of the war, have left an immense number of poor workers without occupation—I have been assured that in the city of Dublin alone there are more than twenty thousand of them. A committee of well-known persons undertook the duty of distributing the funds collected for charity, and while the amount distributed reached a sum of about four hundred pounds per week, the number of applicants was so great that it was never possible to give more than fivepence at a time to any individual. Such a miserable pittance, however, was sufficient to attract to Dublin poor people from all parts of Ireland. The number of disgust-inspiring beggars seen daily is unimaginable.

Everybody speaks of the laziness of the common people in Ireland, but nobody tries to cure it. The charities, small though they may be, are sufficient to draw to the capital more miserable creatures than are to be found in the whole of the remainder of the kingdom—the great object of the administration ought to be to disperse them. It is not the need of the moment which should be considered, so much as the means by which recurring need can be prevented. Industry should be encouraged, not laziness.

The industrious class is certainly the one more worthy of public assistance. The spinners, for example, who, lately, have been selling their yarn for almost the price of the dressed flax out of which they spun it, deserve consideration, and should receive help in order to encourage them to continue at work. To sum up, although the almsgiving of Dublin is extremely creditable, and, in some part, necessary, I believe it would be better if it were spread over the country.

However, I must admit that it would be difficult to say too much in praise of the zeal and activity of the kind persons who have done their best for the suffering humanity of this city. The number of charitable institutions is inconceivable—it would take too much space to attempt to describe them. The one which, to me, seems best designed is that called the Sick Poor's Institution, to which anyone paying a guinea a year can send a poor sick person, who will receive medicine gratis, and visits at home from the doctor when these are necessary.

I revisited the House of Industry, finding it to be still carried on as I have described at the beginning of this volume. The changes and improvements recommended by Count Rumford have not been made—in great establishments like this it is difficult to persuade the governing body to change the methods to which they have been accustomed. As a matter of fact, the economical heater and hot pipes which the count constructed are suited only for a small building with twenty or thirty inmates. There are here over seventeen hundred.[1]

The drunkenness which prevails among the lower classes contributes much to their degradation, and to perpetuate poverty. There is nothing more disgusting than the spectacle of rag-covered women coming out of the public-houses, carrying two or three nearly-naked children and begging for alms. At such too frequent sight the heart's door closes, pity and compassion disappear, leaving behind only feelings of disgust and horror, and a desire to fly from the unpleasant company. Some people have told me that, formerly, drunkenness was just as common in England, but that since ' *The Gin Act*,' which, by a heavy duty, has put strong liquors beyond the purchasing power of the people, they drink now only porter, or ale, healthy and strengthening drinks on which one could hardly manage to get drunk. A ' *Whisky Act* ' for Ireland would be a great benefit to the country, and would soon destroy

[1] The room in which Count Rumford placed his furnace did not allow, perhaps, for a large size. The installation is only a model one.—*Note by Author.*

this odious vice which kills the industry of the poor and keeps them in idleness, dirt, and the most abject poverty.

As I have spoken in the course of this work of manners and customs which seem to me to be different from those of England, I do not propose to recapitulate these. Every county, nearly, has its own peculiar customs, and this diversity makes a journey in Ireland much more amusing for the minute and careful observer. The traveller by coach cannot observe these peculiarities. Generally it may be said that all the reports which have occasioned English prejudice are either false or much exaggerated.

The infatuation for ancient descent exists certainly, but to much less extent than asserted. It is the adventurer who leaves his country who boasts himself of, and terrifies you with, the great names in ' *Mac* ' and ' *O.*' In the country itself no attention is paid to such things. It is quite true that the Irish still distinguish the old families from the new (so-called) —these latter being all who arrived in Ireland since the time of Strongbow, six hundred years or more ago— but this is more by way of remembrance of independent times than from pride. Here it is possible after such long lapse of time to see the peasants, in certain districts, pay ceremonious respect to the representative of their ancient prince. He who is perhaps the most extraordinary is Roderick O'Connor, descendant of the kings of Connaught and of the last great monarch of Ireland at the time of the English invasion in 1171. I have been told that his domestics serve him kneeling, and that no one may sit down in his presence without his permission. When he is addressed or written to one must say *O'Connor*, without any style or title whatever.

I am very sorry that I did not see him ; I was not within forty Irish miles of his house. The crown of gold of the last monarch is said to be in possession of his family, although there are those who think it has been disposed of to a jeweller. I suppose I shall be considered very barbarous, yet I must avow that I find something touching and honourable in these ancient usages.

There are many persons of the name of O'Neill— the O'Neills were kings of Ulster—O'Briens, and MacDermods, which are old royal names of Munster and Leinster, but I have not heard whether there be any living representative of these royal families ; at any rate I have heard of none receiving homage such as I have described.

The changes which the moderation of the Government has brought about, of late years, in Ireland, permit the hope that, in the absence of violent crises, the whole of the inhabitants, no matter what may be their religion, will soon come to regard themselves as one people, and will cease to look on each other as conquerors on the one side, or vanquished on the other. The landlords who, until lately, feeling their position insecure, tried to draw the most they could out of their estates, without troubling about the misery of their compatriots, see, at last, the prejudices arising out of the manner in which their ancestors acquired the estates weakened and dying—they feel themselves real owners. On the other side the people have become accustomed to see them occupy the place of the ancient families. Out of this mutual desire for forgetfulness of the past, it results naturally that the rich, no longer looking on themselves as usurping proprietors, take an interest in the affairs of the country which furnishes their riches, and now, far from wishing to drain the wealth of an estate which they are certain of passing to their children, they strive to improve it and make life more easy and comfortable for the peasants who cultivate it.

Out of such happy change of the state of affairs we may expect prosperity to come to this land, and I have no doubt that, if such measures as have been adopted of late years are continued, and if the Government succeeds in extirpating the seeds of sedition and in preserving peace, Ireland will become a nation, happy and prosperous, and as much respected as in former times she has been despised and misjudged.

FURTHER READING

Baldensperger, F. 'Le Touriste de l'Emigration Française; Le Chevalier de La Tocnaye et ses Promenades dans l'Europe du Nord', *Bibl. Universelle et Revue Suisse*, May 1914, vol. 74, pp 225–257

Kerviler, R. *Répertoire Général de Bio-Bibliographie Bretonne*, vol. 5, 1891

La Tocnaye, le Chevalier de *Promenade autour de la Grande Bretagne par un officier français émigré*, Edinburgh, 1795

Les Causes de la Révolution de France et les efforts de la noblesse pour en arrêter les progrès, Edinburgh, J. Mundell, 1797

Promenade d'un Français dans L'Irlande (with 4 plates), Dublin, M. et D. Graisberry, 1797

Promenade d'un Français dans la Grande Bretagne, Dublin, (printed at the author's expense), M. et D. Graisberry, 1797 (Not in the British Library Catalogue)

Rambles Through Ireland, by a French Emigrant (translated by 'An Irishman'), 2 vols., Cork, M. Harris, 6 Castle Street, 1798 (Not in the British Library Catalogue)

Rambles Through Ireland, by a French Emigrant (translated by an Irishman), 2 vols., London, G.G. & J. Robinson, Paternoster Row; and Bristol, J. Norton, 1799

Promenade d'un Français dans L'Irlande, 2nd edition, Brunswick 1801

Promenade d'un Français dans la Grande-Bretagne, 2nd edition, Brunswick, 1801. (German editions: Riga 1797; Leipzig 1801)

Meine Flucht nach Irland (translated from the French), 2 vols., Erfurt, 1801

Promenade d'un Français en Suède et en Norvège, 2 vols., Brunswick, 1801

Meine Fussreise Durch Schweden Und Norwegen... (translated by H.W.E. Henke), Leipzig, 1802

Resa Genon Irrland Aren 1796, Och 1797 (translated by Samuel Odmann), Stockholm, Johan Pfeiffer, printed by Carl Schrostrom, 1803

A Frenchman's Walk Through Ireland, 1796–7 (translated by John Stevenson), Belfast, McCaw, Stevenson & Orr, 1917

Maxwell, Constantia *The Stranger in Ireland*, London, Cape, 1954

Stevenson, John *Pat McCarty, Farmer of Antrim; his rhymes, with a setting*, London, E. Arnold, 1903

A Boy in the Country (Illustrated by W. Arthur Fry), London, E. Arnold, 1912

Bab of the Percivals, London, Wells Gardner, 1926

Two Centuries of Life in Down, 1600–1800 (with maps and plates) Belfast, McCaw, Stevenson & Orr, 1920

INDEX OF SELECTED PLACE NAMES